D0812833

WITHDRAWN FROM
THE LIBRARY

UNIVERSITY OF
WINCHESTER

KA 0249772 7

Education in an Age of Nihilism

The issue of 'educational standards' is at the centre of government policy and at the heart of the contemporary educational debate. There is widespread anxiety that academic students are failing, yet there is a new machinery of accountability and inspection to show that they are not.

This timely book addresses concerns about educational and moral standards in a world characterised by a growing nihilism. The authors state that we cannot avoid nihilism if we are simply laissez-faire about values, nor can we reduce them to standards of performance, nor must we return to traditional values. They argue that we need to create a new set of values based on a critical assessment of aspects of contemporary practice in the light of a number of philosophical texts that address the question of nihilism, including the work of Nietzsche.

Education in an Age of Nihilism relates philosophy and theory to policy and practice. It will appeal to students and academics studying education and the philosophy of education, providing a much needed analysis of the asumptions underlying the debate on educational standards.

Nigel Blake works at the Open University and is Chair of the Philosophy of Education Society of Great Britain. **Paul Smeyers** is Professor of Education at the Katholieke Universiteit, Leuven, Belgium where he teaches philosophy of education. **Richard Smith** is Reader in Education at the University of Durham and Editor of the *Journal of Philosophy of Education*. **Paul Standish** is Senior Lecturer in Education at the University of Dundee and is Assistant Editor of the *Journal of Philosophy of Education*.

Education in an Age of Nihilism

Nigel Blake, Paul Smeyers,
Richard Smith and Paul Standish

London and New York

First published 2000
by RoutledgeFalmer
11 New Fetter Lane, London EC4P 4EE

Simultaneously published in the USA and Canada
by RoutledgeFalmer
29 West 35th Street, New York, NY 10001

RoutledgeFalmer is an imprint of the Taylor & Francis Group

© 2000 Nigel Blake, Paul Smeyers, Richard Smith and Paul Standish

Typeset in Baskerville and Gill Sans by
Exe Valley Dataset Ltd, Exeter, Devon
Printed and bound in Great Britain by
Biddles Ltd, Guildford and King's Lynn

All rights reserved. No part of this book may be reprinted or
reproduced or utilized in any form or by any electronic, mechanical,
or other means, now known or hereafter invented, including
photocopying and recording, or in any information storage or
retrieval system, without permission in writing from the publishers.

British Library Cataloguing in Publication Data
A catalogue record for this book is availabe from the British Library

Library of Congress Cataloging in Publication Data
Education in an age of nihilism / Nigel Blake . . . [et al.].
      p.   cm.
   Includes bibliographical references (p.) and index.
      1. Education—Philosophy.   2. Education—Standards.   3. Moral education.
   4. Nihilism (Philosophy).   I. Blake, Nigel.

   LB14.7.E393 2000
   370'.1—dc21   00–056031

ISBN 0–750–71016–0 (hbk)
ISBN 0–750–71017–9 (pbk)

KING ALFRED'S COLLEGE
WINCHESTER

370 LBLA   02497727

And if he's kind and gentle too,
And he loves the world a lot,
His twilight words will melt the slush
Of what you have been taught.

Oh, you know what you could be –
Tell me, my friend,
Why you worry all the time
What you *should* be.

The Incredible String Band
You Know What You Could Be
(lyrics by Mike Heron)

The front cover reproduces Matisse's painting 'The Dance'.

Nietzsche's impact on the thinkers of the early twentieth century was extensive. Wittgenstein and Heidegger, Lawrence and Gide, Strauss and Stravinsky, the Cubists and Futurists all registered his liberating influence. A Nietzschean 'culte de vie', a celebration of the sensual, the vibrant, the instinctual and the profane of life – a celebration of 'what is' – pervaded the aesthethics and secular ethics of the decades before the First World War. Its special expession was found in a renewed and liberated culture of dance (we think of Nijinsky and Diaghilev, Isadora Duncan and Loïe Fuller).

It is above all in dance – in its spontaneous order, alertness and poise, energy and style – that we are absorbed most intelligently in the flow of experience. In dancing, Apollo and Dionysos, *logos* and *eros*, meet. In Matisse's 'The Dance' they come together in harmonious ecstasy and naked elegance.

Contents

Acknowledgements

We are grateful to Random House for permission to include extracts from A.S. Byatt's novel *The Virgin in the Garden*, published by Chatto & Windus, to International Music Publications for permission to include verses from Mike Heron's song *You Know What You Could Be*, and to Penguin Books for permission to quote from their editions of the translated works of Nietzsche: *The Antichrist, Beyond Good and Evil, The Birth of Tragedy, Ecce Homo, Thus Spake Zarathustra,* and *Twilight of the Idols.* The extract from *Equus* by Peter Shaffer is reprinted with the permission of Scribner, a division of Simon & Schuster; © 1973 Peter Shaffer.

List of abbreviations

We have used the following abbreviations for Nietzsche's works.

A	*The Antichrist*
BGE	*Beyond Good and Evil*
BT	*The Birth of Tragedy*
D	*Daybreak*
EH	*Ecce Homo*
GM	*On the Genealogy of Morals*
TI	*Twilight of the Idols*
Z	*Thus Spoke Zarathustra*
GS	*The Gay Science*
WP	*The Will to Power*

We have used the latest Penguin editions in all cases except for *The Gay Science*, where we have used the Vintage books edition (trans. and ed. W. Kaufmann, 1974); for *The Will to Power* we have used the Vintage Books edition (trans. and ed. W. Kaufmann, 1968); for *The Genealogy of Morals* we have used the Oxford World's Classics edition (trans. and ed. Douglas Smith, 1996). For *Thus Spoke Zarathustra* we have used the Prometheus edition (trans. T. Common, revised with an introduction by H. James Birx, 1993); for *Daybreak* we have used the Cambridge University Press edition (trans. and ed. R. J. Hollingdale, 1982).

Wherever possible we have referred to the section of the text. Otherwise the page number of the relevant edition is indicated.

Introduction

In *The Will to Power*, Nietzsche writes that 'The highest values have devalued themselves. There is no goal. There is no answer to the question, "why?" '. He believes this is the state of affairs of his time. Values have become merely conventional: they are experienced as external to us, as things we do not recognise ourselves in or identify ourselves with. Political programmes proceed under their own momentum. It is the smooth running of the system which thus becomes, by default, the chief goal and end. This, the devaluation of value, is one kind of nihilism.

We have written this book in the conviction that education, in much of the English-speaking world, and particularly in the UK, is characterised by a similar nihilism, by a lack of commitment which we conceal with devices such as orthodox mission statements or programmes of docile 'values clarification'. Perhaps the most glaring sign of our devaluation of value is the reduction of complex educational aims and purposes, of the whole question of what education is *for*, to a matter of *raising standards*, understood as a matter of children, schools or whole educational systems (local authorities, for example, or nations internationally competing at mathematics) moving from lower to higher positions on league tables, entirely as if educational achievement were no different from that of a football team pulling clear of the relegation zone or becoming a contender for promotion. A standard, we should recall, is in one of its meanings a single scale, like Celsius or Richter, on which all temperatures or earthquakes can be ranked. The standard, and thus the goal and values, are one and the same for all. (All, that is, must be *commensurable*.) Absurd to object that you were trying to do something *different* with your pupils or students – perhaps enlarge their horizons or give them insight into their own experience. As well excuse your football team's relegation on the grounds that the players have been fine role-models to the community.

Along with this reductionism comes a positive refusal to devote real thought to questions of the aims and purposes of education. It is striking that the official documents and reports of the last twenty or so years, from many countries and organisations of the western world, either contain only the most perfunctory statements of such aims (often treating them as eminently establishable by *fiat*) or declare that discussion of ends and purposes is now redundant: a nostalgic practice which we have finally grown out of. Of course we should expect nothing else where the triumph of the market has declared individual subjective choice sovereign and *deliberation*, by corollary, pointless. If the consumer is supreme, educational values are simply what the consumer happens to want, and it makes no more sense to undertake any great inquiry into those values than into preferences in the matter of cars or brands of chicken tikka. Between them the league tables, which announce the score or position as the supreme good, and the market, which deifies choice (of course the logic of the league-tables is to reduce the scope of choice: otherwise people might start thinking about what they really want), appear to exclude the possibility of thinking about educational values altogether.

Into this vacuum spurious or ersatz values readily enter. Mission statements advertise excellence or world-class status, as if this meant that the institution was committed to something substantial, as if this meant that you might know, when you went to this or that university or school, what made it different from any other. The university department may be exemplary (by the standards of quality assurance), the school may be a beacon (having come out of its inspection better than most): but a beacon or example of quite *what* it is generally hard to say. There is a sense here that what is valuable is defined by contradistinction to its opposite (the merely satisfactory, or even the failing). It was this formulation of value as *the opposite of its opposite* that Nietzsche – again – saw as the core of nihilism. What do we stand for? We are no longer sure: only that it is not what these others represent. We are the reds, which means that we are definitely not the blues – them we abhor and would not be mistaken for; once more as if the values of education were no different from those of the most mindlessly partisan football supporter. Governments may encourage this moral immaturity by naming and shaming those who do not come up to the mark. Our values are acknowledged in that we find it is not ours but the neighbouring school which is thus stigmatised, closed and re-opened under new management (existing staff may re-apply for their jobs). In the same way a child's sense of his worth is confirmed when he is told that he has done well enough not to be sent early to bed *today*.

It comes to seem that the only sure value of education lies in the maintenance and extension of the system itself. Better education means more education – shorter holidays, a longer school day:[1] education, education, education, as Mr Blair expressed his new government's priorities in 1997 (see below, p. 184). 'Efficiency' and 'effectiveness' have long been shibboleths. A *school effectiveness* industry of researchers and consultants proclaims that there is no limit to the speed with which the vehicle may proceed (so to speak), irrespective of the state of the road. No school is so bad, so the orthodoxy runs, but that a good headteacher (a superhead, as we must now call him or her) cannot turn it round via the effective management of change. The proponents of school effectiveness are our new educational Taliban, intolerant of philosophical debate or diversity of values, for the most part incredulous at the idea that their approach is not simply common sense. All rush to improve schools, showing how standards can be raised by the teaching of thinking skills, by the judicious use of information technology, or by re-arranging the desks in a horseshoe.[2] A degree of misgiving, a lurking sense of the inadequacy of all this can perhaps be seen in the note of desperate, insistent reiteration: Mr Blair's three-fold 'education', the stream of publications bearing titles like *Really Raising Standards*.[3]

Educational policy, we are told, should henceforth be evidence-based. Social scientists should put themselves at the service of government in the quest for 'what works'. But this idea, apparently so innocuous – who can be against what works? – bears a little examination. All kinds of things may work without being the solutions which, given a broad view of things, we would choose. What 'works' may be morally repugnant (in one sense the Nazis' final solution certainly worked); its very success as means to an end may encourage us not to consider whether the end is appropriate or desirable. It tells us what to do, and it saves us from *thinking*. Talk of what works, in short, risks leading to short-term solutions for problems which may not, in the terms in which they are conceived, be problems at all. Being a question wholly about means, such talk forecloses on questions of the ends which are proposed. The bland confidence that 'what works' labels an unassailable educational good is one of the most worrying signs of the moral void in which education now founders. What if a literacy or other strategy 'worked', raising children's reading scores, but at the cost of ensuring that few of them ever read for pleasure or ever thought very much again?

To many these arguments, and no doubt this whole book, will seem perverse. At a time when governments are committing themselves to education to an extent not seen for many years (and we do not question the genuineness of their fervour), why do we choose this moment to publish a book such as this? We shall probably be dismissed, if we are noticed at all, as moaners, cynics, conservatives or even elitists (an interest in Nietzsche, after all, is often considered suspect). Conceivably we shall be ourselves regarded as nihilists: just as Nietzsche is sometimes, absurdly, thought to glory in the very moral emptiness that he exposes in his own time.

Yet what if the earnest efforts of the undoubtedly well-meaning – of Ministers of State, school improvers, heads of Standards and Effectiveness Units, listers of competences and outcomes, and all the rest – rest on standards of thin air? The very reasonableness, as it may seem, of the terms in which education is currently conceived is what should worry us here. Our contemporary educationists (in committee, task-group or working-party: how well-focused they are!) display a gimlet-eyed certainty, a confidence in talk of planning and targets, transferable skills and outcomes, that speaks loudly of *repression*. Perhaps a facility with the new terminology is not altogether healthy. Whatever the benefits of our New Model Education there is a shadow side here. The targets, standards and benchmarks become the latest nostrums and settle (for all that they like to pose as part of the radical new broom sweeping away the forces of conservatism) into a complacent and nihilistic orthodoxy.

One purpose of this book, then, is to disrupt the new conventionalism: to make what has become familiar and over-familiar in our educational world look a little more odd. This, though, is not easy. The authors of this book are themselves of course not immune to the siren voices, the lure of the accepted commonplace. This after all is where we work; these are the times we live in. To stand back from the assumptions of our time requires support and suitable resources. We have found these above all in the writings of Friedrich Nietzsche, whose presence may be felt throughout our book even where we do not draw on or refer to his work explicitly.

What is it about Nietzsche that suggests to us his usefulness to thinking about education now?

The revival of interest in Nietzsche in the second half of the twentieth century and the current proliferation of books and articles underline the fact that there is not one Nietzsche available to us but many, some of them radically different (and Nietzsche himself, it should be noted, is many Nietzsches). Heidegger's Nietzsche, for instance, is the author of a coherent (if latent) doctrine which constitutes the last word on western metaphysics; Kaufmann's is a recognisably Enlightenment figure whose chief concern is to liberate us from the constraints of authority and superstition;[4] the Nietzsche of the post-structuralists (to use this opaque term for the sake of convenience, and thus to designate Foucault, Derrida and Deleuze amongst others) foregrounds the connections between power and knowledge, the centrality of desire and affirmation, and a certain creative playfulness of philosophical style. We have not attempted to position ourselves carefully here with respect to these various Nietzsches. We owe the reader some account of what we understand by *nihilism* and other crucial concepts, and we go some way towards supplying this in the chapters below. However the reader who looks for a systematic interpretation of Nietzsche will be disappointed. We are less interested in interpreting Nietzsche than in fruitfully *using* him for our own purposes. In fact this seems to us the Nietzschean thing to do.

It would be wrong however to proceed further without mention of the one book in recent years that attempts to bring Nietzschean perspectives to bear on education: David Cooper's *Authenticity and Learning: Nietzsche's Educational Philosophy* (1983). Cooper undertakes a far more systematic and scholarly exposition of Nietzsche than we have attempted here. We have learned much from his book, even where we would not follow his account. In particular we would differ from him in his characterisation of the authentic individual that education should produce. The real difference between Cooper's book and ours, however, is in the sense of the educational climate to which he and we are responding. He was properly concerned by the failure of the kind of education often thought of as 'progressive' or 'child-centred' to achieve anything other than a parody of authenticity. Less than twenty years on, however, the issues are not the same. The triumph of the political Right has ensured the defeat of progressivism, in the debased and sentimentalised form that Cooper attacks, and the rise of quite different educational values, questionable on different grounds.

One way Nietzsche is useful to us is in releasing us from overly narrow conceptions of philosophy. This, if it must be categorised, is a philosophical book; at any rate it is written by four philosophers of education. Philosophy can be a dry and technical business, and philosophy of education has in the past often seemed to want to assert its philosophical credentials by burlesquing the worst kind of analytical aridity. Nietzsche on the other hand makes available to us a richer and less limited notion of what it is to do philosophy. As is well known, his procedure is less to undertake conceptual analysis or to construct tight arguments than to undermine and discredit perspectives that he finds unsound: to reorient our thinking in different directions. In order to do this he is prepared to employ different styles and different voices – aphoristic, fragmentary, apocalyptic, ironic. Thus he takes us beyond existing frameworks of expression and interpretation and suggests the possibility of new ones. And this, we believe, is a valuable approach in a world where the dominant frameworks (and especially of course the nihilistic, performative framework of educational thinking) show an enduring capacity to resist the onslaught of more traditional forms of analysis.

Nietzsche makes us question the easy distinction between philosophy and more literary forms of expression. He reminds us that we must take *language* seriously: that the range of our language and the quality of our thinking are not two separate matters. Language is not to be treated as a box of disposable tools whose function is simply to help us get to wherever we want to go; or, if we do treat language like that, we should not be surprised to find ourselves enmired in the instrumentalism that results from unconsciously foregrounding means-towards-ends. His famous description of truth as a mobile or flexible army of metaphors (*TI*: 374) points to the ineradicably figurative nature of language.

> Truths are illusions which we have forgotten are illusions; they are metaphors that have become worn out and have been drained of sensuous force, coins which have lost their embossing and are now considered as metal and no longer as coins.
>
> (Ibid.)

When we suppose language to be offering us direct and unmediated access to reality we have probably failed to notice the particular metaphors we are using (or, more accurately, which are using us). Educationists' ready talk of *effectiveness* and *what works* supplies examples. That is how we come to think that the only sensible way to interpret the world is by 'counting, calculating, weighing, seeing and touching, and nothing more' (*GS*: 373); and that is both crude and naive.

Above all, it is Nietzsche's perspective that is helpful when we consider what may reasonably be called the crisis of values (or demoralisation) in education. To take this view of education is not to complain that 'the values dimension' has been left out, as if it were something familiar that had unfortunately been omitted, such that some earnest working-party could put matters right by drawing up a set of guidelines. It is emphatically not to make out a new case for 'moral education' as that is generally understood. The problem is both deeper and more interesting than that. The point is precisely to ask what is the value of the kinds of values that currently inform education. And where those values, upon examination, appear discredited and inadequate, where are we to turn? We must find new ones, or nihilism will rule. We must create fresh values, precisely as Nietzsche tells us, in that spirit of dynamic vitality and affirmation which lies at the heart of his notion of the 'will to power':

> A virtue has to be *our* invention, *our* most personal defence and necessity: in any other sense it is merely a danger... 'Virtue', 'duty', 'good in itself', impersonal and universal – phantoms, expressions of decline, of the final exhaustion of life. . . . The profoundest laws of preservation and growth demand the reverse of this: that each one of us should devise *his own* virtue, *his own* categorical imperative.
>
> (*A*: 11)

Anything less than this, Nietzsche would have us understand, is life-denying, and, so far from reinvigorating our moral lives, 'is virtually a *recipe* for *décadence*' (ibid.). In education it is the difference between raising standards as a matter of unfurling banners beneath which one will whole-heartedly march, and raising standards in terms merely of ensuring that the children score more marks this year than last.

In an earlier book, *Thinking Again: Education after Postmodernism* (1998), we also examined the state of education, arguing that instrumentalism, particularly in its latest guise as performativity, has brought about a kind of intellectual paralysis, a condition in which it is difficult to move from vague unease with the educational climate to substantial critique. There are similarities between that book and this. Both attempt to unsettle established thinking about education; both draw on thinkers generally uncongenial to the Anglo-Saxon mind (there we used in particular Foucault, Lacan, Lyotard and Derrida) in order to establish radical lines of criticism and re-open the possibility of creative thinking. This book is rather more closely focused than the earlier text. It is the product of our belief that the roots of the 'postmodern condition', as Lyotard (1984) described it, go deep, and are to be found in that radical negation of values that Nietzsche, and we, call nihilism.

The book is organised in the following way. In Part 1, *Working without Values*, we show how various aspects of our world, especially but not only the world of formal education, are essentially nihilistic. We argue that this is manifested most vividly in some of the best-known attempts to improve education, such as the school effectiveness movement and even the interest in 'emotional literacy' which promises to redeem the schooling that commits itself too narrowly to purely cognitive or intellectual goals. An important theme of this Part is *work*. Clearly education must in some sense prepare children for work, and it is a naïve and perhaps irresponsible philosophy that severs that connection altogether. But the same nihilism that infects education has also come to colour our idea of work, we argue, with disastrous results.

Part 2, *Overcoming Nihilism*, explores the theoretical resources available for addressing the problem of nihilism. Here we offer our most explicit interpretation of those aspects of Nietzsche and of the perspectives he makes available that seem most pertinent to our concerns. The 'revaluation of our values' seems to require a radically new approach to the ethical life in general. We go some way to position our reading of Nietzsche against other influential recent readings, and focus on Nietzsche's contrast between Apollo and Dionysos as a fertile source of insight. Here too we emphasise the crucial role that conceptions of language and literacy play in modern understandings of education, arguing that an impoverished notion of literacy cannot but lead to an impoverished notion of the whole educational enterprise.

In Part 3, *Raising Standards*, we make a case for some unfashionable educational aims and approaches. Education is all about communication, isn't it? – but perhaps there is distinctive educational value in a certain kind of silence, in withdrawing, in listening. Moral education, meanwhile, might concern itself at least as much with cultivating a sense of affirmation, a relish for the zest of life, as with the humble virtues (patience, forbearance, tolerance) derived from the Judaeo-Christian, and mediated through the Kantian, tradition. Nor is it entirely clear that proper relationships between teacher and taught should be a model of distant and disembodied formality. Authorities as far back as Plato, as well as more recent ones, have suggestive things to say on the matter. Education inculcates knowledge, but there is a sense in which ignorance too has its educational value. There are perhaps disturbing ideas here, but ones which we believe must be taken seriously if education is to be reconnected to learning, to vitality and to responsibility.

Lastly, nothing is more certain in the world of education than that good management is the key. The management of change, indeed, may be said to be at the heart of educational reform, as it is in the other public services and perhaps in all aspects of our rapidly changing world, particularly in what is increasingly recognised as the knowledge economy in an age of lifelong learning. It is good organisation and management that make the whole more than the sum of its parts, that help us to formulate aims and objectives and thus to move from where we are now to where we want to be. How could this be doubted? Accordingly we have ourselves tried to draw helpful connections among the different parts and chapters here by including our own reflections on management and in particular on its connections with education and learning. We have kept these short, in deference to the reading habits of the age, and have interspersed them as handy *Fragments* throughout the book.

Notes

1 'Primary school pupils are to be given more rigorous preparation for their move to secondary school, and a nine-to-five school day when they get there, the government will announce this week', *The Guardian*, 13 March 2000.
2 All are real examples: the last may seem a burlesque, but can be found in, e.g., D. McNamara (1994).
3 P. Adey and M. Shayer (1994).
4 Both Heidegger and Kaufmann give a particular emphasis to Nietzsche's notion of the 'Overman' that does nothing to dispel the charge of subjectivism and arbitrariness so often levelled against him.

Part 1

Working without values

Chapter 1

Education without risk

School effectiveness and school improvement have become mini-industries in educational research in recent years with their own dedicated posts and postgraduate degrees. These endeavours are characteristic of current preoccupations with the management of teaching and learning and of an increasingly technical conception of education. School effectiveness researchers, we are told, are 'the first to point out the technical and statistical difficulties in drawing firm conclusions about an "ideal school"' (Lynn Davies, in White and Barber 1997: 32), yet the vocabulary of these approaches to education is characterised by 'test instruments', 'operationalising', 'mechanisms', 'mapping' and above all 'outputs'. The 1997 Government White Paper *Excellence in Schools* promotes the idea of 'Laboratory Schools' (DfEE 1997: 47). Writing in the *Times Educational Supplement* about teacher education in Taiwan, David Reynolds remarks, with some approval, that teachers in Taiwan are 'proud to be applied technologists, not philosophers' (Reynolds, 1997a: 21).

In recent years school improvement has turned in a new direction. Here is Reynolds again: 'We all enjoy pushing up the ceiling of good practice – raising the floor is less popular'. And, varying the metaphor, he argues that school effectiveness needs perhaps to move from its focus on effective (or well) schools to the consideration of ineffective (or sick) schools. This, he suggests, constitutes a radically different agenda. The way forward, it seems, is the Highly Reliable School (or failure-free school), currently being promoted by Reynolds himself. Let us consider his (grammatically infelicitous) characterisation of this:

> *What are the characteristics of the Highly Reliable School?*
> * limited range of goals which require total success
> * recruit proactively and train extensively, pre-service and in-service

- formalised logical decision making
- include measures to identify flaws and generate changes, for example, the simulations which test human and physical components in the nuclear power industry
- pay considerable attention to evaluating performance
- alert to lapses and pay considerable attention to detail to prevent any minor error cascading into major system failure
- highly co-ordinated and interdependent
- crucially data-rich organisations which continuously monitor their decision-making

(*Times Educational Supplement*, 19 January 1996: 10)

It is reasonable to see the Highly Reliable School as a logical extension of more general trends in educational theory and in practice. Reynolds' current project with Avon schools – one of several – involves three annual cycles. It is proposed

- in year one, to use in-service training days to bring to the schools the world's greatest knowledge in school and teacher effectiveness, and school improvement
- in year two, to use the information systems to help the schools to make internal comparisons between their own departments and external comparisons against best practice elsewhere
- in year three, and beyond, to move trailing edge practice ever closer to leading edge practice.

Sam Stringfield, Reynolds' collaborator in the United States, explains how the approach is based on examples of organisations where failure must be eradicated at all costs – for example, air traffic control and the nuclear power industry. This requires a highly rational institution that aims at clearly specified, realisable outcomes and which, crucially, is data-rich. Stringfield suggests that the performance of such High Reliability Organisations provides – the metaphor is significant – 'a lens through which to revisit' schools' educational improvement efforts. Such organisations are required not to engage in trial and error improvement: they are expected to operate 'trials without errors' (Stringfield n.d.: 20–1), and they 'extend formal, logical decision analysis, based on standard operating procedures (SOPs), as far as extant knowledge allows' (ibid.: 23). When the first *Handbook of Research on Teaching* (Gage 1963) was published, a sufficient body of educational research did not exist to guide rationally the development of standard operating procedures for schooling. Since then the situation has changed considerably and 'the rudiments of a science of education' now exist (Stringfield n.d.: 24). This new confidence leads Reynolds to say: 'We believe we "know" [*sic*] that some practices actually work, yet this knowledge is not reliably spread' (*Times Educational Supplement*, 19 January 1996: 10). Failure-free schooling then, as their slogan has it, is now clear for take off.

If these developments seem surprising, it is worth saying that Reynolds is not voicing some heresy here but rather highlighting tendencies that are already very clear in (competence-based) teacher training, and in the concern for underachievement and school failure he is nicely responding to the political moment.

We want to acknowledge highly desirable elements in the approaches in question: the sharing of good practice in different schools; collegial decision making, close interdependence, and readiness to side-step hierarchies: relationships that are complex, coupled, and sometimes urgent; the very laudable aim of improving schooling for those who benefit least from the system. A number of questions arise at this point, however – concerning the logical relationship between failure and success (cf. examinations without failure grades), and concerning the aim of moving 'trailing edge practice ever closer to leading edge practice' and the levelling effect this would have. We shall not address these questions but will confine our discussion to the related issues of the technical conception of education and the removal of the risk of failure.

The objections to the Highly Reliable School are obvious, it might be said. Education just is not like air-traffic control. No doubt some would like schools to run with the efficiency and precision provided by air-traffic control or the nuclear power station but there are good reasons why they should not. Most obviously these industries deal with predominantly physical processes while education deals with human development. Physical processes are predictable in a way that human development is not. Nor is this simply a complicating factor regarding means. For the ends of the activity in each case are markedly different: those of the industries easily specifiable, those of education notoriously controversial, and this difficulty is bound up with the unpredictability and depth that there is to human life. So, if the objections are obvious to some, the intriguing thing is why they remain opaque or insignificant to others. To understand something of this we need to look carefully at the implications of taking teaching or the running of a school to be something technical, and we need to say something about the nature of technology.

Teaching as a technology

It is quite commonly held that technology is applied science. (Knowledge of physics is applied in the nuclear power station.) Teaching as technology might then be understood in terms of the kind of approach promoted by behavioural psychologists in the past. The theoretical insights of the research psychologists were applied in the practice of education. With the failure of this, and as the influence of behaviourist psychology waned, pretenders to scientific status came forward – for example, in 1980 David Pratt claimed the near-scientific status of curriculum theory and design (Pratt 1980). (Of course, physical science is the model here, not the broader conception implied by *Wissenschaft*.) The current conception of teaching, however, is not well understood in terms of the application of scientific theory to practice; rather it is characterised by its use of instruments of measurement. If instrumentation is foregrounded, it exposes a different relationship between technology and science. Rather than technology being applied science, and hence derivative of science, it comes to be seen as (in part, at least) what makes modern science possible. To a considerable extent the development of modern science has depended on the instruments at its disposal, and these have in turn been developed in the light of the kinds of research that they made possible. To some extent, as in medicine, for example, the development of the technology has driven what is done. Modern teaching as technology then may perhaps be understood not as the application of science, but rather as the utilisation of various instruments or quasi-instruments.

Just as scientific theories are taken to be 'objective' in the sense not only of being 'value-free' but also of relating to the world as something other, so too an instrument is neutral, it is assumed, and can be put to good or bad uses in operating on that world. If we consider the relationship between instruments and world in a little more detail, however, these conceptions of neutrality and 'objectivity' come to seem less clearly determined. Let us try to see if anything can be said, albeit in the broadest terms, about the effects of instrument use. Technical instruments, it might be argued, refine or extend our sensory perceptions. Sometimes the process of fining down can have explosive effects. To take examples given by Don Ihde (1979), the dentist's probe enables the dentist to register fine differences in the surface of the tooth of a kind that would not be evident to the fingers directly. It amplifies the sense of touch. The microscope and telescope enable us to see with clarity objects which otherwise would be invisible because of either their small size or their distance from us. But just as this amplification occurs, so too there is a reduction in other aspects of our normal perception of the world such that what might otherwise be available is concealed. The probe does not register the wetness of the tooth; the microscope and the telescope alike present things to view in a kind of flat, homogenised, and framed near-distance that is strangely insulated from us, both limiting in curiously identical ways the visual field. The amplification that is achieved, undoubtedly fruitful in so many ways, brings with it a reduction or concealment of certain aspects of our ordinary experience of the world.

(Of course, many instruments do not directly amplify a sensory perception but provide analogical information; this correlates nevertheless with such a narrowing – as, for example, in seismography. Virtual reality supplies a rich sensory field but through simulation, with interesting implications regarding risk.)

As the similarities between the telescope and the microscope show, there is a kind of levelling of perceptions as a result of the severance of the experience from its ordinary sensory accompaniments or background. The importance attached to the observation effectively downgrades or even erases the embeddedness that is a feature of our normal experience of the world. It prioritises what can be made explicit and in effect denies the ineffable. Most strikingly, as the senses of sight or hearing are amplified, the sense of touch is concealed, as for example where we might examine something too hot to touch. Moreover, where the sense of touch is itself amplified (the dentist's probe) it is one aspect of that sense (rough/smooth) that is enhanced at the almost total expense of others (wet/dry). Touch in its normal complexity perhaps shows better than other senses something of our complex locatedness in the world, and it relates most closely to our vulnerability.

Modern science has not developed solely as the disinterested contemplation of nature. Its development has been determined at least in part by its instruments. In some ways the process this generates is self-fulfilling and self-perpetuating. Instruments provide improved access to those aspects of the world that they were developed to explore and they point to ways in which their improvement or refinement could further amplify our perceptions. Their development is guided by a tacit assumption that the refinement of the instrument and the amplification it provides will progressively give access to the way things really are, and progressively offer completeness of view. This comes to be understood teleologically in terms of the kinds of things the instrument is designed to reveal. One reason that this concealment is difficult to recognise is that the instrument generates its own criteria for correctness. Truth becomes a matter of correctness. The microscope is designed to magnify and greater magnification constitutes greater accuracy. There is no doubt that judgements of correctness can be made in this way. The very justifiability of this, the confidence it gives us, stands in the way of recognition of the concealment that successful use of the instrument effects (cf. bewitchment by IQ testing and psychometry). But this brings with it a kind of myopia, as David Cooper puts it (Cooper 1995), or tunnel vision, one might say. Wittgenstein talks of the way thinking then runs on railway tracks. Technology uniquely has the power to displace other possible ways of revealing the world to us, and it fosters the illusion that things can be viewed in their totality. Technology overcomes the stubborn resistance of things to facilitate access into a world that, in losing its recalcitrance, loses its depth.

It is clear that the kind of technology involved in running schools or teaching does not involve the use of instruments associated with conventional technology. Rather it seems to involve the implement-ation of systematic procedures and the extensive use of information technology. Highly Reliable Schools crucially are data rich. These data relate primarily to the measurement of performance within the school, but they also facilitate extensive comparison between institutions and across the system. This technology should be considered then in relation to the technology of instruments con-sidered above.

The astonishing success of new technology in providing inform-ation storage and processing is one of its most striking features. This success gives further impetus to the desire for information and the structuring of organisations around this. If there is an instrument here it is the computer. But it is not clear that this stands to what is being thought of as the technological in the way that conventional instrumentation does. It does not provide an amplification of perception but digitalisation and coding. The user relates to the machine not as to a conventional instrument but as to a quasi-other in the manner of communication.

The advantages of this availability of information are obvious. It offers controllability and predictability and precision in a way admirably suited to accounting and planning practices. It makes possible the mapping and targeting of populations and client groups so that changing products, information and demands can fill the experience of people, at the same time instilling in them commensurate desires, knowledge and capacities. So in education there is the promise of a tidiness of fit between curriculum, the student and the larger world beyond the institution.

There is no doubt that the gathering and processing of data have a powerful appeal, not least to those who have an interest in the efficient and effective management of an institution. For teacher and student alike – not to mention the manager, the inspector and the potential employer – there is an attraction in forms of learning that divide what is to be studied into clear and readily identifiable units. We should recall also the appeal, associated with technology, of completeness and correctness. How readily this dovetails with the current concern for accountability.

On the strength of the successful use of new technology in so many respects, it is now widely held that businesses and schools should themselves become 'learning organisations'. Thus, Reynolds explains: 'The Highly Reliable School aims, simply, to transform education by generating schools which can "think", based on high quality performance data, and which can "act" upon a knowledge of what constitutes their own and the world's best practice' (*Times Educational Supplement*, 19 January 1996: 10). The scare quotes in this sentence – on 'think' and 'act' – have a double derivation perhaps, borrowed not directly from human life but from that quasi-other, the thinking machine. It is artificial intelligence that comes to shape the social space of the institution and to define what it is for a person to think and act. Reynolds' scare-quotes concerning his own usage suggest that something is adrift here.

The amplifying effects of this technological approach to education have as their correlate the concealment of something of the embeddedness in the world of manager, teacher embeddedness-in-the-world and learner. In the technology of air traffic control or nuclear power stations this is readily justifiable, it might be said, in terms of the clear purpose of the activities. In education in contrast the activity is itself constitutive of the end, and ends are not so clearly defined. In fact, in general education, at least, they depend on a recognition, on the part of teacher and learner, of the multi-faceted involvements of that embeddedness-in-the-world. Concealing this is then deeply at odds with education.

With the concealing that this new technology effects there may also be deeper metaphysical shifts. As Albert Borgmann has put it:

> Of course, even in a nineteenth-century railroad company there were plans, maps, schedules, bills, and books that captured and pictured the past and present of the organisation. Without such texts, as it were, the railroad would have been mired in collisions and confusions. Electronic texts, however, contain vastly more information. And while traditional texts provide coarse-grained snapshots, electronic texts can provide a densely structured moving image of a corporation, an image, moreover, that can be stopped, accelerated, magnified, reduced, and approached from different angles at will.

> The electronic text of a business enterprise is so rich as to constitute a surrogate reality of the operation, and not merely a pale and imperfect copy of the real thing but a counterpart that exceeds its original in perspicuity and accessibility. Finally the electronic text is even more than a brilliant image or model of reality; it is a superior reality. For to manipulate the electronic model is to manipulate the underlying reality. The electronic brain directs the mechanical body of the entire operation.
>
> (Borgmann 1992: 68)

The educational manager sits in his office and devises his streamlined plan. The plan is circulated (for others to implement). His job is done. The 'surrogate reality' hints at an ideal realm of forms of which the institution is but a shadow, and it may partially explain what seems to be a fetishism with data: data assume an importance that displaces any deeper sense of what the given might mean. Unlike the amplified perception of an aspect of the real offered by a conventional instrument, the surrogate of the formal system entices us away from the stubborn messiness of everyday life.

Of course, much of what has been said applies generally to technicist approaches to education. The distinctive thing about Highly Reliable Schools is the way they extend control through information to the eradication of failure. It is this that now needs to be questioned. Yet, what objection can there be to removing risk – in education any more than in air-traffic control? It would take a brave politician to advocate the provision of less information or less accountability, and a plain crazy one, we might imagine, to advocate failure. So where do we go from here?

It is perhaps a paradox that information technology thrives on occasions of crisis and change: so often it seems to be self-evident that more information is needed if there is to be the responsiveness that a rapidly changing world requires. Information technology provides a kind of security by helping us to manage risk: it helps air traffic control to make air travel safe. The risk society is precisely one where danger is taken as something to be managed. Increasing strains on the education system must prompt us to think that more information is precisely what education needs. How hard it is to resist the good sense of this.

But in education it is not clear that this lessening of risk is achieved without cost. Does it not seem that the risk that is faced and the effort expended alter the character of what is learned? Might someone's PhD come too easily perhaps? And this indicates something about teaching also. It might perhaps point to a conception of teaching more closely allied to another kind of *techne* – not technology but art. But we can be too hasty here. Reynolds dispenses with this possibility without any nonsense: 'there is a particularly British view that teaching is an "art", not a science, and therefore it is personal factors and qualities, often idiosyncratic and difficult to judge, which are the key factors' (Reynolds 1997b: 107). And he laments the general failure of teachers to embrace new technologies of practice even though virtually all have been exposed to school effectiveness research at some stage in their careers. To remedy this situation, what may be needed, it is suggested, is evolution of school effectiveness into a craft-based activity disseminated through the accounts and the work of 'exemplary practitioners'. Thus, Chinese cookery has become popular here as a result of the example set by Chinese migrants. But then the 'technology' of teaching starts to sound not unlike whatever it is you pick up by sitting next to Nelly, who is, of course, an exemplary teacher.

Writing about the tensions between technology and art, Anthony O'Hear quotes Ruskin's view that 'it is only for God to create without toil; that which man can create without toil is worthless' (O'Hear 1995: 156). It is precisely in its imperfection, in its unfinishedness, that great art allows for creativity and expressive lapse. Good teaching and good learning are imperfect, incomplete and prone to lapses, and in these respects they live with risk and failure. The multiple ways of revealing, which they share with the work of art, are essential to any richer conception of education. But there are limits to the analogy here. Ultimately, while teaching is not technology, neither is it art. There is nothing in teaching that corresponds with the productive aspect of art. It is understood better in terms of practical reason.

It is fashionable in some quarters to advocate a revival of Socratic method, conceiving of this as a systematic technique. But it is not clear that this is true to Socrates' goading of the learner: Socrates is the bee, gadfly, snake and sting-ray – ambivalent creatures whose effects can be to anaesthetise and to vivify, suggestive of the closeness of a kind of danger. While the technological approach would muffle the sense of crisis, it is the critical edge in Socrates' teaching and learning that seems most essential.

What is at issue here then clearly goes well beyond what some may imagine to be purely methodological questions. Kierkegaard draws attention to the way in which the whole apparatus of planning and control is at odds with the kind of ethical depth with which our lives otherwise confront us. In a passage oddly appropriate to the present discussion, he attacks the preoccupation with outcomes. Cut off from the convulsions of existence, 'lecturers', as he calls them, have lost sight altogether of the fact that

> ever since the Creation it has been accepted practice for the outcome to come last, and that if one is really to learn something from the great it is precisely the beginning one must attend to. If anyone on the verge of action should judge himself according to the outcome, he would never begin. Even though the result may gladden the whole world, that cannot help the hero; for he knows the result only when the whole thing is over, and that is not how he becomes a hero, but by virtue of the fact that he began.
>
> (Kierkegaard 1985: 91–2)

In contrast to the hero our common inclination is to shy away from 'the fear, the distress, the paradox' and to flirt aesthetically with the outcome, imagining that by so doing we are therefore improved.

Just as Kierkegaard sardonically exposes the rift between these ways of thinking, so Heidegger – in more offensively portentous terms perhaps – spells out the metaphysical background: he explicitly links the foundationalist demand for security (associated especially with Leibnitz) and the suppression of risk with the reduction of language to an instrument of information:

> 'Information' at one and the same time means the appraisal that as quickly, comprehensively, unequivocally, and profitably as possible acquaints contemporary humanity with the securing of its necessities, its requirements and their satisfaction. Accordingly the representation of human language as an instrument of information increasingly gains the upper hand. For the determination of language as information first of all creates sufficient grounds [*zureichenden Grund*] for the construction of thinking machines and for the building of frameworks for large calculations. Yet while information in-forms, that is apprises, it at the same time forms, that means, arranges and sets straight. As an appraisal, information is also the arrangement that places all objects and stuffs in a form for humans that suffices to securely establish human domination over the whole earth and even over what lies beyond this planet.
>
> (Heidegger 1991: 124)

Derrida's quip on this: 'Information ensures the insurance of calculation and the calculation of insurance' (Derrida 1983: 14).

And in a mischievous parenthesis Heidegger reminds us that Leibnitz, the object of this attack, was also the father of 'life insurance'! If Heidegger is right, there is an essential relation between our two concerns – between the technological conception of education and the idea of education without risks. The Highly Reliable School is a logical extension of the concern with school effectiveness – a symptomatic development, one might say, a working through of its pathology. We need to be goaded to prevent us subsiding into a way of thinking that 'carries an air of harmlessness and ease, which causes us to pass lightly over what really deserves to be questioned' (Heidegger 1968: 154). Is it not significant that in Heidegger's most widely known discussion of these themes, in 'The Question Concerning Technology' (1977), two key examples are the technology of nuclear power and what is in effect air traffic control? Tranquillised acceptance of the technological approach is the real danger zone, the threat a kind of nihilism.

FRAGMENT I

The solution – whatever the problem – of course lies in managing education effectively. Or at least reciting 'effectiveness' as a mantra.

The National Standards for Headteachers can be read on the Teacher Training Agency's website (http://www.teach-tta.gov.uk/ nshead.htm). This document uses the word 'effective' or its cognates (effectiveness, effectively) 45 times out of a total of 3,319 words (four more occurrences than of 'headteacher(s)'); 'effective(ly)' is conjoined with 'efficient(ly)' seven times, to ensure that the techo-rational message is – effectively – conveyed. Under 'communication skills', for example (p. 8):

Headteachers should be able to:

(i)   communicate effectively orally and in writing to a range of audiences
(ii)   negotiate and consult effectively
(iii) manage good communication systems
(iv)   chair meetings effectively
(v)   develop, maintain and use an effective network of contacts.

What an image of clean-limbed, mobile-phoned, executive-brief-cased energy these multiple effectivenesses convey! We shall be in no doubt when such headteachers have communicated with us: their consultations will be minuted, the meetings which they chair brisk and quite possibly bracing. Shall we feel that we have been *heard*? No matter, for we may aspire to join their network of contacts.

But is not effectiveness our latest expression of the will to power? Is the effective manager (of schools, of anything) not the new *Übermensch*, the superior being who has risen above the herd? Effectiveness is rather the most nihilistic value 'lording it under the holiest name'. The highest kind of person, the master or aristocrat in Nietzschean terms, proposes his own ends and affirms his own values. The votaries of the cult of effectiveness, by contrast, are experts only in means (if, of course, they are even that at all). Their ends and values are laid down for them. They need no convincing of the need for change: the temple of Effectiveness has an impressive side-chapel dedicated to the Management of Change.

They would no sooner take part in a dispute on the objectives of education than they would seriously question the latest taxonomy of management styles, or express reservations about Kolb's Learning Cycle.

David Reynolds (n.d.), in the course of recommending an explicitly technicist model of teaching, complains that in the world of education 'High status . . . goes . . . to those who celebrate a values debate and discuss the "ends" of education'. A High Priest of Effectiveness fulminating against the Old Religion.

'The highest values have devalued themselves. There is no goal. There is no answer to the question, "why?" ', Nietzsche, *WP*: 2

Chapter 2

Life skills, teaching skills

> I can foresee a day when education will routinely include inculcating essential human competencies such as self-awareness, self-control, and empathy . . .
>
> Daniel Goleman, *Emotional Intelligence*, 1996: xiv

In this chapter we discuss something which is extremely common in our contemporary world but generally goes unremarked. That is the tendency to call all kinds of human abilities, qualities and capacities 'skills' or 'competencies'. The reader who has read the kind of documents and reports that now make up so much of our literature on education is likely to have come across listening, leadership, parenting, management and assertiveness skills and many others. Of course we do not claim that people cannot become better listeners or better parents. But is this a matter of acquiring *skills*? Readers who do not see that this is problematic might like to consider the kind of relationship they have with their own children. If the relationship is good, is that most significantly to be understood in terms of their possession of certain skills, techniques which they practise upon the children? Perhaps, it will be said, too much weight should not be placed upon the notion of skills here: it simply provides us with a convenient noun for when we are talking about things we can be better or worse at and learn to improve in. We, as will become clear, do not think skills-talk should get off so lightly. We think that calling all manner of qualities 'skills' and 'competencies', and casting the work of teachers, university lecturers and others as primarily the exercise of skills, gets something very badly wrong and is a key sign of the nihilism of our age, of a culture that has lost its sense of value.

Aristotle on anger

Daniel Goleman's influential book *Emotional Intelligence* (1996) promises to release us from too narrow a view of human intelligence and in turn too limited a view of education. He begins with what he calls Aristotle's challenge. In the *Nicomachean Ethics* Aristotle wrote, according to Goleman, that while it is easy enough to become angry, it is not easy to be angry 'with the right person, to the right degree, at the right time, for the right purpose, and in the right way'. This precise wording does not appear in the *Nicomachean Ethics*: we return to this below. As the word 'right' implies, Aristotle is here interested in the ethical dimension of anger, as of the other passions. Some things *ought* to make us angry (injustice, cruelty and deceit, for instance). Other things ought not: we do not praise the man – to put it in Aristotle's kind of language – who gets angry with a child for not knowing the answer which he has never been taught. Goleman's interest is different. Education, he claims, has focused too exclusively on cognition, on knowledge and the kind of intelligence that can be measured by IQ tests. The problems of our individual and collective lives stem rather from our emotions – emotions mishandled and misunderstood – than from purely intellectual ignorance or error. Education should therefore attend to the development of the emotions as much as to any other aspect of learning.

When the matter is put like this we can agree with Goleman. Such a shift of emphasis, properly conceived and executed, seems to offer much to a world of personal conflict and failed relationships. But the crucial point here is that things must be properly conceived if they are not to unravel from the very start. Consider again the quotation that prefixes this chapter, with its talk of 'essential human competencies such as self-awareness, self-control, and empathy'. Elsewhere (p. 269) Goleman writes that Aristotle's concern is with 'emotional skilfulness'. It is necessary to pause, in our enthusiasm for fostering healthy emotional development, and consider how odd it is to talk of emotional skills and competencies. In the sequel, *Working with Emotional Intelligence*, there are some interesting shifts between these and other terms. Goleman begins by talking of a new focus on 'personal qualities, such as initiative and empathy, adaptability and persuasiveness' (p. 3). On the next page he uses *capabilities, abilities, qualities* and *capacities* as if they were interchangeable, and writes that they have been 'talked about loosely for decades under a variety of names, from "character" and "personality" to "soft skills" and "competence"', claiming that 'there is at last a more precise understanding of these human talents, and a new name for them: emotional intelligence'.

Now personal qualities are such things as a disposition to care for other people. A caring person is generally caring: when we know he is caring then we know something about *him*. To have caring skills, or competencies, is rather different. They might be a matter of knowing, for example, that the elderly can easily get confused if their routine is disturbed, and feel the cold more than younger people do. If you have these things as skills then you have the ability, if you so wish, to misuse them as well as to use them well. You will know better than most how to induce confusion or pneumonia in an old person. The skilful doctor, as Plato observed and recent grisly events in Greater Manchester have confirmed, makes an unusually skilful poisoner. But if you are a caring person – if this is one of the characteristics of your personality – you will abhor the misuse of those skills through which your personality expresses itself.

Conversely, something like persuasiveness, if that is understood as a good thing to have, is not a personal quality. Imagine someone who, rather than being good at persuading work colleagues to reach consensus and squabbling children to desist, was just generally persuasive: so that you found yourself agreeing with him when he argued that *Harry Potter* was the literary event of the year, and agreeing with him just as much when he changed his mind and argued for Seamus Heaney's translation of *Beowulf*. Such a person does not have a fine personal quality, on a par with empathy: he is plausible, and you distrust him. He can make black seem white and 'the unjust case appear just' and vice-versa, as Socrates (or Plato) accused the sophists. Persuasiveness is a skill or set of techniques. On its own it is morally neutral: it can be used for good or ill.

To take one last example from Goleman, self-knowledge, or self-awareness as he calls it, is the last thing in the world that could properly be called a competence. For competencies are things we choose to operate, or not; yet with self-awareness it is precisely the quality of our choosing – amongst other, sometimes deeper, things – that is in question. A person who lacks self-awareness believes she is autonomous and chooses for herself (a make of car or a particular career, for instance), but it may seem clear to others that she is the victim of clever advertising or parental expectation. If only she *was* self-aware she would see through these things. You cannot choose to be self-aware today (scrutinising your motives, noting the possible effects of stress on your powers of judgement, carefully identifying your feelings and their sources) and tomorrow decide to take the day off from the whole demanding business ('This Thursday I'm not going to think about what I'm doing and why: if I feel like shouting at my secretary and blaming everything on my husband then I shall just go ahead and do so'). For who is the 'you' that does the choosing?

For Aristotle, the important thing is not to 'turn on' the right kind of anger at the right time at the right person, like a schoolteacher who calculates that a show of indignation at a particular pupil's behaviour will impress the rest of the class. His challenge is not 'to manage our emotional life with intelligence' (Goleman 1996: xii) as if our emotions were a portfolio of stocks and shares but to understand and pursue 'the good for man', a distinctively ethical project which requires a careful examination of the emotions but cannot be reduced to deploying or expressing our emotions in one way or another. 'Emotional intelligence' is not just a modern way of talking about morality, as Goleman seems to think, especially where it involves collapsing those distinctions between character (what a person is) and competence or skill (what a person has or can do) that enable us to mark out the real or true from what is practised – even if from the best of motives – as a matter of policy, artfulness or deceit.

When our personal qualities, as opposed to our skills, are engaged in what we do then there is a commitment and degree of risk, which is perhaps another reason why some people prefer to talk of skills. When a teacher shows that the subject she is teaching, or the novel or the poem, really means something to her (and is not just one more thing about which she manages to muster professional enthusiasm) then she stands to be more hurt than usual by her pupils' lack of interest or scepticism. It is safer, of course, to shelter behind the deployment of skills: they can be held at arm's length, so to speak, and their owner is not so damaged by any inadequacies revealed in them as he is if his personal qualities seem to be wanting. (Consider whether it makes sense to talk of 'sincerity skills'.) If it is John's parenting skills – to revert to an example from the beginning of the chapter – that are at fault then perhaps it is not his fault: he never had the opportunity to acquire them, and anyway he can go on a course to brush them up. But what if – for whatever reason – John has never been able to build a proper relationship with his son or daughter? How is that different from lacking certain skills, and will it be so easy to put right?

If relating to other people, or doing our work, is essentially a matter of exercising skills and competencies, then there is no deeper engagement, no personal commitment: no vital and nourishing immersion. Goleman himself cites Csikszentmihalyi's work on 'flow', the kind of sublime performance in which 'the emotions are not just contained and channeled, but positive, energised, and aligned with the task at hand . . . the hallmark of flow is a feeling of spontaneous joy, even rapture . . . it is a state in which people become utterly absorbed in what they are doing, paying undivided attention to the task, their awareness merged with their actions' (pp. 90–1). It is a state of self-forgetful attunement. One of the areas where we can attain this state, of course, is the domain of genuine craft skills: carpentry, home decorating, gardening, cooking (it must say something about us – British at least – that so many television programmes are now devoted to the last three: *DIY SOS*, *Ground Force*, Delia Smith and the rest). But these are not the domains which are subjected to objectionable skills-talk. The question is what happens to being a parent when we are persuaded to think of it in terms of the exercise of skills rather than the sensitivity and spontaneity of a human relationship; what happens to being a teacher when the possibilities of 'flow' are cut off by the requirement that we see teaching as a collection of skills which we choose from our repertoire and operate.

A Grecian urn

In Chapter 8 of Antonia Byatt's novel, *The Virgin in the Garden* (1978), a young teacher, Stephanie, sits in 'a chill brown classroom, whitened over with chalk dust', and teaches Keats' *Ode on a Grecian Urn* to a group of girls.

> Stephanie's idea of good teaching was simple and limited: it was the induced, shared, contemplation of a work, an object, an artefact. It was not the encouragement of self-expression, self-analysis, or what were to be called interpersonal relationships. Indeed, she saw a good reading of the *Ode on a Grecian Urn* as a welcome chance to avoid these activities . . .

She tries to clear her mind of the 'clutter of mnemonics', the jumble of analytic devices to which the academic intelligence threatens to reduce the poem and which come to represent the poem when she does not have her attention concentrated on it:

> a sense of the movement of the rhythm of the language which was biological, not verbal or visual . . . some words, the very abstract ones, form, thought, eternity, beauty, truth, the very concrete ones, unheard, sweeter, green, marble, warm, cold, desolate. A run of grammatical and punctuational pointers: the lift of frozen unanswered questions in the first stanza, the apparently undisciplined rush of repeated epithets in the third. Visual images, neither seen, in the mind's eye, nor unseen. White forms of arrested movement under dark formal boughs.

She reads the poem out twice, quietly and with as little expression as possible.

The ideal was to come to it with a mind momentarily open and empty, as though for the first time. They must all hear the words equally, not pounce, or tear, or manipulate. She asked them chilly, 'Well?' prolonging the difficult moment when they must just stare, finding speech difficult and judgement unavoidable.

Her pupils are to clear their minds. They must not strain to please teacher, or launch into enthusiastic reminiscence of a holiday in Greece. Here is a kind of death: the antique funerary urn, the verses by the doomed or dying young poet, the cold, brown, dusty classroom. In Keats's poem the urn or classical vase is addressed as 'bride of quietness', 'foster-child of silence and slow time'. Whatever the vase tells us it is not something that can be expressed explicitly. 'What the poem is trying to say is . . .' – that formulation, which Stephanie's pupils will no doubt offer her if they are allowed to (with knowledgable talk of 'hidden meanings'), gets things terribly wrong, as if there was a message here which the poet has somehow obscured but we modern readers could confidently decode and spell out. This is why the pupils are not to 'pounce, or tear, or manipulate'. They must bring a different and unaccustomed quality of attention to bear. They must *listen*, but of course this is not to deploy listening skills, skills that they already possess. The poem requires a different kind of listening which it teaches us and thus makes possible: 'Heard melodies are sweet, but those unheard/Are sweeter . . .'. The poem speaks 'Not to the sensual ear' but 'to the spirit'.

The vase defies our analytical understanding. There is no answer to those questions in the first stanza: 'What men or gods are these? What maidens loth?/What mad pursuit? What struggle to escape? . . .' Cause and effect are not to be looked for here. We shall not come to understand when we see that first this happens, then that. In the second stanza the fact that the action depicted on the vase will never move to a resolution (there will, we might say, be no *outcomes*) is no reason for regret. The lover will never win his girl '– yet, do not grieve;/. . . For ever wilt thou love, and she be fair!' Stanza three suggests this perspective depends on the jaundiced eye of the dying poet, romanticising the idea of deferral, with 'burning forehead, and a parching tongue'. The next stanza depicts the sacrifice of a heifer and a town 'desolate' with its streets silent; no-one, declares the poem, will ever return to tell us why this is so. From quietness we have moved to the unheard and on to silence, both that of the deserted town and of the vase itself. This silence 'dost tease us out of thought/As doth eternity'. Truth is not to be spelled out, but lies elsewhere: in art, in beauty, in the vitalism that emerges even or especially when life in its most Dionysiac forms (flowery tales, pipes and timbrels, wild ecstasy) is offered and denied.

Of course not all teaching is like the teaching of a poem. Indeed the second sentence of Byatt's chapter reminds us that 'Good teaching is a mystery and takes many forms'. If it is a mystery then we shall pass over it in silence, for a while.

The bed of Odysseus

In the *Odyssey*, the Greek epic poet Homer presents a profound and well worked-out philosophy of the nature of skills and their place in a well-ordered human life. Indeed perhaps the *Odyssey* is above all a reflective treatment of the skills and capacities through which individuals may bring order and harmony to their world. Odysseus is announced in the most emphatic word of the first line as *polutropos*, 'the man of many ways'; elsewhere he is *polumechanos*, 'the man of many devices'. He is, in short, consummately skilled, a by-word for skill and cunning. (He was sometimes credited with the invention of the wooden horse, the device through which the Greeks gained entry into Troy.) The epic is full of descriptions of skilled activities such as weaving and boat-building, as we shall see, and of peoples such as the Cyclopes at one extreme and the Phaeacians at the other who exemplify the possession of certain kinds of skill or capacity and the lack of others. And it is through his contact with them that Odysseus refines his own understanding of what would now no doubt be called the skills of being civilised: 'he saw the cities of many men and knew their minds'.[1]

In the world of Homer there is no shortage of opportunity to exercise what we shall call genuine or craft skills, and our judgement of individuals and whole societies is formed in large part through seeing what skills they have and how they exercise them. Our first direct sight of skilful Odysseus is in Book 5 weeping on Calypso's beach, and our sense of his desolation is increased by the rich description immediately before of Calypso's island, Ogygia, and the order she has brought to it, and of the goddess herself weaving and singing, two of the *Odyssey*'s pre-eminently skilful activities. After the god Hermes intervenes to tell Calypso she must let Odysseus go, our sense that he is being restored to life and to the world after his seven years hidden away on Ogygia is conveyed by the detailed description of him building a boat:

He threw down twenty [trees] in all, and trimmed them well
with his bronze axe, / and planed them expertly, and trued
them straight to a chalkline . . .

(Book 5, ll. 244–5)

These words will be significantly echoed later as Odysseus describes
how he constructed the bed in his palace in Ithaca. Odysseus is a
craftsman and a man of skills, and for him to recover the use of
those skills is to be restored to life. It is sometimes said, and was
implied earlier in our discussion, that calling abilities or qualities
'skills' is a way of denying that they say anything very important
about us. That this is not true in the case of Odysseus is due partly
to the richness of his skills – these are true craft skills, with no
division of labour even, for Odysseus makes the entire boat – and
partly to what he uses the skills to do. Far from disowning
responsibility or avoiding risk he uses his skills to embark on the
sea, the very emblem of risk and uncertainty.

Here perhaps is the first thing that Homer has to teach us about
skills. Where everything is called a skill it is harder to pick out and
recognise the value of true, traditional or craft skills: carpentry, say,
or cooking. Such skills, quite apart from their obvious utility value,
can bring absorption, peace and fulfilment. Working with what is
wholly *other*, which has a distinctive nature of its own and cannot be
forced to comply with our desires and fantasies – the wood that will
split if worked the wrong way, the pastry that will fall apart without
careful handling – gives us a kind of respite from the insistent
demands of our own egos. When we do work that demands craft
skills we cannot wholly impose ourselves on the world of things, yet
as we acquire those skills the gulf between us and the external
world, which often makes us feel clumsy and alienated, diminishes
until we can, as we say, 'put something of ourselves' into what we
do. (Recall the 'flow' that we talked of above.) Thus we learn a
proper relationship to the world, one in which we are neither so
distanced from it that we can only submit to its iron laws nor so at
one with it that, like magicians, like Circe perhaps, we can make the
world respond to our will. This is the value of craft skills: they can
help us find and hold our place as human beings, they can locate us
properly with regard to the world around us.

Before he reached Calypso's island, Odysseus and the reader had
been offered another instructive lesson on the nature of skills. The
Cyclops Polyphemus is not without skill: he is a dairy-farmer,
herding sheep and goats, penning and separating them carefully,
and making cheese. But all this goes on, Homer tells us, on an
island where all kinds of crops grow abundantly without the effort

of agriculture, and across the bay lies another island of still greater fertility and spontaneity in producing fruit and vegetables. Polyphemus' skill is spectacularly misplaced. It is the product of a kind of myopic, stubborn determination to do one thing right at the expense of ignoring the other possibilities around.[2] Circe too, for all her splendid palace with hot baths and silver-studded chairs with footstools, possesses only a limited perspective. Discovering that this is the Odysseus fated to come to her island and be invulnerable to her drugs she can only think of immediately trying to seduce him. Later she expects him to dine without it having crossed her mind that the absence of his companions, turned to swine by her spells, may have an adverse effect on his appetite. We might say she lacks social skills, if we have fallen into the current jargon, but this would miss the point in an important way. She has only skills – skills developed to their utmost in the form of magic – and without the accompaniment of appropriate sensitivity and human sympathy skills are seen to be crude instruments for achieving crude purposes.

It is above all Scheria, the land of the Phaeacians, that gives Odysseus and us the fullest opportunity to reflect on both the potentials and the limitations of human skills. This is a culture of some tact and delicacy, as we see right at the beginning when the princess Nausicaa and her father discuss whether she may have the wagon to take the dirty clothes down to the river to wash. Nausicaa is too sophisticated to mention that she has thoughts of marriage at the back of her mind, and her father is too discrete to let her realise he has guessed her secret. So too Queen Arete is more urbane than to press her question of where Odysseus – newly shipwrecked and stripped naked by the elements – acquired the clothes he is wearing, clothes which she herself made, and of course the ones which Nausicaa had taken to wash.

On his arrival at the royal palace Odysseus notes its marvels and ponders, as well he may. There are bronze walls, with a cobalt frieze, golden doors, silver pillars, extraordinary automatic watchdogs made of gold and silver with an everlasting mechanism (or more literally, if you prefer, immortal dogs made by Hephaestus, 'and all their days they are ageless'). The *pièce de resistance* is the lighting system, an art deco arrangement consisting of 'young men fashioned all of gold and in their hands holding/flaring torches' (8, 100–1). This is to say nothing of the gardens, in which early- and late-ripening varieties of everything from grapes to cabbages are set out side by side so that there is a constant abundance of everything. It is commonly noted that this is all a sign of a supremely well-ordered community, from which Odysseus may learn the last lessons he has to learn before he can return to Ithaca and restore order to his own community. Thus Norman Austin (1975: 156) comments that the Phaeacian landscape and their palace decor 'mirror the complexity of their social economy . . . [they] can work in any material – stone, metals, or wood – can build ships and palaces, carve statues, sail the seas, turn night to day. They are supreme artisans. The polychromatic, polymorphous scene in Alkinoos' palace reveals an organically functioning community, the first *polis* Odysseus has seen since leaving Troy'.

A modern sensibility may well be attracted by a society which, as Alkinoos tells Odysseus, loves feasting, dancing, the lyre, changes of clothing, hot baths and bed (8, 249f.). But these Phaeacians should make us uneasy. The palace is overdone, the Phaeacians self-indulgent in their exercise of skills. This society is tranquillised, docile, tame. (It is certainly incestuous: Alkinoos has married his niece.) They take pleasure and pride in their skill in sailing, to the point of giving conveyance to all and sundry despite the prophecy that the sea-god, Poseidon, will one day drop a mountain on their city in resentment. They disdain to use their skills in utilitarian ways: the worst thing Euryalos can say when trying to goad Odysseus into joining in the footraces and the wrestling is to accuse him of being a merchant seaman, one 'careful of his cargo' (8, 159f.). And there is something tiresome in the Phaeacian insistence that Odysseus, whom they know to be suffering from exposure and exhaustion, should test his athletic skills against theirs.

Is this a culture very like ours is in danger of becoming, one where skills are raised to pride of place with too little regard for the values that should direct them, where facility with what should be *means* has been elevated to the status of an end in itself? It is striking that when Odysseus takes up the athletic challenge he finds it necessary to remark on the impropriety of competing with one's host. What is also striking is the story that the bard, Demodocus, sings. It is the story of Ares and Aphrodite, caught in adultery by the great craftsman god, Hephaestus, and pinned down in the net he made so that all the other gods could laugh at them in their embarrassment. Of course this prefigures the possibilities that Odysseus must face in Ithaca, where he, another great craftsman, must test the loyalty of his wife. This is the dramatic effect of the story at this point in the *Odyssey*. But we might also note that the Phaeacians admire a story in which the ethical issue of Aphrodite's adultery is met with a purely technical solution, a mechanical contrivance. Away from the rituals and subtleties of the palace, when the Phaeacian men can let their hair down after an afternoon's sport what they really like is a ribald story with a technical twist (something like science fiction with a dash of pornography, perhaps). Their education – their education for citizenship, we might say – and their skills training have between them not touched their moral sensibility. Although Odysseus can learn much from the Phaeacians they are surely not meant as an unqualified model. Skills purely for skills' sake are a sign of moral immaturity; worse, they get in the way of growing up morally at all. We have said that what are commonly called skills are not activities to which we give anything of *ourselves*. It is notable that Odysseus's odyssey takes him from coping with his trials through brute force and cunning to the exercise of subtler qualities where he must call on everything he is in order to prevail. Impressive though his defeat of the Cyclops is, in its grisly way,[3] there is something of the test for becoming an army officer about it: three poles, a rope and a mallet to make a bridge with and get your men across. Or perhaps the Boy Scouts are a better parallel, particularly in view of the gratuitous curiosity that landed Odysseus in the scrape in the first place and the triumphant taunting of Polyphemus with which the chapter ends. Brute force alone, however, cannot overcome Circe, and some see in that episode and especially in the turning of men into pigs the acknowledgement of humankind's propensity to brutishness that Odysseus must make if he is to grow from a man of skills and tricks into a man of wisdom. Whether this is so or not, the journey to Hades, the Underworld, must surely be seen as in some sense emblematic of an inner journey to self-knowledge. And self-knowledge is the last thing in the world that can sensibly be called a skill, as we pointed out above.

What gets Odysseus home after his visit to the Underworld is less strength, skills or cunning than memory. This sounds strange, but it is so. He explicitly attributes his survival, as he begins to tell his tale to the Phaeacians, to recollection: 'nothing is sweeter in the end than country and parents' (9, 34–5). He has the capacity to be motivated by memory without forgetting (the temptation offered by the Lotus eaters) or relapsing into mere reminiscence (only Odysseus could listen to the Sirens' song of the past without being seduced by it). He turns down Calypso's offer of immortality, which is conditional on forgetting his home (1, 57). The insight that important forms of learning may be more like remembering than acquiring – 'taking on board' as we now say in tribute to the superficiality of the process – and particularly than acquiring *skills*, is of course developed in Plato in the doctrine of *anamnesis*. What Homer and Plato both understood is that because skills relate to means whose ends are predetermined there is something limited and limiting about a conception of learning that makes it essentially a matter of skills acquisition.

One climax of the *Odyssey* is of course Odysseus's killing of the suitors who had coveted his wife and kingdom, but if we see the *Odyssey* as more than a story of revenge and much more than a loose bundle of sagas, if it is the story of Odysseus's *learning*, and the place of skills in his journey towards a kind of wisdom, then another and more satisfying, more moving climax is his recognition by Penelope. For her the question is: is this the same Odysseus that left home all those years ago? Has he been brutalised by war and wandering to the point where he is no longer relevantly the same person? In a crude sense of course this is him, he is not an impostor. The scar Eurykleia, his old nurse, discovers when she is washing his feet guarantees that. But this is not quite what Penelope and the reader want to know. What, then, persuades Penelope that this is Odysseus restored to her, whole and sound? Which of the many secret signs known only to the two of them is powerful enough to act as a guarantee? 'Make me up a bed out here,' Odysseus tells Eurykleia, 'since my wife will not acknowledge me.' 'Yes,' says Penelope, 'make up a bed for him outside our bedroom, using the very bed that he made himself.' Odysseus expostulates: the bed cannot be moved. He fashioned it around a growing olive tree. In the following lines he describes in detail how he made the bed:

> There was the bole of an olive tree with long leaves growing/ strongly in the courtyard, and it was thick, like a column./I laid down my chamber around this, and built it, until I/ finished it, with close-set stones, and roofed it well over . . ./ Then I cut away the foliage of the long-leaved olive,/and trimmed the trunk from the roots up, planing it with a brazen/adze, well and expertly, and trued it straight to a chalkline,/making a bed post of it, and bored all holes with an auger/. . .
>
> (Book 23, ll. 190ff.)

On one level of course Odysseus simply reveals that he knows the secret of the bed and is therefore who he claims to be, that is, no other person. But on another level he reveals himself in this marvellous description to be still the impassioned craftsman who made the bed all those years ago: whose skill is rooted in home and marriage as the bed which is their symbol is rooted through the flourishing olive tree, the tree of Athene, goddess of wisdom; the bed which Odysseus inlaid with gold, silver and ivory, working it intricately – *daidallōn, the* word for craftsmanship, the skill of Daedalus. Only now can Penelope see that this is the true Odysseus, his humanity guaranteed by his continuing pride in exercising skill wisely in the service of home and family, ends which are worth serving.

This climax to the epic develops entirely as it should. It is not a botched job on the part of a committee of bards who failed to see that Book 23 preserves elements of two incompatible endings, one where Odysseus is recognised by his scar and one where he is recognised by the device of the bed. The two recognitions are of a different order, and the one is not enough to do the job of the other. Such irony that this epic about the recovery of moral integrity and of real values should be thought to have its own integrity fractured in this of all ways. Perhaps it is a natural outcome of seeing Homer as merely the name for a tradition of *skilled* story-tellers, juggling their epithets to make up the hexameter and moving elements of the tale around with the oral equivalent of cut-and-paste. If we thought of the *Odyssey* as merely the product of such skills, how could we ever understand that it is, amongst other things, a brilliant, sustained examination of the place of skill in a well-ordered life?

Conclusion: learning and teaching

If we reduce all human qualities and capacities to a matter of skills and competencies, then, we shall be slow to recognise the profound limitations in our current notions of teaching and learning, and of education in particular. In particular, because characteristically we know what counts as a skill in advance, learning skills is inimical to the richer forms of learning which involve personal development and creative variation. The point is well made by Wright Mills in *The Sociological Imagination* (1970: 232–3):

> The sociological imagination . . . in considerable part consists of the capacity to shift from one perspective to another, and in the process to build up an adequate view of a total society and of its components. It is this imagination, of course, that sets off the social scientist from the mere technician. Adequate technicians can be trained in a few years. The sociological imagination can also be cultivated; certainly it seldom occurs without a great deal of often routine work. Yet there is an unexpected quality about it, perhaps because its essence is the combination of ideas that no one expected were combinable – say, a mess of ideas from German philosophy and British economics. There is a playful-ness of mind back of such combining as well as a truly fierce drive to make sense of the world, which the technician as such usually lacks. Perhaps he is too well trained, too precisely trained. Since one can be trained only in what is already known, training sometimes incapacitates one from learning new ways; it makes one rebel against what is bound to be at first loose and even

sloppy. But you must cling to such vague images and notions, if they are yours, and you must work them out. For it is in such forms that original ideas, if any, almost always first appear.

The *mystery* of good teaching is disturbing, however. Whatever are we to do if we cannot articulate the skills of teaching, its competencies and sub-competencies? We shall have the greatest difficulty, shan't we, in training the next generation of teachers, and even more in holding them, and those who train them, to account. Talk of vitalism is all very well; but there is a *system* that needs to be operated here – set out, approved, monitored and inspected. And that requires measures (call them competencies, standards or what you will) that are specific, explicit and assessable. If something is lost in the process then it looks rather elitist anyway. We are interested in the many and not the few, and are not to be deterred by talk of the Nietzschean 'herd', by airy-fairy ideas about teaching Keats in what looks suspiciously like a single-sex old-fashioned grammar school, or by reflections on Greek Epic. Of Sociology and its imagination the least said the better.

Accordingly, those seeking to be awarded Primary Qualified Teacher Status (QTS) must, when assessed, demonstrate that they:

(a) understand the purposes, scope, structure and balance of the National Curriculum Orders as a whole and, within them, the place and scope of the primary phase, the key stages, the primary core and foundation subjects and RE;

(b) are aware of the breadth of content covered by the pupils' National Curriculum across the primary core and foundation subjects and RE

(c) understand how pupils' learning is affected by their physical, intellectual, emotional and social development.

(Teacher Training Agency, Standards for the award of QTS)

– and so on, to the extent of several hundred competencies or 'standards'. Now we are in business!

Notes

1 Book 1, l. 3. All references are to the translation by Richmond Lattimore.
2 Not for nothing is he one-eyed. The world is full of his descendants.
3 The Cyclops traps Odysseus and his companions in the cave where his sheep spend the night, and places in the exit a great stone which no man could move. Odysseus gets the Cyclops drunk, puts out his one great eye with a sharpened stake, and then escapes by strapping his men and himself under the sheep when they must leave for their pasture in the morning. Polyphemus, groping around to ensure no men are leaving with the sheep, does not think to feel their undersides.

Chapter 3

Choice, narrative and work

In his *The Corrosion of Character* (Sennett 1998) which he subtitles 'The personal consequences of work in the new capitalism', the sociologist Richard Sennett describes contemporary work in a Boston bakery. Formerly an 'Italian' and Italian-owned bakery, staffed mainly (with rich East Coast irony) by Greek Americans, the bakery is now owned by a food conglomerate, and high-tech automation has replaced the hot, noisy, smelly, mildly dangerous hubbub of former times:

> Computerised baking has now profoundly changed the balletic physical activities of the shop floor. Now the bakers make no physical contact with the materials or the loaves of bread, monitoring the entire processs via on-screen icons which depict, for instance, images of bread colour derived from data about the temperature and baking time of the ovens; few bakers actually see the loaves of bread they make. Their working screens are organised in the familiar Windows way; in one, icons for many more kinds of bread appear than had been prepared in the past – Russian, Italian, French loaves all possible by touching the screen. Bread had become a screen represent-ation.
>
> (Sennett 1998: 68)

Sennett tells us he found the bread 'excellent' and that plenty of Bostonians plainly agree – the bakery does well. As for the 'Greek' bakers of former times, all family men,

> Craft pride [amongst the Greeks] was strong, but the men said they didn't enjoy their work, and I believed them. The ovens often burned them; the primitive dough beater pulled human muscles; and it was night work, which meant these men, so family-centred, seldom saw their families during the week.
>
> (Sennett 1998: 66)

Why on earth, then, will so many of us react to the passing of the old bakery and the story of the new bakery with unease and distaste? Should we do so? Do we even have any right to do so?

Sennett tells a story about the new bakery, complemented by other observations and by reference to other working milieux throughout his book, of superficiality and 'illegibility'. For the new bakery workers, the ones who have replaced the Greeks, a 'bouillabaise of ethnicity, gender and race' (p. 67), are unhappy in their own way. Yet this is not the familiar problem some call alienation. Sennett comments of the new workforce, 'In place of alienation, their sense of daily life in the bakery was marked by indifference' (p. 70).

Why should this be? It has a lot to do with a life of button-pushing, but that's not the essence of it. After all, in some sense most of us academics now spend a life punching buttons on a keyboard too, but this hasn't diminished the quality of our own working lives. As Sennett himself points out, 'At higher levels of technical work, the advent of the computer has enriched the content of many jobs' (p. 73). It has to do rather with the role the bakery button-pushing plays. For one might at first ask: if any aspect of the process is automated, why not all of it? And if not all of it, doesn't that mean there is some significant role for human judgement and expertise here?

Well, yes and no. Sennett isn't clear on this point, but automation seems to be entailed by the need to produce large batches. On the other hand, the computer process doesn't actually work very well. (No surprises there, then.)

> Automated bread is no marvel of technological perfection; the machines frequently tell the wrong story about the loaves rising within, for instance, failing to gauge accurately the strength of the rising yeast, or the actual colour of the loaf. The workers can fool with the screen to correct *somewhat* [my emphasis] for these defects; what they can't do is fix the machines, or more important, actually bake bread by manual control when the machines all too often go down.
>
> (Ibid.: 68)

To say the process is illegible is to say that at quite a deep level these workers just don't understand what they're doing. But in that case, what's in this regime for the owners of the bakery? Sennett is clear here: it allows them to hire workers at lower wages, 'even though now all have higher formal technical qualifications' than their Greek predecessors (p. 72) – a point to give pause to all of us concerned with education.

Note in particular that the workers' scope for intervention is limited, even in those respects which are their responsibility; and that the inevitable waste and failure which follows from this is accounted for in advance by management. This is an almost inevitable concomitant of the conglomerate's 'post-Fordist' strategy of flexible specialisation – asking the bakery to switch frequently between small batches of different products (bagels, baguettes and so on). As Sennett points out, in a flexible regime difficulty is 'counterproductive'. Yet without difficulty and resistance, 'we create the very conditions for uncritical and indifferent activity' (p. 72). And Nietzsche would appreciate his observation that 'When things are made easy for us, as in the labour I've described, we become weak' (p. 74). (Teachers and educators may take this to heart, not least when next they are told that the criterion of good teaching is that it 'facilitates' learning.)

But why is the condition in the new bakery not properly described as alienation? For in Sennett's view, this word does arguably describe the condition of the new black foreman, Rodney Everts. Everts is the sole survivor of the earlier 'Italian' regime, and in some ways a benefactor of the new one, which is less racist. But he also understands the rationale of the new regime in its contrasts with the old and the moral harm it does to the other workers, manœuvered into uncritical indifference. 'That clarity is what a humane Marxist used to mean by alienation, the unhappy dis-associated consciousness which reveals, however, things as they are and where a person stands' (p. 70). But in the nature of the new work, in its 'illegibility' as we shall see, the others lack this understanding. They are not even alienated. As Sennett observes, in Victorian and early modern factories nothing was hidden from the workers. But in contemporary conditions a great deal may be hidden from them. 'Detachment and confusion' are Sennett's epithets for their responses (p. 74). He describes their work identities as weak. One of the new workers (actually Italian, this one), says 'I go home, I really bake bread. I'm a baker. Here, I punch the buttons'. He explains why he didn't bother to attend a seminar Everts gave on baking: '. . . it doesn't matter; I won't do this for the rest of my life'.

Sennett has a rich moral tale to tell about new work and modern society, organised partly in terms of the inadequacies of older Marxian sociologies in grasping the specificities of the new psycho-social order of contemporary – we shall say 'postmodern' – capitalism. The Boston bakery is not the only paradigm for this new capitalism, but it fits together with others to form a new pattern. But a valid story of any complexity allows other questions than its author's own to be put as well. And it seems to us worth asking how Nietzsche's categories of affirmation and nihilism can be used to describe the difference between life in the old bakery and in the new.

Nihilist perspectives on postmodern work

In an important commentary on Nietzsche, Gilles Deleuze (Deleuze 1983: 147–8) defines two or maybe three ideas of nihilism in Nietzsche's *oeuvre*: the negative, the reactive and, as the nadir of the reactive, the passive. In negative nihilism, value is attributed to some form of the transcendent – Deleuze mentions 'God, essence, the good, truth'. To refer to belief in God or commitment to truth as nihilism will sound perversely paradoxical to most people. After all, what better sources or guarantors of value might one wish for, what could be less negative, less nihilistic than these? Nietzsche's objection is that in locating value somehow 'outside the world' we rob the world of any value itself. We deprecate the life we actually live as incapable of any self-justification; and therefore we live lives which are actually not worth living, whether or not they measure up to some transcendental paradigm.[1]

In the next stage of nihilism, the reactive, people go beyond this negativity towards their own perspective on 'appearances' and reach disillusionment with regard to all 'transcendentals', such as God or 'the good' as well. But rather than affirming value in life itself instead, they slide into a dull despair. If there is no transcendent value, in particular if 'God is dead', then there is no value at all; for value can only be transcendental or nothing at all. (It is this view, thinks Nietzsche, which must somehow be repudiated (Danto 1980: 19–35).)

Nietzsche finds a certain initial ambiguity in reactive nihilism. Its precursor, negative nihilism, as a form of nay-saying to 'life' in deference to the 'transcendental', is at least an exercise of will to power, inasmuch as it is 'will to deny' (Deleuze 1983: 148) – to deny that value can be found in life itself. And at first, the angry rejection of the transcendent which is reactive nihilism also seems to share this vehement wilfulness. But Nietzsche believes that, in its totalising despair, reactive nihilism eventually loses even the positivity of the will to deny. It is will itself that eventually withers in reactive nihilism, and passivity – passive nihilism – must ensue.

Nietzsche uses here a potentially instructive grammar of ethical categories with his three forms of nihilism. Do they help us articulate our unease with the postmodern bakery and its workers? At first sight, the question is unpromising. We do not seem to be dealing here with either faith in the transcendental or the loss of such a faith. But as it is clear that both the old and new stories of the bakery are set in overtly secular and disenchanted worlds, a Nietzschean would wish to find affirmation of life in their activities, yet cynically expect a passive nihilism. But even so, this latter might seem a more appropriate category for the attitude of the postmodern shift-worker than for the Greeks. The Greeks at least found solidarity in the bakery, a solidarity grounded in shared ethnicity and shared work. And here 'shared' meant more than just 'the same':

> Good worker meant good Greek. The equation of good worker and good Greek made sense in the concrete, rather than the abstract. The bakers needed to co-operate intimately to co-ordinate the varied tasks of the bakery.
>
> (Sennett 1998: 66)

> The character of the workers was expressed at work in acting honorably, working co-operatively and fairly with other bakers because they belonged to the same community.
>
> (Ibid.: 67)

This community was characterised by strong families, as we have noted, and also, uncomfortably, by the racism of the lowly towards the 'lowest'. These Greeks despise the poor and 'scrounging' blacks. So this is not an idyllic picture. But it is, in significant degree, a meaningful one – which is central to Sennett's own argument. The lives of the Greek bakers seemed not to be those of resignation to vacuity, of passive nihilism. Their resentments and mutual demands still betray some live, informing will. Can the same be said for the lives of the 'postmodern' bakers? It is hard to think so.

But we need to be cautious here. It would be culpably naïve to 'read off' the moral character of particular workers by reference to their work situation. What people actually do is determined in part (though never wholly, of course) by what they themselves think they are doing. (Remember the man quoted earlier who thinks he's 'a baker' at home, but not at work.) And this in turn will inevitably be influenced by the other things that they are doing, the context of their broader lives. It is significant that the postmodern bakers are nearly all part-timers. Some are single mothers balancing demands of children and work. Others combine two or more part-time jobs, which may have little or nothing to do with one another. Some have commitments other than paid work – 'resting actors', for instance. Only some are just under-employed. To ascribe a passive nihilism to them all would be crass.

But one can, nonetheless, ask sensible questions about what a context such as the postmodern bakery allows within its own domain or positively encourages or discourages amongst its workers. We get a clue to this in a further comment from Sennett:

> In order to be hired now, the people on the shop floor have to prove that they are computer-literate. However, they won't use much of this knowledge on the job, where they are simply pushing buttons in a Windows program designed by others. "Baking, shoemaking, printing, you name it, I've got the skills," said one of the women on the shop floor with a laugh . . .'
>
> (Ibid.: 70)

What she means, of course, is that she actually has no skills specific to any of these activities. (Indeed, she cracks her joke as Sennett and she survey the trash cans full of waste and misfires, which the Greeks would never have tolerated.) She is, tellingly, a paradigm of the beneficiary of 'transferable skills' who constitutes the current ideal of further and even higher education in the UK and in much of the rest of the developed world. And yet she is no substitute for the skilled operator.

It seems, then, that the question we need to ask is whether this button-pushing work can be conceived as a locus for the assertion of value in one's life, and since this is plainly unlikely, precisely why not. If this activity is trivial, just what is it that constitutes its triviality (a question only a philosopher would ask)?

Nietzsche's famously all-encompassing scepticism about objectivity in values might suggest that value can be attached to or witheld from absolutely anything one chooses; yet in so many passages, with a familiar apparent inconsistency, particular choices and ways of choosing or deciding suffer Nietzsche's aristocratic disdain or contempt. So what might make the difference between choices credible and not credible, if objectivity has no place in the realm of values? We might suggest – and Nietzsche the professor of philology might sympathise – that an analogy with language can help. If an action or activity is to constitute an affirmation of value, it seems that one might minimally require it be 'meaningful' or 'pointful' in some sense, at least for the agent, even if for him or her alone. To say of some action or activity that it has no conceivable point or meaning as far as one is oneself concerned and yet to insist that one performs it in assertion of value in life, seems abject bad faith, a vapid blast of verbiage. So can we formalise, in any helpful way, the idea of a pointful or meaningful action? If this is to help with a Nietzschean analysis, we must formalise this concept of meaningfulness without reference to the 'point' such action might have for others than oneself or within some context alien to one's own concerns (such as instrumental activity). Linguistic analogy gives a hint as to how to do this. In the *Tractatus Logico-Philosophicus*, Wittgenstein introduces a metaphor for sense and senselessness in linguistic propositions. A meaningful proposition may be thought of as an arrow, pointing in a particular direction – as Frege puts it, a proposition has a 'sense' in that it 'points' to either the True or the False (Frege 1984). The usefulness of the metaphor becomes clearer when we ask what a meaning-less proposition is like. Wittgenstein likens it to an arrow pointing in two opposite directions at once – to both the True and the False, in Frege's terms. In the face of a meaningless proposition, we don't know which way to turn. (And thus a covertly pragmatist element appears in the *Tractatus* which is brought out more vividly in the 'use-theory of meaning' of the later *Philosophical Investigations*.)

Can we think of a meaningless action or activity in a comparable way? For the bakery worker who facetiously claimed possession of all the possible skills of any kind of work, pushing buttons and manipulating Windows icons might well be thought of like a dysfunctional arrow. The 'arrow' of a proposition, when meaning-less, points in two opposite directions at once. Actions, by contrast, obviously don't fit into any such dichotomy. But they may, as here, point in so many directions at once as to seem comparably 'pointless' in their own way. Pressing buttons in response to an icon of temperatures has as much – but also as little – to do with firing pottery, producing steel mouldings, controlling greenhouse temperatures or monitoring the temperature of a patient in intensive care, as to do with baking bread.

But what does it mean, in turn, to make this last remark? For instance, why should we not say rather that this button-pressing is not meaningless but, on the contrary, a wonderfully meaningful operation precisely because it's meaningful in so many different contexts?

Here, another linguistic idea may be helpful, that of narrative. In a narrative, a collection of events and states of affairs are strung together in a temporal order, and one which suggests, if it does not explicitly state, various kinds of connection between them (cause, coincidence, reaction and much else). In a credible narrative, the 'and then . . . and then . . . and then . . .' structure strongly suggests non-arbitrary connection between the stages, not just mere adventitious chronological sequence. And arguably, what gives 'sense' to an individual action, a direction of some sort, is its legible or comprehensible place in a sequence of antecedents and consequences. But what we want to suggest about the button-pushing in the bakery is that it doesn't actually fit any credible narrative for the individual 'baker'.

Of course, it would be foolish to deny that pressing the buttons fits into any narrative at all. For the technologist who designed the system, for the bakery's owners, indeed for its bank or shareholders even, the button-pushing activity plays a vital role in a chain of activities and for them it is indeed rich in meaning, financially or perhaps technically. And more generally, this polyvalent kind of button-pushing fits snugly into a huge range of possible narratives of making and earning.

But for the individual worker who actually pushes the button, things are different. For on the one hand, the button-pushing does not, for him or her, fit into some longer sequence which is, in Sennett's word, 'legible'. Remember how much of the process is hidden from the worker in such a factory, how 'illegible' everything becomes. Between activity and payment there is an ill-comprehended, certainly disregarded gap – what does this activity say about me? Can I tell how my activity fits into the broader narrative of this workplace? How detailed an account can I give of the whole commercial process and my place in it? Why does pressing these buttons constitute an activity worthy of the particular wage I get? The workers may not usually see the bread or the ingredients, so they may have only a minimal idea what they are doing – little sense of the material antecedents or consequences for their actions, which only barely depend on them at all. And it is what happens in this space of antecedents and consequences that should also, but actually doesn't, show the new bakery workers just how their own narratives intertwine with those of others: other workers, the owners, the customers. The button-pushing requires no co-ordination with other workers, whilst the customer is, for the worker, just a statistical index, not a real person musing over what to buy today or passing an opinion on yesterday's badly baked loaf. This meaninglessness of the actual activity, its disembeddedness from antecedent and consequence, becomes vivid at moments when the system breaks down. The Greeks had enough understanding of the system they worked with to make a serious attempt of their own at fixing mechanical breakdowns. But such is the complexity of the new computer architecture that, with the best will in the world, the 'new' bakers just have to sit passively (for hours, sometimes) and wait for an outside 'expert' to come and fix things for them. When the machine breaks down, their own skimpy narratives come to a halt as well.

Thus their work is different even from that of the 'piece worker' tightening one or two screws on a Ford model-T assembly line in the 1920s. That man, at least, could see where his work had come from and where it was going, and understand why. His relations, economic and social, with fellow workers were to some degree governed by his place in a structure, particularly the narrative structure of producing a car, a structure at least partially legible to him. And of course, car workers come to think of themselves as car workers: making cars becomes part of their own personal narratives, even if not necessarily a particularly enjoyable or valued one. Whereas in the bakery, social relations are at best adventitious: 'I won't do this for the rest of my life'. This young student might just happen to move in with that young single mother. It might just have to do with being in the same place at the same time. But that's about all it has to do with work.

Marx thought that work on assembly lines was alienating because it could not but be meaningless. Of course, there's a lot wrong with such work, but the comparison above shows that in this respect, if not in terms of immiseration, things could get far worse than in Marx's day. Marx's error lies not in mistaking the humane disaster of meaningless work, but in overlooking the small redemption of meaning made possible in narrative – the very kind of narrative which resistance in the labour movement could be organised around. A fortiori, he could not imagine a world in which even this was nullified. (Is it any coincidence that the labour movement is today moribund?)

So we begin to see, perhaps, why the assertion of value in the givens of life seems impossible in the context of the kind of indifference to work such as that found in the postmodern bakery: we can see what constitutes the triviality of this work. Almost nothing significant in the individual narratives of these workers leads to or depends on their work activity in this bakery. The nature of the system robs them even of the embeddedness of the line-worker, revealed in the thinness of their responsibilities in the bakery. (In the 'Italian' bakery, the Greeks viewed waste as a scandal and knew how to minimise it.) Sennett himself emphasises the problem of the collapse of narrative structures for workers today. What we try to do here is to give added philosophical weight to the insight by relating it to problems of authenticity and nihilism, without begging ontological questions about the status of the subject (for instance as the 'sovereign subject of experience', unmediated by discourse). If an individual is to escape a charge of bad faith in asserting value in what they do, there needs be some test of authenticity to apply to the activity, a test that this kind of work cannot but fail. We suggest that it is the ability to fit the choice into some narrative 'of one's own' which makes the difference between authentic assertion and bad faith; and that this becomes barely possible in some postmodern forms of work.

Autonomy in the context of capitalist narrative

There are those who may accept the need for narrative to make sense of choices but resist the diagnosis that none is available here. There is at least one way in which contemporary workers are positively encouraged to 'make sense' of their work or assert some secular value in it. Workers these days are expected to view the meaning of their lives in terms of the ideals of the free market.[2] But is such a project, of exhorting workers to think of their lives in terms of a free market narrative, credible? Was it ever? Arguably, at one time yes, it was credible – yet precisely when least insisted upon, up until the conservative counter-revolution of the 1980s.

The political theory of the free market is seared, these days, into our every practice. The market is the economic project of individual freedom, instantiating the effects of unrestricted or unrestrained free choices. It ratifies individual freedom in the unparalleled material wealth and success it supposedly brings wherever it reigns. Any institution which constrains free individual choice demonstrates its ethical unacceptability in its invidious effects on market success and the prosperity of the commonwealth, and by thus further inhibiting free development for both society and the individual.

In what sense, though, could free market ideology be said to have constituted a narrative – not just a set of ethical and economic doctrines, but some kind of story which individuals could relate to, precisely as a story? The free market is assumed to be progressive – both expansionary and innovative, and thus a project extended and elaborated through historical time. In that sense, it has a story it can offer to the individual and may invite his or her participation in that story, in some way or other. In early capitalism, one supposedly exciting form of participation was to take a role in colonial expansion, if only as part of 'the poor bloody infantry'. Another was to 'rise' through an organisation to some position of responsibility within it, great or small. At the very least, it said to those who gained nothing of substance that their work had meaning because it subtended the lives of their 'betters', whose wealth expanded with the success of their workplaces, thus making 'the nation' greater – a tawdry story, but not without an ugly truth. In later and less oppressive capitalism, industry often had the ability genuinely to engross its workers in technical innovations, whatever their complaints about working conditions. (One of us lives in a former aircraft manufacturing area which also boasts a historic race track, where transport technologies remain the mainstay of eager male conversation in the local pubs.)

Insofar as the progress of the free market rested on industrial development, it had a story which was a narrative of ever-elaborating instrumental rationality, the technical rationality of choosing means to ends, rather than that of deliberation on what the ends should be. And though educational theorists often regard instrumentalism with deep misgiving, this was a story in which most people could find a role to play, whose part in the story was more or less perspicuous, at least to themselves. Thus, people could give meaning to their lives by aligning their own narratives with the Grand Narrative – the over-arching social narrative[3] – of capitalist progress. If this sounds unconvincingly abstract, it may help to notice the important role of 'intermediate institutions' here. More specifically, under capitalism people learned to relate their lives more immediately to particular institutions which in turn defined their own roles first in relation to each other and second to the capitalist Grand Narrative itself. Important roles have been played by the institutions of the firm, the union, career, industrial neighbourhoods, employment rights, management, vocational education. It is in these terms that the Grand Narrative of the market has presented itself to people as something other than a doctrinal abstraction – something to which one might relate the narrative of one's own life in concrete ways.

By such means, capitalism provided a background supportive of projects of individual autonomy. Precisely because there was a Grand Narrative, a 'big story' unfolding in one's society, and yet one compatible with democratic freedom, one could construct a story of one's own, even one inimical to or committed against that very narrative, such as a socialist story. This is not at all to say that capitalism is itself a precondition for socialist commitment, for instance. Capitalism is not the only or thus the necessary background for socialism. The point about Grand Narrative and autonomy is more simply that Grand Narratives provide contexts for 'making sense' of one's life, without necessarily determining what sense one chooses to make. The lives of the industrial agitator, social reformer, or bohemian 'dropout' also make more vivid sense against a backdrop of some Grand Narrative, capitalist, socialist or other.

Instrumentalism, nihilism and narrative

However, critics of capitalism, both socialist and traditionalist, Leftist and conservative and even politically liberal, have often discussed capitalism in terms of a commonsense conception of nihilism. The standard complaint is precisely that the instrumental rationality characteristic of the industrial order, and which becomes socially pervasive under capitalism (and State Socialism, too), distracts both individuals and social groups from any informing sense of values, without which instrumental rationality makes no sense. One might readily reconcile oneself to the vast elaboration of tools and techniques in modern society if there were some clear sense, if only for particular individuals, of where this was all going – some sense of what we need our improved production processes, better transport, labour-saving devices, efficient telecommunications, better training or our more efficient financial sector, and so on, for. Instrumental rationality requires a rationale, which it cannot supply in and of itself.

This kind of critique has informed most traditions of educational theory. It is made explicit in the classic analytic philosophy of education of Hirst and Peters, which argues to the primacy of intrinsically worthwhile activities in the social sphere, and thus for the educational sphere. Deweyan pragmatism elevates democratic ideals over instrumental activities, whilst educational progressivism explicitly puts individual emotional and social development before vocational aims. And the Critical Theory of education today draws primarily on the most developed of all critiques of instrumentalism, that of Jürgen Habermas. What's more, each of these theories of education tends as much to liberalism as to a socialist or traditionalist politics.

But our analysis of the potential of Grand Narrative to provide means for making sense of one's life, in particular here of one's working life, should give educationists pause. Notoriously, educational theorists have lacked success in persuading their communities of the superior insight into values and their importance which they claim for themselves. The theory of intrinsically worthwhile activities, for instance, may occasionally enter journalistic or political debate in some form, as an ad hoc expression of puzzlement, unease or dismay at the direction of educational practices, but has failed to inform many serious projects of educational action, either locally or politically. Yet if social life under instrumental rationality is as pervasively nihilistic as value critiques typically claim, this is surely puzzling. How is it that society and its individuals 'get by' so easily in this supposedly nihilistic culture?

Two points arise here. First, insofar as the primary task facing any individual is to make sense of her life in some way, to be able to act meaningfully, this is conceptually a task prior to that of making life worthwhile. So it should not be too much of a surprise if 'a sense of values' is not the only or perhaps even the most important endowment for the individual seeking some sense of meaning. The possibility of making an understandable narrative for one's life, good, bad or indifferent, seems at least as necessary to us as any sense of values. And as we have just seen, a pathologically instrumentalist society such as our own does nonetheless offer many such possibilities for making sense of life. Against that background, it is perhaps less surprising that so many people seemed unmoved by laments or accusations that their lives are nonetheless uninformed by a sense of values.

Second, and perhaps more interestingly, the construction of a personal narrative inevitably takes place under social constraints. Value theorists might deplore too much talk of personal narrative as inherently egocentric; but this is in fact not the case. Almost any credible personal narrative involves other people as characters in one's own story. For most of us, and most importantly, it cannot but involve our 'significant others', typically partners and family members. And human development into and through adulthood is in part the elaboration of one's narrative to include more and more people in increasingly elaborate patterns. But of course, we do not control others (and should not try to do so), so the task of working out our own narratives is a task of intermeshing them with, and adjusting them to, those of others. This influence of others in our own lives is in no way deterministic, but neither is it arbitrary. It requires of us negotiation and renegotiation, typically at a subliminal level. This in turn implies that your attempt to make life meaningful is inevitably intertwined with mine, but in unpredictable ways. (This is not just metaphorically but literally true. As you read this chapter, your career intersects with mine if only momentarily, whether we know each other socially or not. I write for you, and what you read at this moment depends on how I live.)

This suggests a lack of social and psychological realism in value-theoretic approaches to education. Such approaches typically emphasise our potential for autonomous deliberation, to stand back from the stream of ordinary life, contemplate questions of value – either in solitude or better, we now think, in dialogue with others – and evaluate the way we live or wish to live and adjust our way of life accordingly, if we can do so. Theories which prioritise rational autonomy imply at least the possibility of some kind of equivalent moment of intellectual or spiritual abstraction. The objection to this had better not be, moreover, that this abstraction is impossible. To think it impossible would be to subscribe to a social determinism which would posit too many problems of its own anyway. But what we can suggest, with some plausibility, is that such a programme of autonomy perhaps asks more of people than the autonomy theorist acknowledges. Of course, autonomous deliberation is never intended to be easy. But the difficulties are typically expected to be intellectual, emotional and above all ethical. But what we want to suggest here is that the real difficulty is perhaps epistemological.

Deliberating values or elaborating narratives?

Insofar as the practice of autonomous deliberation is a radical practice of abstraction, it is not just morally and intellectually risky, but puts in abeyance or in question those very narrative constructions which have hitherto served to provide a context for action meaningful to ourselves. Moreover, if we are then to rebuild or remould our lives in the light of autonomous deliberation, to reconstruct meaning in our lives, we must return from deliberation to the task of narrative construction. In doing so, we may indeed pick up the same narrative where, metaphorically, we 'left off'. But we must redirect or reconstruct it in ways which also take our new values into account, considerations less concrete and specific than the intermeshing of our narrative with those of others. This is likely to disrupt any prior existing canon of meaningfulness, whilst nothing guarantees success in any novel narrative construction. Our social relations, which hitherto have informed our attempts to 'make sense' of our own lives, are now complicated, if not compromised by extraneous considerations, and they may break down. (This is a tale of modern 'alienation' – from partner, family, work or background – following reflection and reconsideration of one's life, familiar in the fictional narratives of modern drama, film and literature, of course.[4]) The exercise of autonomy promises the danger of a loss of achieved identity and meaning, whilst guaranteeing nothing in its place. Even if one's new sense of values seems secure, the attempt to reconstruct our narratives accordingly may be quite insecure.

Immediately many will respond, quite rightly, that of course autonomous choice does not preclude a concern for shared activities, relationship and experiences. Indeed, the whole rationale for autonomous deliberation is perhaps typically to think through problems arising within this shared life. Autonomy is not a recipe for individualism. And this is quite so; but it misses the point. The point is precisely that there is a mismatch, a disjunction, a rupture between two kinds of process or personal exercise; an epistemological difference between rational deliberation on the one hand and the construction of narratives on the other. Constructing a coherent argument (a criterion for rational deliberation) and constructing a coherent story (or narrative) involve two quite different kinds of coherence. The relations which matter in the former are those of logical validity; in the latter, those of plausible human relationships. And the trouble is that success in the one has little or nothing to do with success in the other.

Accordingly, the two exercises bear quite differently on the task of making sense in one's life. Of course, the autonomy theorist knows perfectly well that deliberation is some kind of abstraction from everyday life. She may even think this abstraction is a necessary precondition of 'making sense' – stepping outside entanglements and confusions. And if we are talking of making sense of values, then she is probably right. What she overlooks, however, are the ways in which the quotidian internegotiation of narratives itself already constructs some kind of meaning to life. To engage in deliberation on values is not necessarily to ignore other people, but it is nonetheless to put aside the elaboration of narrative. It is to step out of story-telling into (what moralists call) practical reason. Dangerously, it may tempt one to assume that where deliberation has not yet happened, there is, as yet, little, morally or intellectually, which the individual has reason to value as 'her own', as authentic. Yet from a narrative point of view, autonomous deliberation is not just an attempt to construct meaning in one's life. On the contrary, it begins to look more like an interruption of an already ongoing process of authentically making sense of one's life.

From this point of view, the apparent social and political failure of value-theoretic educational theory begins to look easier to explain. So far from offering the student or the teacher a helping hand in making sense of their activities, deliberation on values begins to look like a disruption of that very process of making sense. Making sense sometimes occurs not only without deliberation on values, but possibly even despite it. And autonomous deliberation may begin to look like a kind of negative nihilism, in Nietzschean terms: turning one's back on the sense already made in one's 'authentic' choices, and substituting a fetish of abstract values in its place. And by contrast, 'fitting in' with a society governed by instrumental rationality begins to look like some kind of pre-reflective assertion of authenticity, though probably not one which Nietzsche the ethical aristocrat would much admire.

We may gain here another ray of illumination on the widely acknowledged inadequacy of individualism and its prioritisation of the autonomous exercise of freedom under market conditions of unaccountable choice. Individualism does not account credibly for how we make sense of life in the maelstrom of negotiated interaction with others, prioritising, as it does, market relations over communicative interaction more generally. Thus it presupposes, by default, a picture of the individual making sense of life by her pursuit of privately held abstract values – the negative nihilism we have just described. But perhaps the narrative account may be more valuable for the light it may shed on communitarianism. The narrative approach will obviously reinforce the communitarian perception that we cannot but make sense of our own lives, and a fortiori our own moral lives, except by reference to the lives of those others we live with and live among. But it is arguably a failing of communitarianism to characterise this interconnectivity in abstract terms of values and principles, rather than in terms of interlocking and sometimes mutually interfering narratives. In emphasising supposedly shared abstractions rather than the concrete projects of making sense, in and amongst each others' lives, communitarianism risks becoming yet one more variety of negative nihilism, positing some kind of transcendent sense of the good, over against meaning and value immanently constructed by ourselves.

So at the very least, we may suggest that value-theoretic approaches to education are intrinsically patronising, to a degree, an imposition on authenticity even when emphasising the priority of the values of ordinary people and their autonomous assent to them. In seeking to 'educate' this assent in various ways, value-theoretic approaches disregard the more complex and psychologically vital constructions of meaning which sustain people prior to any reconsideration of values. And in doing so, they propose the priority of extra-mundane abstractions over lived commitments. To say this is not to deny any role at all for values. But it is to suggest that their relevance is limited to occasions of under-determined choice in life rather than as the containing frameworks for living which they are typically taken to be. And to say this is to demote their guiding importance for educational practice. The very theory of intrinsic value may take the form of negative nihilism if its relevance is mistaken for fundamental.

This should not surprise anyone familiar with the well-known problem confronting Peters' Transcendental Argument to the priority of intrinsic values (Peters 1965). Peters grounds the argument in the hypothesis of an interlocutor who asks why she should take supposedly intrinsically valuable pursuits at all seriously. (The

answer Peters gives is that to ask the question is in itself to take
those values seriously in the first place.) 'But what do you say to
someone who never asks the question anyway?', the familiar
objection asks. For such a person, the question is probably not one
which has a role in their narrative. The difficulty with this objection
has seemed to be that it meets a logically rigorous argument with a
contingent pragmatic difficulty, however serious. But the problem is
not simply the problem of 'getting the argument going', the
difficulty that the Argument might be valid but subjectively un-
interesting to many. The deeper problem is that there are reasons
for some people, probably for most in fact, which positively count
against asking the question. To do so would be to abandon their
already ongoing project of making sense of their life, in socially
more compelling and epistemologically prior ways. And this
difficulty arises not just with Peters' Transcendental Argument but
in response to any philosophical intervention concerning values. To
repeat, people might need recourse to reflection on values at
difficult points in their lives – points were there is no one obvious
direction in which their narratives would most coherently go. At
such points, perhaps they will ask Peters' question, or some similar,
or be glad to be reminded of such considerations. But to predicate
an entire education on insights principally necessary in emergencies
is patently a very strange strategy indeed.

The future of education under the failure
of instrumentalism

The guiding impulse behind attempts to theorise education in
terms of values has always been, of course, a fundamental commitment to rational autonomy. Without some political commitment
to the value an education might have for the intelligently educated,
the hegemonic criteria for education would be those determined by,
and functional for, social agencies (governments, firms and so on)
indifferent, if not inimical, to the good of the individual. In our own
society, these would be primarily the criteria of competence and
efficiency in technical pursuits, and secondarily the demands of
social control. In questioning the pertinence of value-theoretic
approaches, we question at least how such autonomy might best be
promoted. But moreover, we question whether autonomy is the
most helpful concept for organising an approach to education
which is other than merely functional for 'the powers that be'. It is
not clear that rational autonomy itself makes much sense except in
its 'grammatical' relations to the values functional for autonomous
rational decision. In a world where a value-theoretic approach

seems unhelpful, so too do analyses of education in terms of autonomy, even if autonomy remains for educationists a value.

We suggest that a more credible guide to educational practice is the obligation of realism, of a Nietzschean attention to the way things really are, stripped of illusion and delusion: of acceptance of reality and assertion of what value one may hold in this worldly context, without reference to transcendent abstractions. Of course, realism in the realm of truth is also one of the requirements of rational autonomy. But rather than disclosing to us the values which we can meaningfully accept within our world 'as it is' but without any guarantee that these will make life easier for us, rational autonomy presupposes that there must be values which would supposedly guide coherently our choices in a properly understood world. By contrast, a Nietzschean realism does not covertly constrain values to the requirement of providing criteria for coherent choice but accepts that our values may be no less compelling for us even when they nonetheless create difficulties too. Indeed, it may disclose a world in which coherent choice itself turns out to be a severely constrained prospect. Those who find such an idea simply foreign in its perversity might well compare it with the 'tragic pluralism' proposed by Sir Isaiah Berlin (in many writings, e.g. Berlin 1990: 1–20) – the claim that even within a single culture, human values are typically many and incommensurable, such that coherent choices between them are often impossible, and leave us with the tragic necessity of inevitable failure in regard of some set of values versus others.

A Nietzschean realism need not entail collusion with the social or political status quo. In pointing to the ways in which work in the context of a larger economic narrative can and does sustain personal narratives, we do not, as we have made clear, suppose that all succesful personal narratives must be complicit with hegemonic social and economic values. Relations between personal and larger narratives are more supple and less deterministic than that. The implications of a narrative-oriented approach to education might be to educate students more richly in the details and complexities of the dominant narratives of their society and the range of personal narratives, both complicit and reactive, which individuals construct in relation to those which are dominant. If value is to be found, as Nietzsche suggests, within life and not outside it, then it's a richer and more detailed appreciation of 'how it is' that we need, not schooling in the negative nihilism of transcendental values. If talk of 'how it is', however, shades too easily into covert ideological distortion, one would need to treat circumspectly Nietzsche's call to accept 'the given' in life. The question is not whether to accept the given, but to distinguish what actually is 'given', and what merely adventitious or ruthlessly imposed. Nonetheless, it remains very doubtful whether schooling in values would shed much light on such a question.

But if the theory of intrinsic value is itself a form of negative nihilism, postmodern instrumentalism begins to seem something even worse, a decline into reactive nihilism. This chapter began with a story of new ways of work which seem to indicate a collapse of even the instrumental rationality which, we have argued, has informed many peoples narratives hitherto.[5] Whilst this story is unaccommodating to the negative claims of intrinsic value, it also confounds even personal attempts to find a narrative meaning intrinsic to patterns of work. To a degree, this helps to explain the current vogue for educational reassertions of 'values' in State-coordinated crusades in 'raising standards'. Patterns of work become less reliable, less rooted in localities, less hospitable to coherent constructions of career, less sociable and so on. (All these themes are taken up in other chapters of Sennett's book.) The less capitalism has to offer in terms of narrative possibilities, the more insistent are political and business leaders on its abstract doctrinal justification – negative nihilism becomes necessary, locating value in particular and tendentious analyses of freedom, rather than in life as lived. Insistence on the virtue of the values of the market comes hand in hand with revival of values rhetoric in education.[6]

But notwithstanding our official commitment, as a society, to the educational goal of rational autonomy, it is in fact instrumental expertise on the one hand and the requirements of social control on the other which dominate the curriculum at school and increasingly even at the level of higher education. We educate as though autonomy were no real aim or value for us at all. So what might we expect for the future of either side of our current educational enterprise as instrumentalism itself increasingly fails to sustain the construction of personal narratives? In the short term, little will change. Most of us have our narratives already, however badly they may be strained in the postmodern context, and parents and teachers still attempt to induct youngsters into some narrative-based sense of purpose. But in the longer run (and perhaps Sennett and other commentators see the early stages of such processes), we may anticipate a double irony, dangerous if not lethal for education.

On the one hand, we cannot be surprised if projects of revitalising education for social control ('raising moral and spiritual standards in schools') begin to fail quite badly. Consider the kinds of discipline or school subjects that we look to as crucibles of those values we want to cultivate in the young – literary studies, history and historical aspects of geography, sports and performance activities, and not least of course, religious studies. All of these are concerned not just with values but with narratives. Even in sports and performance, for instance, there is a concern with the role these activities play in the shape of a meaningful life (apart from their value in terms of physical or mental health, for instance). And central to them is a concern for the internal narrative structure of sporting and performance events, unfolding across a span of time. A clever move on the football pitch, a particular way of singing a particular chorus, such things get their point and purpose from their place in a narrative structure. And this is why such activities are appropriate for teaching the young to make their own personal narratives whilst intertwining them with those of others; in sport, we call it 'team spirit'. And in literature and history, this intertwining of different levels and kinds of narrative is ideally made patent. But it is only within such complex narrative contexts that any considerations of value even begin to make sense as concrete realities rather than philosophical abstractions – and even then, as we have seen, only marginally. No wonder then that narratives, such as the Bible stories, are central to all the world religions and thus to religious and spiritual teaching of any kind. How else are teachers in these areas to engage the young in thinking about values than in relation to the narratives of their own young lives, both past and anticipated?

But what future can there be for these kinds of educational activity if we move towards a world in which work loses its potency to sustain credible personal narratives across a lifetime? Once the penny begins to drop with the young, that theirs are to be 'portfolio careers' – no careers at all but an incoherent sequence of projects, often desperate, at simply keeping going in life, but with no overarching, informing purpose (because no success in such purposes is plausible any more) – once the message gets through that even commitment to life in a particular locality and the kind of narrative localities can sustain (as in commitment to a local sports team, for instance), what plausibility will literature, history, music, religion or sport, amongst others, have for the young? What potency in the 'real world' might these kinds of knowledge and awareness have? For this sense of rootlessness and lack of direction is increasingly not just something education policy responds to, but something it positively and intentionally promotes. Once we look beneath the gung-ho economic rhetoric to the actual curricular realities, how else do we interpret demands for the maximum possible vocational flexibility and the spectre of Lifelong Learning?

If the young are increasingly born into a world in which their elders themselves have lost a sense of narrative, how will they even understand attempts to give them a sense of values when they increasingly lack exemplars of structured, well-constructed lives in which values might have sense or purpose? (Sennett opens his book with the story of an acquaintance who lives the nomadic, rootless, socially superficial career of a technology consultant, and who feels acutely his inability to provide for his own children the example of a coherently constructed life which his own father had provided for him – notwithstanding that his father's life was restricted and limiting and that his own was outwardly far more succesful.) In such a world, the negative nihilism of values education would become quite vivid. And the idea that values education could fill the gap left by loss of narrative is just logically incoherent. It is the idea that an educational project could compensate for the gap left by the failure of its own inescapable preconditions.

What then for the future of education in instrumental activities, pre-eminently in technology but also in the sciences, mathematics, economics and business studies which also contribute to it? These will be taught, of course, with a modicum of success. But those educational reformers with an eye and a half firmly on global competition, demand more than a modicum. Nothing less than world-beating excellence will do. And yet this will not happen, subverted by the very complicity of their intentions with the narrative vacuity of postmodern careers.

In education for expertise in instrumental activities, motivation and interest are just as important for achievement as anywhere else. The question then is what motivation or interest might be found in instrumental activities which lack a narrative context. Moral theory has an elementary argument, and up to a point a good one, against the coherence of a life uninformed by any sense of values whatsoever. It points out that an instrumental justification of an action or activity refers to the desirability of some further action or activity, for which it is functional. It then points out that these further aims can also be questioned, but that it would be absurd if these too were indefinitely referred to other actions or activities. The result would be infinite regress and thus pointlessness. Only some ascription of 'value in itself' can stop the regress and inform a life with . . . well, with what? It is valid to say that only this can inform life with value. But as we have seen, value seems marginal, if not unnecessary for informing a life with meaning. An acceptance of a narrative structure to one's life can give us meaning, and this in turn, for good or ill, can keep questions of value at bay.

But it is when narrative itself fails that the problem of regress really begins to bite. For psychologically, it is not values but narrative which dictate motivation and interest. In the saddest of

Sennett's chapters, former senior technical staff from IBM, now redundant because of IBM's inattention to new directions in information technology, reflect on the blindness to new developments (primarily the personal computer), which flowed from their absorption in engrossing technical problems of their work on mainframe machines. But though they have suffered from this in the new world which has overtaken them, their lives are testimony to the richness and commitment which was possible for them within a context of narrative coherence and quite without reference to any abstract exercise of reflection on values. They are the opposite pole to the 'new' bakers, whose stance to their own instrumental activities is sheer indifference ('. . . it doesn't matter; I won't do this for the rest of my life'). The new bakers are amongst those for whom the pointlessness of regress really hits home. They can do effectively enough what little is required of them to earn and survive. They might also have the personal capacity to become 'world beaters' in the industrial sphere, but plain as day, this is not going to happen for them within their current context of narrative vacuity. When Rodney Everts, the foreman, offered to give them an optional a seminar on baking just to help them understand what they were involved in, none showed up. For these people, flexibility does not extend to any deeper and thus transferable understanding of their own instrumental sphere. For there is little likelihood that they will stay within that sphere anyway. Their flexibility is nothing more nor less than their very indifference.

But do we really believe that we can readily ignore indifference to what is being taught? What quality of knowledge and understanding do we expect without commitment to the study? Yet what else than indifference do we expect from students in a world where the only narrative context for instrumental learning is to stagger from one insecure career niche to another? And what commitment to 'transferable skills', where these are precisely conceived in context-free, purposeless terms and even valued by government and business as such? We are beckoned to a world in which the price of avoiding failure is sustained mediocrity. Beating the world is a hollow joke. There is only one consolation for this prospect (if such it be), and that is the mediocrity that others are also destined for in a globalised, postmodern economy.

Notes

1 Notice that, for Nietzsche, 'truth' means 'the Truth' – some reality supposedly deeper than 'appearance'. Like most modern philosophers, he has no use for this idea in any other than its scientific form. As for the mundane 'truths' of 'appearances', in his view these have nothing

more than perspectival, hence relative validity. But one does not have to subscribe to this relativism to agree that there is a problem about deriving value from mundane truth – to say so is merely to agree that the Naturalistic Fallacy really is a fallacy, which is a commonplace of contemporary ethics.

2 This quasi-Nietzschean secularism is perhaps no accident either. In Britain, the first major post-war political apologist for the free market was Enoch Powell, a determining influence on Margaret Thatcher. But Powell was also the only British politician of substance who could seriously claim an intelligent commitment to Nietzschean ideas, notwithstanding his traditionalist religious commitments. As we shall see, the relation between *laissez faire* and nihilism is rich in irony.

3 We have discussed Grand Narrative and the ways in which the narratives of individual lives can relate to it in Blake *et al.* 1998: 91–110.

4 An example well known in the UK is the play, later filmed, *Educating Rita* – a story of a young working-class woman dubiously emancipated though participation in higher education as a mature student.

5 For a further discussion of the gathering failure of instrumentalism which examines the role of globalisation in the process, see Blake 1999.

6 See, for instance, the work of the former SCAA on moral and spiritual education, which it aimed, by merely rhetorical means, to detach from any philosophical critique. For an analysis of this work, see Blake 1997.

FRAGMENT II

Consider again how *the list* has become almost the standard means of casting written material about education (item vi: Headteachers should be effective constructors of lists.) This partly reflects the fact that government and its agencies have their hand in education and its publications as never before; it does not explain *why* they, or anyone else, should employ to excess the bulletted, lettered or numbered (especially the decimally numbered) paragraph, sentence or phrase. We might think of various reasons for this. Such formatting

- seems eminently scientific (para. 2.13: now doesn't that suggest a fearsome degree of precision?)
- is businesslike (you can easily tick off bulletted or numbered points as you go down them, should you want to for some reason)
- is a ready product of the new technology's toolbar and so cannot be resisted
- saves the trouble of coherent thought or writing, especially when listed items appear 'in no particular order'
- looks nice on the o.h.p. or flip-chart.

Yet the most seductive thing is this: the list can seem directly to mirror the world of action, on a certain view of human action. It appears the very model of clear, transparent writing, in which without the occlusion of any of that figurative nonsense we can see straight through to the reality beneath. You chaired this meeting and that meeting and the other meeting effectively: therefore 'chairs meetings effectively' can, in your case, be ticked.

In our desperation to exclude the poetic we do not notice that *clarity* is itself coloured by metaphor.

One day they will write treatises on the prevalence of the list in the late twentieth-century. We are slow to notice how odd this practice is and what it says about us and our world.

FRAGMENT III

In the university Faculties of Business and Management – representatives of the world which education is so ready to copy – there is a widespread view that existing versions of management and management theory are inadequate in our changing world.

We are often said to be in the midst of a frenzied search for new approaches to management (Eccles and Nohria 1992; Hamel and Prahalad 1994). Many writers (e.g. Kets de Vries 1995) identify as the basic flaw in current paradigms of management the essentially rationalistic or Cartesian cast of mind which thinks in terms of linearity, quantification, and command and control organisation. Techno-rationalism, that is to say, is perceived to be an exhausted paradigm. Dehler, Welsh and Lewis (1999) write:

> *The tenets of management orthodoxy served practitioners and academics fairly well from its founding as a 'discipline' of scientific study in the mid-1950s. Grounded in Weberian concepts of hierarchy and bureaucracy, command and control, and the efficiency principles of Taylorism, such initiatives suited a lengthy era based on the manufacturing orientation of the industrial revolution . . . the organisational struggle of today seeks to overcome this techno-rational model of organising and managing.*

Sometimes identified as 'Second Wave' management thinking, the techno-rational model is often compared unfavourably with 'Third Wave' theory in which issues of learning and knowledge management are taken as central (Toffler and Toffler 1997). Thus Hamel and Prahalad (1994) argued that companies cannot be defined by what they do, but by what they know . . .

We can write like this, if we like; this is the stuff of a thousand articles in the numerous journals on management. Academics produce it in huge quantities in order to satisfy the demands of research assessment, to seek promotion, or merely to appear productive.

There remains the question whether such writing falls under the paradigm whose demise it announces.

This style of writing is much aided by the new technologies – access, download, cut and paste. Efficiency and effectiveness re-enter by the Windows after we have shown them the door, for this is the communication society, the knowledge economy: speed and efficiency of knowledge exchange, effective use of cyberspace.

No-one thinks to submit a handwritten *haiku* to the academic journal. Even use of the first-person pronoun may bring a rejection letter.

Chapter 4

Education and the Last Man

Early in *Thus Spake Zarathustra* Nietzsche introduces the discourse on the Last Man. How does Zarathustra characterise this the most contemptible of men?

> Lo! I show you *the last man*.
> 'What is love? What is creation? What is longing? What is a star?' – so asks the last man and blinks.
> The earth has become small, and on there hops the last man, who makes everything small. His species is ineradicable like that of the ground flea; the last man lives longest.
> 'We have discovered happiness' say the last people, and blink thereby.
> They have left the regions where it is hardest to live; for they need warmth. One still loves one's neighbour and rubs against him: for one needs warmth.
> Turning ill and being distrustful, they consider sinful: they walk warily. He is a fool who still stumbles over stones or people!
> A little poison now and then: that makes pleasant dreams. And much poison at last for a pleasant death.
> One still works, for work is a pastime. But one is careful for fear that the pastime should hurt one.
> One no longer becomes poor or rich; both are too burdensome. Who still wants to rule? Who still wants to obey? Both are too burdensome.
> No shepherd, and one herd! Everyone wants the same; everyone is equal: he who has other sentiments goes voluntarily into the madhouse.
> 'Formerly all the world was insane' – say the subtlest of them, and blink thereby.

They are clever and know all that has ever happened: so there is no end to their ridicule. People still fall out, but are soon reconciled – otherwise it spoils their stomachs.

They have their little pleasures for the day, and their little pleasures for the night, but they have a proper regard for health.

'We have discovered happiness' – say the last people, and blink thereby.

(Z: 40–1)

This is a levelled world – not difficult to recognise today – where the will of the people is so enfeebled that it is directed only towards a life of ease and freedom from discomfort. It combines utilitarianism with a naturalistic ethics, the regulation of desire and its satisfaction, normalisation and Macdonaldisation. Culture itself is watered down and made easier to digest. Can we even dignify these Last Men as egalitarian? Are they not rather free-loaders from the welfare state, too puny of spirit even to realise how they are living off the system? Notice also that no-one wants to rule now – because people want a stress-free death-in-life. We do have, it is true, our aspiring managers, career-advancing, portfolio-building, box-ticking professionals, but they just follow the rules. Management is conceived as something where you don't think beyond the rules, so they don't want to rule. And there is a respectable face to this also: the Last Men acquiesce in the tranquillisation that the modern world progressively brings them and that is amongst its rewards. We have here not just the beneficiaries of the welfare state but the well insured, the securely pensioned, the life-policied and health-planned: the life insurance advertisement promises 'security and complete peace of mind', bourgeois world of the Moral Majority.

If this is Nietzsche's passive nihilism, the way for it has been cleared by nihilism's uglier forms. We are tired, no doubt, of hearing of the way the world has changed (with the fashionable talk of the management of continuous/discontinuous change), of the loss of former certainties, of the way former values have devalued themselves, of the death of God. This is the reactive nihilism that Nietzsche identifies. Who is to say that this is better than that? All is down to personal opinion. And, of course, any talk of absolute values, or even objectivity, is just a rationalisation of the power of the ruling classes. We have seen a fashionable laid-back radicalism (Howard Kirk fashions history[1]), popularly misconstrued as Nietzschean.

Institutionalised in educational practice, such assumptions lead to the 'democratisation' of the curriculum, to an egalitarian political correctness, and to a hostility to the measurement of results or the passing, so it sometimes seems, of any judgement. In educational theory, they are enshrined in the work of David Cooper's 'Reckers' – 'radical egalitarian critics of knowledge and educational reality' (Cooper 1980: 106). Relativism, it seems, is rampant, and we have the morality of 'anything goes'.

Reaction and *ressentiment*

Within the last decade a certain *fin de siècle* anxiety has been reflected in renewed and widespread public interest in moral education, and this has been manifested in many ways. In the UK it has been given a particular impetus by the publications of the Schools Curriculum and Assessment Authority on this topic and on spiritual education, while the provocative book *All Must Have Prizes* by the journalist Melanie Phillips plainly tuned into a widespread belief that standards were in decline (Phillips 1996). Those publications in their turn were in part responses first to the 1988 Education Act's intention of placing education in a context which includes the spiritual, moral and cultural development of pupils and of society, and second, and paradoxically perhaps, to the reduced emphasis on moral education that has been argued by some to be an effect of the National Curriculum. There is no doubt that the Schools Curriculum and Assessment Authority and Melanie Phillips both tapped into and fed public perceptions of what was going on in schools and in society at large. There is no surprise that recent policy and practice in education have been dominated by an anxiety about standards. Sometimes there has been an almost knee-jerk reaction and resentment at the ethos and effects of progressivism: what we need is a return to discipline and traditional methods, the story goes, though the style and substance of this traditional education are sometimes conceived in the crudest of terms – teach them the facts, obedience to authority, skills for jobs and smart uniforms.

There are, of course, many robust critiques – of the effects in education of the reactive nihilism identified above – that eschew such easy solutions. These can be sensitive to the different guises nihilism can take, to the darkness at the heart of our otherwise earnest but technicised conception of education. Consider the following as representative of the liberal tradition:

> We talk endlessly of raising standards. We are preoccupied with what constitutes an effective school and how schools can become more effective. Our enthusiasm for value-added increases by

the minute. But what standards do we want to raise? What, thinking about educational ends rather than management means, do we want our effective schools to be effective at? What value do we want to add? In education, as in every other sphere of human activity, it is the integrity of the ideas that guide our actions which really matters. If those ideas are woolly, simplistic or otherwise corrupt, no amount of energy and dedication will stop the process of educational reform running into the sand.

Of course, we do need to think, long and hard, about the skills and personal qualities young people will need to secure worthwhile jobs, but there is a deeper responsibility still, namely to be crystal clear about the true ends of education. And, as this speaker points out,

> Oakeshott could not be clearer. His greatest fear is that what he calls 'socialisation' (by which he means 'systematic apprenticeship to domestic, industrial and commercial life') has been substituted for education. Education is the disinterested study of the best that has been thought and said. It has no extrinsic purpose. 'Socialisation', on the other hand, can only be justified in terms of the goals external to itself which it is meant to achieve: be they goals of social engineering or manpower planning. Writing in 1972, in terms not so much intemperate as apocalyptic, he saw the substitution of 'socialisation' for education as 'the most momentous occurrence of this century, the greatest of the adversities to have overtaken our culture, the beginning of the dark age devoted to barbaric affluence'.

Contrary to the current preoccupation with effectiveness, what is at issue here is not primarily a matter of method or technique:

> Early on in his essay Oakeshott states that he will have little to say about 'the procedures, methods and devices' appropriate to the educational engagement. In fact, no doubt because in recent years arguments about procedures 'have imposed themselves upon our understanding of the transaction itself, with unfortunate consequences', his comments on pedagogy are as powerful and relevant as they are deeply unfashionable. His starting point here is that education 'is a difficult engagement of learning by study in a continuous and exacting redirection of attention and refinement of understanding which calls for humility, patience and courage'.

One of the ways in which the drive to raise standards has gained its highest profile in England and Wales is through the Office for Standards in Education (Ofsted). Its influence has in its distinctive way shaped the perceptions of both the general public and the politicians themselves about what is to count as a standard. Its recent head, Chris Woodhead, Her Majesty's Chief Inspector of Schools, has at times seemed to portray himself as the very incarnation of such values. And sometimes as something more: as a man inspired by a higher vision, a man uniquely in the know about what is required, a man who has seen it all before and who is really rather tired of it now. His actions and the operation of Ofsted have had an undoubted effect on the running of schools, especially in terms of the amount of attention given to performance indicators, to marketing and to inspection. As Woodhead himself would recognise, teachers commonly perceive themselves to be suffering from stress, low self-esteem, poor rewards and lack of praise for their efforts, and he is the man they love to hate.

It may come as something of a surprise then that the Oakeshottian words above are none other than Woodhead's own (Woodhead 1995: sections 25, 22, 16). These aspirations have not always coincided with the operations of Ofsted. And something of the incongruity is already evident in the title for this lecture: Woodhead's 'Education: The Elusive Engagement and the Continuing Frustration' turns Oakeshott's 'Education: The Engagement and its Frustration' (Oakeshott 1989) to banality, the apocalyptic become peevish, the magisterial merely tetchy. The frustration, it should be clear, is Woodhead's own.

We have then this Woodheadian Oakeshott-*lite* but also another Woodhead who seems only too ready to underwrite the performativity in the system. And with the latter that tone of condescension and resentment at the way that Ofsted is repeatedly maligned, the tone that teachers have come to know so well. Consider the following paragraphs from the 1998 Annual Lecture, the voice now addressed to something grand:

> A couple of weeks ago, the Chairman of the Select Committee, Margaret Hodge, reprimanded me for the intemperance of my language – polemic, I think, was the word she used.
>
> I am unrepentant. The lesson of the last ten years is as bleak as it is clear. The Government of the day can reform each and every element in the educational enterprise, but if these reforms do not challenge the orthodoxies which have dominated classroom life in too many schools for the last forty years, then they will do little or nothing to raise standards. There is no point in tinkering with the means, if you do not have the courage to think about the ends. These things need saying, loudly, clearly and, at times, intemperately.
>
> (Woodhead 1998: sections 12, 13)

This is Woodhead against the world of falling standards, Churchillian *gravitas* in the name of right. Woodhead takes upon himself the mantle of saying untimely things. (You wouldn't expect *me* to do the popular thing.[2]) But there is a deeper conformism here, to the demands of a certain authoritarian persona. It is not just the familiar emphasis on spelling and grammar and the like (for much of which there is much to be said): it is the grudging acknowledgement of the difficulties teachers have, the recriminations against 'failing' schools, the apparent fawning before politicians and the ritual public humiliation of progressivism. The celebration of the cultural inheritance in Oakeshott is here tainted, to say the least, by the negativity, by something like *ressentiment* – 'carping guardian of the established order, watchdog of current values', in Deleuze's words (Deleuze 1993: 55).

Active forces are stifled in the Last Man. One can never have done with anything, never set aside or forget:

> The slave revolt in morals begins when *ressentiment* itself becomes creative and ordains values: the *ressentiment* of creatures to whom the real reaction, that of the deed, is denied and who find compensation in an imaginary revenge. While all noble morality grows from a triumphant affirmation of itself, slave morality from the outset says no to an 'outside', to an 'other', to a 'non-self': and *this* no is its creative act. The reversal of the evaluating gaze – this *necessary* orientation outwards rather than inwards to the self – belongs characteristically to *ressentiment*. In order to exist at all, slave morality from the outset always needs an opposing, outer world; in physiological terms, it needs external stimuli in order to act – its action is fundamentally reaction. The opposite is the case with the aristocratic mode of evaluation: this acts and grows spontaneously, it only seeks out its antithesis in order to affirm itself more thankfully and more joyfully.
>
> (*GM*: 22)

The triumph of the slaves as slaves is something we all succumb to: it is the negativity that eats away at an ordinary human life, with its (self-)recriminations, regrets and resentments. Suspicion, the inexhaustible capacity for disparagement, and then self-reproach, self-deprecation – these conceal a hatred or desire for revenge, and a reduction of things to mediocrity. Moreover there is a peculiarly disengaged perspective here – the stance of the onlooker and indeed of inspection. Morality requires the standpoint of the passive third party, the objectifying gaze and neutral stance. Nietzsche, in contrast, wants us to grow tired of the words 'reward', 'retribution', 'punishment', righteous revenge': 'That *your* Self be in the action, as the mother is in the child: let that be *your* maxim of virtue!' (Z: 120).

Passivity ensues where reaction, in ceasing to be acted, becomes *ressentiment*. 'This', for Deleuze, 'is the great resounding event: the reactive man in place of God. We know that the result of this is – the last man, the one who prefers a nothingness of will, who prefers to fade away passively, rather than a will to nothingness' (Deleuze 1983: 174).

Affirmation

What we need is the transvaluation of all values. This is not, it must be clear, the cynical debunking of all values as if they were nothing, it is not nihilism, but the debunking of those settled and stale values that stupefy and dull us, values that become simulacra of values. And the recognition is that there can be no abstract detached evaluation of values: to judge the worth of the values someone lives by you need to judge how she came by those values. What kind of striving led to them? Or how readily did she just take them as read? This will be their pedigree. Aristocratic values are not created *ex nihilo*: one must raise the standard for oneself and follow it, in an actualisation of energy and enthusiasm. They require a rejection of that dwelling on the negativity that has characterised and shaped so much of our thought: negativity of moralism, of lack, of 'consolations called *spontaneity* and *creativity*' (Lyotard 1993: 116), of the subjectivist preoccupation in the creation of one's own values.

We are coming close here to what is needed, but consider the various ways in which laudable commitments can nevertheless go awry.

- We see that the fact that values have been striven for is a mark of their authenticity: as active evaluations, they release energy. But aren't we tired of hearing of the aim of authenticity, and hasn't our tiredness picked up on something important here: the authentic becomes invested with a mysterious essence – 'the real thing'? Sometimes, as in Heidegger's Nietzsche, this can seem like the substitute for the god that has died.
- We see that values require personal assent. So, we imagine, values can be agreed, they can be the product of consensus. But this opens up what Lyotard calls 'the nihilism of reasons' (ibid.:

25), the modern positivism of the free-thinkers. Surely you must see reason. Surely you cannot deny the facts. But how far do these facts even make sense without some prior evaluation? The modern myth is of an objectively viewed world to which values can be subsequently and contingently attached.

- We recognise Oakeshott's good teacher as a living exemplar of what it is to study the subject, to be energised and enthralled. But Oakeshott's teacher is sentimentalised and displaced by the cult of personality. Emulation degenerates into a kind of mimicry.
- We recognise the best that has been thought and said and advocate initiation into the intrinsically worthwhile. But a strange halo can hang around such pursuits. Canonisation leads to deference – or to that hollow kind of aesthetic reverence where people cultivate good taste as a social attribute. Real engagement with learning can give way to dry scholarship or to the English disease of gentility (Alvarez 1962). And worse, there can be a deep, if scarcely conscious, cynicism in learning (even where the curriculum is of the best) where one goes through the motions, perhaps with great 'success'.

It is not that these orientations are inherently bad but that they are liable to subversion by the negativity that culminates in the Last Man.

In the face of this, a conversion is needed. Exuberance in the nursery school, fascination of the engineer with the machine's precision, rapt contemplation of the work of art, puzzling over an equation in mathematics, peculiar turbulence excited by a philosophical problem – all are typified by an intense absorption. What we want, as Lyotard has it, what we want is intensity. With something like electric illumination, the teacher must conduct intensities.

Enthusiasm in a lesson might be like absorption in a game, not the final stages where the outcome is becoming clear and you coldly clear your opponent's pieces from the board, but when in the middle, where it still could go either way, the game begins to pick up speed. Stick to your well-planned lesson if you want to be assured of successful outcomes, but lose the engagement and its intensity. To enter into this intensity the lesson must make manifest the confident experience of the good. 'To understand, to be intelligent, is not our overriding passion. We hope rather to be set in motion. Consequently our passion would sooner be the dance, as Nietzsche wanted . . .' (Lyotard 1993: 51).[3]

We speak not of social rank but more of an aristocracy of the self. Some have the mettle for this more than others; but the Last Man allegorises debilities within oneself. We do not really know what someone totally without *ressentiment* would be like. We come to see the actuality of resentments and recriminations, a clinging to negativity and a refusing to let go, but also possibilities of affirmation and intensity. If Nietzsche is right, we must look for and overcome these negativities in ourselves, and there can be no doubt that these are crucial for education. The strong – those who can affirm life – need to be protected from the life-sapping nihilism of the weak, and this is not to be realised through the nostalgic restating of values, through the monitoring and rubber-stamping of standards, for these are only guises of the Last Man. It must reach its completion by passing through the Last Man, but going beyond him to the one who wants to perish, to have done with that negativity within himself: relentless destruction of the reactive forces, of the degenerating and parasitic, passing into service of a superfluity of life (*EH*, 'The Birth of Tragedy': sections 3, 4).

Notes

1 Howard Kirk, the anti-hero of Malcolm Bradbury's *The History Man*, is a professor of sociology at a new university in the late 1960s.
2 When Margaret Thatcher used these words, they proved popular with voters.
3 On this Lyotardian reading of Nietzsche we have benefited from discussions with both Gordon Bearn and James Williams.

FRAGMENT IV

Management theory is in crisis. If the governing values of management are not supplied by effectiveness, where are they to be found? *Learning* is the new candidate. Good management places a premium on the learning of the workforce. All organisations shall be learning organisations. Every failure is a chance to learn, but of course there are no real failures or problems anyway, only opportunities.

Recall the software company manager. He summoned the employee who had just made a mistake costing $10 million. Expecting to be fired, the nervous employee was told: 'Why would I fire you? I've just invested $10 million in your education!'

The *Reader's Digest* catches the right tone here. Endless optimism, unconditional positive regard and unshakeable faith in capitalism.

Management will love learning because organisations are leaner and people have to take on more diverse responsibilities; because the pace of change means that the skills required for any job don't stay the same; because in the future we shall all

- change careers every two months
- build a portfolio of work
- situate ourselves in a network of possibilities
- work from a deckchair on the moon with a computer and a modem

– because this is the knowledge economy in which 97 per cent of the workforce deals not with things but with concepts, and in which all but three of the top *Fortune 500* companies are in the business of producing not artefacts but ideas. We have of course made these figures up, but the reader will find the general picture familiar.

If learning is to be the fundamental value of management then we are in worse trouble than we thought. For it is all up with learning already. In the world of formal education the Priests of Performativity have ensured that learning amounts to getting results: more of them, got faster, means better learning. More GCSE passes at grade C and above means a better school. A National Curriculum for the unborn child, and GCSEs to be taken at nine years by those who can manage it. The first year of undergraduate study to be franchised to school sixth-forms, the one-year undergraduate degree (originally we wrote two-year, but that is nearly upon us in the form of the 'Foundation Degree': you cannot make these things up), the five-semester academic year.

In *Emile, or on Education* Rousseau writes that 'the most important, the most useful rule of all education . . . .is not to save time but to waste it' (*la plus grande, la plus importante, la plus utile règle de toute l'éducation? ce n'est pas de gagner du temps, c'est d'en perdre*, para. 271).

To think that trainee teachers were once permitted to read stuff of this sort!

FRAGMENT V

The learning society, meanwhile, and the enterprise of lifelong learning, have turned out to mean accreditation, the accumulation and validation of skills. Really the only learning we are interested in is the kind that can be entered to the account on our personal swipe-card: Internet for Beginners, Assertiveness Skills, Intermediate Time Management. It is a sign of how wary we are of learning that we want to think of it in terms of skills – something we *have* rather than part of what we *are*. There is Personal Growth, of course, its expanding shelves some distance from the Education section and worryingly close to the texts on Nostradamus and the Real Meaning of the Eclipse.

The truly exciting thing is that in the new emphasis on learning we are urged to take responsibility for our *own* development.

Managers – and their companies – now realize that developing managerial skills and techniques is not simply the responsibility of the company. Managers, too, have a role to play in being proactive and identifying areas in which they need to develop. Today, instead of being pawns moved around by corporate might, managers are increasingly encouraged to examine their own strengths and weaknesses to develop the skills necessary for the future. Rather than having their own development mapped out for them, managers are managing it for themselves.

(Crainer 1996: 212)

The key value in management is learning, and learning must be managed. Perhaps the key value in learning is precisely that – like an effective research project – it should be well-managed. The key value in learning is management. You will manage your own learning, and if things do not go well with you no doubt it will be because you lacked the relevant management skills. Do not despair: there are courses for such things.

Part 2

Overcoming nihilism

Part 2

Chapter 5

Nihilism, Nietzsche and education

> Indeed, we philosophers and 'free spirits' feel, when we hear the
> news that the 'old god is dead', as if a new dawn shone upon us;
> our heart overflows with gratitude, amazement, premonitions,
> expectation. At long last the horizon appears free to us again,
> even if it should be bright; at long last our ships may venture out
> again, venture out to face any danger; all the daring of the lover
> of knowledge is permitted again; the sea, *our* sea, lies open again;
> perhaps there has never yet been such an 'open sea'.
>
> (*GS*: section 343)

It is fashionable these days in the wave of the criticism of post-
structuralism and postmodernism, to blame Nietzsche for nihilistic
tendencies in educational theory and to reproach nihilism for being
subjectivistic and relativistic, thus condemning it in essence as
indefensible. In his reflections on liberal education, Arcilla for
instance describes the Nietzschean subject as one who simply does
not care about justifying her beliefs and actions to others and
concerns herself exclusively with self-centred desires or values:

> Although Nietzsche calls on us to create and organize our own
> worlds, he appears to demand that we live only by the rule of
> whim. Are there to be no guides for the will? Is everything
> permitted? Is all external constraint to be considered simply an
> enemy will, fit only to be resisted and overpowered? Under such
> conditions, is it possible to create a culture that can be
> commonly affirmed? With these questions, which threaten any
> conception of social order, we begin to appreciate the cost of his
> renunciation of the problem of reason, a renunciation that
> makes him, in the eyes of many, the prophet of nihilism, or at
> least of the quintessentially postmodern question: Whose
> values?
>
> (Arcilla 1995: 45)

As indicated, this criticism is not uncommon. Thus Johnston (1998) too argues that a total break from education as it is currently practised is what would be needed if one were to adopt a thoroughly Nietzschean stand on education. And he further holds that Nietzsche castigates the interpersonal values that education promotes in favour of an intrapersonal, intrasubjective, and individual emphasis.

> For Nietzsche, though, there is no question of a reconciliation between the realms of the individual and social. One simply has to overcome the social if one desires in turn to self-overcome. To propose a democratic Nietzsche requires one to somehow fashion a compatible solution that does not give too much control, too much weight, to either the social or the individual. A democratic Nietzsche cannot exist in this respect and at the same time recommend to the individual a radical turning away from society and the social in favor of oneself. Nietzsche chooses . . . [A]nd the choice he makes is the individual.
> (Johnston: 1998: 81)

Clearly, it is easy to show that Nietzsche has been misinterpreted in ways both sinister and potentially dangerous, for instance where he was posthumously adopted as the approved philosopher of the Nazi Party, but the fashionable criticism concerning his subjectivism and relativism is another and equally important matter.

In this chapter we will first deal with nihilism in general and the particular position Nietzsche holds concerning this. Then we will sketch the way Nietzschean ideas have been used in the context of educational theory. Finally we shall focus on the inadequacies of some of these and indicate in what sense Nietzschean nihilism holds out a prospect of re-conceiving education.

Nihilism

It is not until the late eighteenth century, and thus with the emergence of the Enlightenment, that the term 'nihilism' appears on the philosophical scene,[1] partly as a result of the implicit tendency of transcendental idealism to dissolve the reality of the external world in the nothingness of consciousness, by focusing on the subjective conditions for the possibility of knowledge. It was in debates about the implications of early nineteenth century German idealism that Jacobi criticised the idealism whose untenability was shown in his view by its culmination in chimerism or nihilism. The literary realm too had its own version, a poetic nihilism which was attacked as the romantic fascination with the privacy of individual consciousness. In these discussions too the term was used to signify the loss or dissolution of an independently existing world external to consciousness. In the second half of the nineteenth century nihilism tended to be linked to moral, religious and political anarchism, usually grounded in loss of belief in God. Arrival in the popular consciousness was mainly through the activities of a group of Russian political dissidents who labelled themselves 'nihilists' and the presentation of their views in the novels of Dostoyevsky and Turgenev. Evidently Nietzsche too played a role in this. For him nihilism is generally used to describe a negative, life-denying interpretation of the world (such as Christianity or Buddhism) or the absence of any meaningful interpretation of the world due to the collapse of the prevailing one (see further below).

Carr (1992) distinguishes different strands of nihilism. Epistemologically it is characterised by the denial of the possibility of knowledge with the result that 'All knowledge claims are equal or equally (un)justified' and no standards exist for distinguishing warranted from unwarranted belief, or knowledge from error. Alethiological nihilism denies the reality of truth: metaphysical or ontological nihilism is the denial of an (independently existing) world. In ethical or moral nihilism the reality of moral or ethical values is disclaimed. It is not denied that people use moral or ethical terms, rather it is claimed that these refer to nothing more than the bias or taste of the agent making the assertion. Finally, existential or axiological nihilism refers to the feeling of emptiness and pointlessness that follows from the judgement 'Life has no meaning'; probably this is the most commonplace sense of the word. In practice the various senses tend to overlap and intermingle. They are all related to the last kind, since we describe life as pointless, meaningless or our existence as without value precisely because we believe that there is no truth, that knowledge is mere illusion, or that there is no moral fabric in the universe. The despair of this kind of nihilism is thus parasitic on one of the other logically prior forms. Nihilism which makes a negative assertation about the nature of the world is different from the related position of scepticism, as the latter merely expresses doubts about the possibility of knowledge or the reliability of our senses and reasoning faculties. Neither is it identical with all forms of relativism:[2] epistemological relativism does not commit one to epistemological nihilism. One could believe that while ethics are contextual, there are some elements common to all ethical frameworks.

Nietzsche's particular kind of nihilism

The author *par excellence* to whom nihilism is ascribed is of course Friedrich Wilhelm Nietzsche, who violently proclaimed that 'God is dead', which he calls in the section quoted at the beginning of this chapter 'the greatest recent event'. The nihilist despairs because he longs to value something but in good faith cannot, for he believes that only values believed to be objective can in good faith be professed (and he no longer believes in objective values – incidentally, the claim that only objective values can be legitimate values is itself a value judgement). The particular form of nihilism in which Nietzsche is interested should however be understood as the state one may be in when nothing truly matters to one. Overcoming this nihilism is not so much a matter of replacing old values with new ones, as it is of coming to value something where previously one valued nothing. Roughly what he means is that we must take a certain sort of responsibility for what we say about the world and accept that we cannot lean on something else when values are concerned. Sense can no longer be made of the idea that the ways in which we view the world are justified by something standing above, beyond or behind the world itself. Neither nature, nor reason, nor revelation can provide the moral standards for the governance of life. He holds that as there are no objective values, as all values are the creation of human beings, they typically serve the needs of their creators – understanding why they were created requires therefore investigating the (historically and psychologically conditioned) needs of their creators.

Nietzsche teaches that we are free to adopt the perspective that proclaims the value of creating subjective value.[3] This creation should not be understood as a kind of subjectivism, as if the subject could create values *ex nihilo*, could impose or project values into the world. What Nietzsche means is that we have to take responsibility for having to take responsibility, rather than trying to deny the fact of such responsibility by means of a fantasy of access to the world's nature that would be wholly independent of our 'human, all too human' interests and aims. His interest lies in the loss of the world: more specifically how humans create and do not find a world. He wants to transcend the reaction of those who seek compensation in imaginary revenge (instead of a real reaction, i.e. a deed) or those who nostalgically restate values (see further below). Whoever can afford to tell the truth about himself, will come to find unintelligible the idea that the sense he makes of the world is either inherent in the world or imposed upon it from the outside – a criticism particularly directed against the lie, as Nietzsche maintains, that

Christian moral values are objective. Failing to take responsibility characterises what he calls 'the herd' and threatens the very possibility of individuality in the present age.

No, life has not disappointed me. On the contrary, I find it truer, more desirable and mysterious every year – ever since the day when the great liberator came to me: the idea that life could be an experiment of the seeker for knowledge – and not a duty, not a calamity, not trickery. – And knowledge itself: let it be something else for others; for example, a bed to rest on, or the way to such a bed, or a diversion, or a form of leisure – for me it is a world of dangers and victories in which heroic feelings, too, find places to dance and play. 'Life as a means to knowledge' – with this principle in one's heart one can live not only boldly but even gaily, and laugh gaily, too.

(*GS*: section 324)

There is no magical action or event that binds interpretations to their objects, nothing in this sense that might justify our interpretation of the world, yet there is no radical freedom either. We go on intelligibly with our concepts in the ways that we do, as members of the particular culture that we live in. According to Nietzsche, Socrates however asks what justifies interpreting one's concepts in the way one does and demands that the justification be articulated in terms wholly independent of the actual conditions of the interpretation in question (cf. *TI*, 'The Problem of Socrates'). Socratism presupposes a standpoint that is completely external to culture as a whole; its aim is not to achieve critical independence from this or that tradition in particular, but rather from any and all traditions whatsoever. This stems in Nietzsche's opinion from a desire not to see ourselves as members of a community at all and he diagnoses behind this an urge to give up altogether on the attempt to make sense. Socrates' failure comes down to not understanding the role that the authority of culture plays in the practices of judgement, that is to say the constraint that one's culture exercises on one's judgements. It is about intelligibility as opposed to making meaning which is fundamentally a practical matter.

Every morality is, as opposed to *laisser aller*, a piece of tyranny against 'nature', likewise against 'reason': but that can be no objection to it unless one is in possession of some other morality which decrees that any kind of tyranny and unreason is impermissible. . . . The essential thing 'in heaven and upon earth' seems, to say it again, to be a protracted *obedience* in *one*

> direction; from out of that there always emerges and has always
> emerged in the long run something for the sake of which it is
> worthwhile to live on earth, for example, virtue, art, music
> dance, reason, spirituality – something transfiguring, refined,
> mad and divine.
>
> (*BGE*: section 188)

And also:

> Wherever authority is still part of accepted usage . . . one does
> not 'give reasons' but commands.
>
> (*TI*, 'The Problem of Socrates': section 5)

What Socrates is calling for is precisely a justification of obedience to
such authority, as mere obedience is never enough to guarantee
intelligibility. 'Authority' as in the passage above from *Twilight of
the Idols* refers to something we might call the 'constraint' that one's
culture exercises on one's judgements. The error that Nietzsche
thus diagnoses at the root of Socratism is a matter of treating
obedience as interpretation, as accepting one's culture's interpretation of itself, of its members, its world, as something that presents
itself as a candidate for philosophical justification (a demand which
only makes sense in the context of a collapse of culture). Unless we
have good reasons to rule out alternative interpretations we cannot
be said truly to mean anything at all by our moral judgements,
since judgements guided only by instinct are blind. Though he is
not trying to rule out the possibility of all rational inquiry
whatsoever, he is concerned to understand the nature of what he
thinks of as specifically philosophical resistance to the ordinary
conditions that govern the employment of any concepts at all. In
other words his claim is not that we must learn to live without
reasons but rather that we must come to see where it no longer
makes sense to ask for reasons, because a search for reasons ends in
discovery of the conditions for whatever we want to explain.

From this it follows that 'perspectivism' cannot be a view with
which Nietzsche intended to replace the traditional epistemology
he rejected. In the same vein there is his denial of the thing-in-
itself: this presupposes a particular essence, a metaphysical system
or ontology that gives once and for all the *eidos*, the nature of
something and associated normative implications. One should be
careful here: we do not impose interpretations on the world so that
we are responsible for the meaning we make of the world in this
sense; rather what is at stake is a fundamentally practical matter. As
he denies that we can make good sense of the idea of the object of

such an imposition, the concept of imposition itself makes no sense. Two different senses of 'responsibility' are at work here. On the one hand responsibility is a matter of articulating one's (Socratic) standards of judgement, standards which must be sufficiently independent of one's actual practices of judgement to have the required kind of objectivity and justificatory status. On the other hand there is responsibility in an existentialist vein, where one either accepts or disowns responsibility for what one says and does and is, just because there is no one and nothing else to bear that responsibility (this would constitute an absence of standards). But for Nietzsche the conception of standards being appealed to here is incoherent, and he therefore finds the notion of responsibility incoherent. Rather than claiming that we should take responsibility for the meaning we impose on the world, Nietzsche seems to show us how we resist the meaning we find in the world and how we are inclined to hide in the herd. Thus he seeks to replace the Socratic notion of responsibility, which in his view expresses philosophical dissatisfaction with life, with a notion of responsiveness understood in terms of the notion of commitment, a form of passivity, an openness to what matters to us.

Nietzsche intimates the possibility of a new relation to things, a relation in which we have learned to leave them be. On the one hand we accept them in their pristine and unsayable integrity, on the other we transform them through continually renewed mythic and artistic renderings. The tragic form of art is for Nietzsche a way to overthrow nihilism by the discovery of the special value of what is near to us, the value of what seemed to be unimportant.

> My formula for greatness in a human being is *amor fati*: that one wants nothing to be other than it is, not in the future, not in the past, not in all eternity. Not merely bear what is to endure that which happens of necessity, still less necessary, still less to dissemble it – all idealism is untruthfulness in the face of necessity – but *love* it.
>
> (*EH*, 'Why I Am So Clever': section 10)

The things around us are wonderful because they are fragile. One can love them, they can become precious and things we care for, because they are not immune from the uncertainties of life. When we realise this, the little things of life acquire a new significance for us and this may lead to a better attunement to the world. The latter is however not to be taken as equivalent to 'resting in peace': this cannot be reconciled with his idea concerning self-realisation and the emancipation of the creative will. It is, however, meant to temper the ambitions of reason itself by focusing on its limitations and its presuppositions.

Nietzsche claims that we lack a culture, not in the sense of being untutored in the finer things of life (though such a claim may well be true); 'culture' refers neither to mental, nor institutional, nor artistic cultivation but to a form of life in which sense is made, that is in which we take responsibility for what we say. Speech requires a willingness to submit oneself, not to want to stand outside culture if we are to engage in rational criticism. If nihilism is understood as something like a modern crisis of meaninglessness, then Nietzsche's worries are different from the existentialists' worries. The latter claim to have recognised the meaninglessness of life in general, and propose a distinction between those who can face up to this fact and those who cannot. Nietzsche claims to have recognised the meaninglessness of our lives as we now live them, but he also insists on the possibility of rectifying the situation.

Nietzsche's antipathy toward what he calls moral values is aimed at those ways of life that seek to deny life. It refers to whatever it is in our religion, philosophy, and ethical life that gives voice to our need for reasons understood as a demand that our actions be justified by an appeal to something both independent of our interests and opinions and available to everyone, just insofar as they are rational. Thus philosophy too is diagnosed as a spectator's way of making sense of life. The antipathy is against those ways of life that seek to deny life:

> It is clear from the outset that such a self-contradiction as the ascetic priest seems to represent, that of 'life against life', is, in terms of physiology now rather than psychology, simply nonsense. It can be nothing more than *apparent*; . . . *the ascetic ideal is derived from the protective and healing instincts of a degenerating life*, which seeks to preserve itself and fights for existence with any available means; . . . The ascetic priest embodies the desire for another existence, somewhere else, is even the highest form of this desire, its real intensity and passion. But the very *power* of this desire is the chain which binds him to this life; this very power transforms him into an instrument, obliged to work to create more favourable conditions for human life as it exists here . . .
>
> (*GM*, 'Third Essay': section 13)

To affirm life means to affirm one's membership of a culture, but this is simply to make sense, to speak intelligibly; it is about affirming those passions, affects and drives that are condemned by conventional morality, but not about stepping outside the achievement of intelligibility, that is to say that one's perspective on the things around one cannot but be from the perspective of the culture to which one belongs and which is at the same time affirmed. Evidently, the Enlightenment and all that goes with it was for Nietzsche neither a necessary nor a sufficient condition for the justification of a particular individual stance. Like its metaphysical predecessors it had lost its credibility and could no longer convince. Man is part of something from which much traditional thought had excepted him, and his nature is embedded in a wider nature from which it differs in some key respects but shares at the same time elements as well (cf. *BGE*: section 9). Nietzsche's revaluation of values is carried out from a naturalistic viewpoint: 'This [revaluation] requires a knowledge of the conditions and circumstances of their growth, development and displacement' (cf. *GM*, 'Preface': section 6). Living in accordance with nature is living a life that affirms what nature is in us, without dressing it up through morality. It consists of instincts and inclinations, the body, sexuality and so forth. Consequently, customs, institutions and moralities are 'natural' when they affirm the natural instincts of any group of human beings.

> I find those people disagreeable in whom every natural inclination immediately becomes a sickness, something that disfigures them or is downright infamous: it is *they* that have seduced us to hold that man's inclinations and instincts are evil. *They* are the cause of our great injustice against our nature, against all nature. There are enough people who *might well* entrust themselves to their instincts with grace and without care; but they do not, from fear of this imagined 'evil character' of nature. That is why we find so little nobility among men; for it will always be the mark of nobility that one feels no fear of oneself, expects nothing infamous of oneself, flies without scruple where we feel like flying, we freeborn birds. Wherever we may come there will always be freedom and sunlight around us.
>
> (*GS*: section 294)

At a deeper level living in accordance with nature prescribes an ideal of human perfectibility. Schatzki (1994) characterises the *Übermensch*, being the fullest expression of the will to power, by the pursuit of a single goal, freedom (the ability to harmonise the divergent inclinations and instincts within one into a coherent force directed toward one's ruling goal), discipline (the struggle required in order to attain freedom), the creation of values and the affirmation of all elements of reality. The return to nature is thus not a return to an unbridled, instinctual beast of prey, rather '. . . it is a rising up to a harmonised existence that focuses on an achievement, affirms what is, and creates the values according to which it operates' (Schatzki 1994: 158). Evidently this creation of values and ends is not a free arbitrary willing, it is not a matter of whim in Arcilla's sense (above); rather it involves the unrepressed flowering-forth of the necessity that is a person's own nature, one of the products of the overflow of which are the values and goals that govern his life. In the same vein, creativity is neither the apotheosis of the modern idea of individual self-assertion nor an imitation of nature, rather it is the focused expression of the nature in us, which at least partly varies from person to person.

There is to be no devaluation of nature and body, so that we are not cut off from that unique transformative potential which exists within us, in which sexuality and bodily energy is fundamental to the creative possibilities arising from a truly artistic relation to life. Though Nietzsche focuses on joy and happiness as values of the creator, this should be understood in a nuanced way:

> Whether it be hedonism or pessimism, utilitarianism or eudaemonism: all these modes of thought which assess the value of things according to *pleasure* and *pain*, that is to say according to attendant and secondary phenomena, are foreground modes of thought and naïveties which anyone conscious of *creative* powers and an artist's conscience will look down on with derision, though not without pity . . . there are higher problems . . .
>
> (*BGE*: section 225)

Thus he restores natural features into the content and criteria of the good without building ought into is by an essence or *telos* of man. The latter would imply that particular values are justified by a reference to the nature or essence of man, with built-in criteria determining what at a basic level the kind of joy or happiness a human being really longs for is. Moreover, Nietzsche did not seek somehow to supply new values, for instance a concrete specification of some new set of institutions and practices that might give content to modern life. Instead, he provides attractive and inspiring portrayals of human types strong enough to create values without deceiving themselves about their origin.

Being intelligible, making sense, as an intersubjective, third person perspective, is a kind of creation, but not a creation *ex nihilo*:

we talk about the world, but no gap between us and the world is bridged in doing so; only psychologically speaking there is a gap between ourselves and the sense that we make. The cultural obedience dealt with above is different from mere slavishness, which does not tend to produce something for whose sake it is worth while to live on earth (see also *BGE*: section 188, quoted above). Philosophically it makes no sense to hold anyone responsible for this obedience; we do not choose or otherwise decide what constrains us. The freedom Nietzsche associates with this has nothing to do with freedom of choice. The artist knows how strictly and subtly he obeys thousand-fold laws (cf. *BGE*: section 188). Letting yourself be constrained by this kind of obedience expresses more adequately an acceptance of the authority of the culture. And it is this that, according to Nietzsche, tragedy teaches us. It does this however in an indirect fashion, reminding us that only as an aesthetic phenomenon can life be justified.

Socratism thus functioned in Nietzsche's view as a response to a particular kind of suffering which is not that connected with everyday misfortune, nor is it the arbitrariness of human convention. Instead, the tragic Greeks suffered from the meaningfulness of life: its necessary fragility between elevation and destruction. Socratism resists this by saying that life stands in need of justification, of resting on solid foundations of certainty, thus exemplifying a theoretical optimism: the illusion that knowledge can make us happy, the unshakable faith that thought, using the thread of causality, can penetrate the deepest abysses of being, that thought is capable not only of knowing being but even of correcting it. From the tragic point of view culture is no longer seen as standing over or against nature, but instead one is simply obedient to its authority. The possibility of being mistaken provides for Nietzsche no reason to worry whether one has somehow gone astray, does not give one cause to distrust one's instincts. For Socrates what one does is simply not good enough. This reflects the philosopher's desire for something more than our human, all-too-human practices – a desire for something less than what we have already got in the form of our human, all-too-human psychology.

For Nietzsche (the authority of) culture is something to which we are called upon to be responsive, our resistance to which we are called upon to overcome. And his demand on us to transform our life, to make something of ourselves, is not the common idea of self-creation, rather it is a matter of giving one's life style: of overcoming the resistance to recognising the particular life one has. What is 'invented' is therefore a kind of self-recognition, becoming what we are is a matter of finding oneself, of properly under-

standing what we have become. Human life is seen here as a
struggle against our unwillingness to let ourselves be intelligible.
Clearly there is no room for an ostensibly positive philosophical
account of intelligibility.

> We remain unknown to ourselves, we seekers after knowledge,
> even to ourselves: and with good reason. We have never sought
> after ourselves – so how should we one day find ourselves.
>
> (*GM*, 'Preface': section 1)

Finally, Nietzsche rejects the idea that the would-be individual must
stand outside his or her historical or cultural community and view
the world from a radically different standpoint. What is the case in
general also holds for philosophers themselves:

> You ask me about the idiosyncrasies of philosophers? . . . There
> is their lack of historical sense, their hatred of even the idea of
> becoming, their Egyptianism. They think they are doing a
> thing *honour* when they dehistoricize it, *sub specie aeterni* – when
> they make a mummy of it.
>
> (*TI*, 'Reason' in Philosophy: section 1)

Education and the Nietzschean legacy

Many take *Thus Spake Zarathustra* as the text to unlock the hidden
educator in Nietzsche's philosophy. Others focus on a number of
his early writings and on some of his later ones, or on those where
Nietzsche concerned himself explicitly with the state of education in
his time. There are authors who, finding their inspiration more
generally in his philosophical works, and depending on the
particular aspect they are interested in, propose different kinds of
'Nietzschean educational theory'.[4] Johnston (1998) enlists a
Nietzschean interpretation which uses sublimation in an educational manner, another which advocates 'free' education; there is
also a Dionysian 'agonistic' Nietzsche, a metaphysical Nietzsche, a
'pedagogical anthropologist' who ultimately views all cultural
criticism as broadly educative, an aristocratic anti-university anti-
system Nietzsche who purportedly argues for a complete dis-
mantling of the German educational system, and one who
advocates an aristocracy of the self. Aloni (1989) indicates three
pedagogical dimensions: a radical redefinition of the aim of
education (conceived as the recovery of health and worth); a
pedagogical anthropology in the shape of Nietzsche's search for the
favourable conditions under which great human beings and noble

cultures can come into being; finally, his works themselves can be called pedagogical.

One of the themes that attracts attention is the matter of the real essence of man, not to be found deep inside himself, but rather far above himself, and able to be revealed to man by his true educators. The search for freedom is thus a search for man's authentic being resulting from a deep feeling of responsibility on man's part. This is a freedom man can achieve only by himself; only by struggling with himself. It is not to be equated with lawlessness, but rather a 'freedom for'. This involves for man a mastery over himself, and a full responsibility for his own good and bad actions. The heavy price to be paid for this is his loneliness and isolation from society. A person must be willing to burden himself with his personal destiny, a willingness that can be developed by learning to live in solitude and by finding friends who will confront him with difficult truths. It is important to understand this correctly: the idea of 'being' and 'becoming' is not about finding a personal essence or destiny, but about becoming a free, authentic creator of values (understood in other than in subjectivistic terms), purposes, and perspectives for oneself (a version of child-centred pedagogy does not fit with Nietzsche). It is thus about being a destiny rather than having one. Self-overcoming too enters here, seen by some as the means through which an organism exercises her will-to-power and gives form to herself, by seeking out and competing against the most awesome opponents.

Rosenow (1989) rightly argues that Nietzsche's concept of 'self-overcoming' is a revision and revaluation of the traditional concept of self-mastery or self-control. The latter is based on the idea that a human being is of two or more dimensions and that it is her task to subjugate the rival and contesting powers to one of them (her true essence). The task is to struggle with oneself and to suppress instincts and evil inclinations and to subjugate them to the sublime element. As the ability to master one's impulses and inclinations is not inborn, external authority is necessary. Though educational theories differ in the way they design the constraints, they all aim at the internalisation of external authority to become an integral part of man's personality; this is the point of departure for self-education. It is this concept of 'self-mastery' that Nietzsche challenges. A human being is an individual, the essence of which is uniqueness and singularity. A human being has to overcome all that represses her nature and denies her freedom. This includes conventional moral values, but also the reverence for scholars and philosophers with which her education has imbued her. The authentic overcoming of the false idea of self-mastery imposed by the political and religious establishment requires constant exertion and a readiness for renunciation and sacrifice. As Simons argues: 'Less safety, less mutual protection, less kindness and love, less ease and more contests must be welcomed because of what they would produce. . . . The superman will say YES to life whatever life brings and must exist in the constant pain of battle' (Simons 1988: 345–6). Here the focus is on the social and cultural mechanisms, including education, that adapt man to human society, repress his nature and deny his freedom. It explains Nietzsche's rebellion against established norms and values, the overcoming of his socially defined personality and his lack of reverence for scholars and philosophers who advocate the supremacy of reason.

Johnston therefore characterises, in our opinion correctly, the impetus for any Nietzschean education:

> . . . [it] begins and ends not with society, not with democracy, not with the school, not with the teacher, but with the multiplicity of individual characterizations known collectively as the self.
>
> (Johnston 1998: 68)

Nietzsche agrees, so Johnston claims, that social forces play heavily upon the acceptance of truths, but he argues that truths are reducible in the last to the individual. The self-affirming individual creates her own truths in the sense that how she finds herself, what takes hold of her, will be expressed in what she says and does and tested for 'fit' against the predominant truths of the masses. Thus she rejects (exclusively) outward truth-valuations and overcomes other truths in favour of her own. Of course, Nietzsche does not value each and every truth as equal; he is not in this sense what might be called a relativist. He rather takes upon himself the task of being a cultural critic of the age, thus juxtaposing accepted truths with deviant ones in order to expose truths for their contextual nature. Johnston continues:

> Levelling the field allows individual truths to compete with socially constructed ones. And this strengthens the worthiness of the individual, who remains in perpetual conflict with social, cultural, and historical forces.
>
> (Johnston 1998: 69)

One matter of considerable debate has been the so-called anti-social and subjective nature of Nietzschean authenticity. For instance, Rosenow (1973) is sceptical of a Nietzschean education because it is in his opinion inherently antisocial. Another is the emphasis on a so-called aristocratic kind of education that is thought to be implied. Though Nietzsche would surely agree with a rejection of instrumental reason, this does not mean that he is a proponent of an anarchistic education for children. He does value obedience, rigorous study and stern discipline as far as elementary education goes, but ultimately rejects the hegemony of the educational-cultural institutions (of higher education) in favour of one's individual self-overcoming, and it is to this that education is a means. Nothing here implies situating oneself outside the intersubjective level or necessarily setting oneself up in opposition to others.

It will be clear from the above that Nietzsche's position is different from the extreme relativism and scepticism that claims that because all the traditional groundings for value and knowledge were an illusion we are now faced with the 'nothingness' of these values, a position he refers to as 'nihilism' and which in his opinion is the fundamental character of our age. Both modern nihilism and traditional western values have the same logical relation to the world: they judge it negatively and hence devalue it. He wants to reinstate the value of phenomena such as birth, death, human illness and suffering, the sensory, i.e. the human body. By offering a psychological account of notions such as guilt, sin and redemption he tries to undermine the traditionally sharp distinction between human beings and other animals. He argues that the fact that we feel both responsible for what we do and yet ultimately powerless to do other than we do, that we feel, as it were, victims of ourselves, is a feature of our lives that has a complicated psychological and sociological history. Here, speaking is seen as a form of promising, i.e. a social activity. In obeying the laws of the community the individual member is keeping what Nietzsche considers to be a promise, a 'pledge', in order to enjoy the advantages of society. To say of someone that she has the right to make promises then means that she speaks intelligibly, that she takes responsibility for what she says. Where on the other hand the community itself fails to make sense, where talking the way the herd does is in fact a failure to speak, the notion of an individual can be understood differently. To give one's word (as the sovereign individual has the right to do) is to incur an obligation to let oneself be understood, an obligation to overcome one's unwillingness to do so, to renounce one's desire to remain opaque.

The positive task of Nietzsche's educational psychological and unmasking method is to assist us in overcoming repressive culture and to entice us into discovering in and for ourselves the genuine roots of our creative powers. Nietzsche does not admit a radical

(Freudian) psychological determinism; instead he contends that we have the liberty to shape our selfhood and ideals by freely choosing our education and our exemplary figures. By subjecting our intuitive admiration for great individuals to psychologistic self-analysis we come to realise what we value authentically and what we really are. The road towards authentic freedom and spontaneous creativity (essential to self-overcoming and re-creation) requires two stages: liberating ourselves from the external layers imposed on us by institutional conditionings and freely adopting and assimilating moral norms. In a blind, automated, Darwinian world, where all our transcendental goals have disappeared, we must create new immanent aims. But this needs to be done according to the basic Nietzschean intuition of complete immanency, as Golomb argues:

> There is only one world, one nature and its forces, and there are no transcendental or supra-natural powers: there is no 'pure reason', there is no other world, different and better than ours. Hence, everything that belongs to man and his culture – and is related to Nietzsche's moral ideal of the qualitative progress of mankind – must originate from and be explicated exclusively within the human context.
>
> (Golomb 1985: 107)

With this in mind Nietzsche will expose prevailing pseudo-ideals and false values which are deflecting human effort from its utmost goal. His position embodies a particular kind of vitalism (of *amor fati*), a naturalism without ontology.

Nietzsche holds that the child alone can 'create new values' and this creation, unlike the creation often attributed to traditional values, is not given to us fixed and finished all at once in a revelation from heaven. The child is 'innocence and forgetting'. She gives a sacred 'yes' to all existence for she is beyond the resentment of her body and the world which characterised traditional values:

> The child is innocence and forgetting, a new beginning, a sport, a self-propelling wheel, a first motion, a sacred Yes. Yes, a sacred Yes is needed, my brothers, for the sport of creation: the spirit now wills *its own* will, the spirit sundered from the world now wins *its own* world.
>
> (Z, Book I, 'Of the Three Metamorphoses')

The values Nietzsche envisages arise out of the creative process itself, involving an ever-renewed engagement with the flux of phenomena, with perpetual birth and death. Thus we look for the ways to overcome nihilism which enable us to affirm this world. It is not the discovery of a metaphysical truth that is aimed at but the restoration of the integrity of the phenomena. It is art alone that would seem to have the power to do this. Art does not harden and solidify phenomena into new metaphysical determinations. Images, symbols and metaphors can affirm and enhance the presencing of the phenomena in ever new and renewed configurations:

> Art and nothing but art! It is the great means of making life possible, the great seduction to life, the great stimulant to life.
>
> Art as the only superior counterforce to all will to denial of life, as that which is anti-Christian, anti-Buddhist, anti-nihilist *par excellence*.
>
> Art as the *redemption of the man of knowledge* – of those who see the terrifying and questionable character of existence, who want to see it, the men of tragic knowledge.
>
> Art as the *redemption of the man of action* – of those who not only see the terrifying and questionable character of existence but live it, want to live it, the tragic-warlike man, the hero.
>
> Art as the *redemption of the sufferer* – as the way to states in which suffering is willed, transfigured, deified, where suffering is a form of great delight.
>
> (*WP*: 853, II)

To rear great men is according to Nietzsche the highest task of mankind. As only education can provide for the growth of genius, it is the highest duty. He himself assumed the task of educating the educators which is a self-education, that is to say a recognition and removal of the streaks of decadence. He holds that all philosophy originated and was carried out in the service of education. True education always entails the active influencing of the soul. The (in some sense) individualistic nature of education is a consequence of the educator's need to express herself selectively, thus structuring the needs of her students. Education is aimed through devotion at bringing out the very best in everyone. It has, however, everything to do with control, eventually with controlling oneself, being the coordinator of one's own instincts as Nietzsche calls this. Thus individualism in education is just the opposite of unrestrained development:

> All culture begins with the opposite of that which is so highly esteemed as 'academic freedom' with obedience, with subordination, with discipline, with subjection.
>
> (Nietzsche 1909: 140)

Elsewhere in the *Fifth Lecture* he insists that the aim of the public school is to prepare and accustom the student always to live and learn independently thereafter, just as in the meantime he or she must live and learn dependently there. Thiele (1990: 170) therefore concludes, in our view rightly, that for Nietzsche freedom in an educational setting is a euphemism for anarchy. And it should also be recalled that it is for Nietzsche, of course, not the acquisition of facts or skills or technique, but the transmission of passion and will from teacher to student, that defines education.

What the teacher has to teach simply is not transmissible to a crowd. The educator is to serve as a model for her students. Education is not the determination of who the student should be, but of how she might become who she and only she is. It is not about liberating her potential, but instead about confronting her with various demands that enable her to give shape to her life herself. The educator serves as a living exemplar of what this can mean, as a beacon for her student of what it is to be enthralled by a subject. The authority and discipline the subject commands are indeed indispensable. The true educator celebrates success when her students become worthy of demanding their independence. The disciplined training that allows the student to end her servitude to custom (including the custom of morality) ultimately results in the achievement of maturity and individuality and thus in the end of her servitude to higher persons. The true educator is she who successfully demonstrates a solitude to her students. She serves as the model of how one may escape herd life and bear one's individuality heroically. Only she who has attained her solitude is worthy of being an educator, a catalyst in the formation of other solitaries, prompting the sort of response that may foster the enhancement of our life. Throughout she is alone; even the relations she has with others are further affirmations of this and of her independence. But this kind of solitude is not that of the hermit: what has significance in her life, what gives her life meaning, necessarily refers to others. Her relations towards others are therefore not conceived in terms of what is useful (for her), instead they form the necessary background for her own self-overcoming, for her finding for herself an answer to the question of the meaning of life.

Nietzsche's hostility toward education can thus be understood as expressing his battle against all justificatory tendencies based on firm foundations and systems. His warning can be seen as a kind of way to help us to overcome our insecurity and the rationalisations this generates. He makes it clear that we do not operate in a vacuum of power relations but that these are masked by quasi-arguments.

Making sense and over-coming are both a matter of letting things count as they are, of being responsive to them. It is a perpetual task, this struggle against our unwillingness to let ourselves be intelligible. Nietzsche's language is persuasive and necessarily visionary. That all knowledge presupposes experience and that all experience is individual lies for him at the basis.

Education as a process, for Nietzsche, ultimately does not assist a self-overcoming individual to overcome hitherto accepted valuations. It can quite evidently not supply the task of overturning valuations that education itself comprises. A Nietzschean view of education would in the end necessitate a movement away from the social ideal to an individual one, in favour of intrapersonal, intrasubjective and individual values. Such a self-overcoming individual requires something that education as normally understood ultimately cannot provide: 'a moment-to-moment, hour-to-hour, day-to-day self-realization of one's strengths and weaknesses, together with a profound ability to suffer well' (Johnston 1998: 77). This kind of individual cannot be disseminated but rather must be self-taught. This is the reason why it is not correct to attribute to Nietzsche the ideal of an aristocratic education for a few rare individuals. The mission of all education in the end is that it should pass into (what is perhaps not best expressed by the concept of) 'self-education'. Though education holds an important function for the masses (passing on acceptable values from one generation to the next), for the self-overcoming individual this kind of education too has to be overcome. In the end one must be able to distance oneself from the means of one's education, even, as Schacht argues '... if we must initially be seduced and induced to engage with it and take it seriously enough to be affected by it' (1998: 330). As one finds in the connotation of the German word *Erziehung*, the object of this education is to 'draw us out' and up toward becoming what we are, thus providing 'us with a way of facing and coming to terms with the terror and horror of existence.

Notes

1. For a more detailed discussion of 'nihilism', see, for instance, Carr 1992; Edwards 1990; Rosen 1969.
2. For a discussion of this position see in particular Chapter 1 in Blake, Smeyers, Smith and Standish 1998.
3. What this implies is developed further in the chapter on affirmative ethics and integrity.
4. See, for instance, Aloni 1989; Arcilla 1995; Aviram 1991; Cooper 1983a, 1983b; Golomb 1985; Gordon 1980; Hillisheim 1973; Rosenow 1973, 1986 and 1989; Sassone 1996; Schneider 1992; Sharp 1984; Simons 1988.

Chapter 6

Our most holy duty

Language and literacy

Let us start with Michael Barber, head of the UK government's Standards and Effectiveness Unit, who thinks it is all going terribly well:

> We've been gathering evidence all term of the impact of the literacy strategy in primary schools. We played that evidence back to the several hundred teachers who attended the TES-sponsored conferences over the past three weeks. The message is very clear: it's got off to an excellent start. The vast majority of local authorities and schools are working hard to put it into practice.
>
> (*Times Educational Supplement*, 27 November 1998)

This paragraph, itself a highly literate artefact, repays careful reading. The reader is drawn in by the intimacy and informality of the initial 'We've', and disposed to be convinced by the evidence: if it could be 'played back' it must have been firm evidence indeed, the kind of thing you could record on sound or video and play back to an attentive audience. But can you really record 'impact' in that way? Doubts should be silenced. For the message is clear and uplifting. Further informality, in 'it's got off to an excellent start', half suggests Barber is reporting the informal speech of teachers standing up to testify at the sponsored conferences (literacy, like everything else in our commodified world, can of course be sponsored). Here indeed is evidence being played back to us, we may feel. The 'vast majority' – ah, never mind what the vast majority did or thought. We know we can relax when we hear of them, for they represent the normal folk to whose bosom we aspire to be clutched. They are hard-working and we, Barber's intended audience, are busy teachers. We are made for each other.

Suitably relaxed by finding ourselves part of the crowd, we can nod along with Barber's second paragraph:

Teachers are seeing the benefits. Most are asking 'How' questions rather than 'Whether?' or 'Why?' This is not to say that nobody has any problems. A major change of this kind is never without some problems but the balance sheet is extremely positive . . .

Teachers have come to accept their role under the totalising state. They are its instruments, devotedly carrying out procedures. The new educational regime of course is not slow to lay these down, prescribing literacy strategies and literacy hours in unprecedented detail. A technology has been evolved, in which phonemes, graphemes, *haiku*, *tanka*, tautology, tense, text and trigraph whirl in technical complexity satisfying to those disposed to be satisfied by that sort of thing. 'Teachers who have not formerly had systematic training in teaching the crucial phonic/word level work at key stage 1 will need further training to reinforce skills', Barber writes, glossing over what might be thought the crucial question of what *is* crucial to literacy. 'The key to the strategy is that teachers master the skills involved in it. The basic premise, after all, is that this is an entitlement for every primary teacher to know, understand and be able to use proven best practice'. (An advanced course in critical literacy might spend twenty minutes of its Critical Hour on that last pair of sentences.)

Meanwhile the literate child is defined, according to the Literacy literature, by bullet-pointed (of course) criteria of which the second is that he or she should 'be able to orchestrate a full range of reading cues (phonic, graphic, syntactic, contextual) to monitor their reading and correct their own mistakes'. A DfEE Web page tells us that 'Most children learn to read by putting letters together that match up with the sounds that they remember hearing. They learn the sounds that letters make. They learn how letters join together to make words'. The balance sheet is positive: problems in one column, but a list of teacher skills and literacy skills – putting letters together, learning the sounds that letters make – in the other.

Those who construct these technical edifices are often hurt and puzzled by criticism. 'Research has shown', they say, 'Best practice. Vital not to be deflected from the way ahead'. A major question hangs over the research basis for the Literacy Strategy, but this is not an issue we want to explore here. Nor do we intend to discuss just to what extent literacy *requires* various abilities that could be called technical skills. In fact we are entirely sympathetic to the idea that readers benefit from understanding what might be called the nuts and bolts of language, although this is not to concede – nor to deny – that literacy is best taught via the acquisition of such elements. Whether that is so will only be known after much more empirical research has been conducted: perhaps more empirical research than one can imagine ever being completed. As for knowledge of the 'building blocks' of language, its lexis, morphology and syntax, we are among those who find such knowledge absorbing, though we draw no inference from that about what may or should interest anyone else, even if it is made part of the 'fun' of the Literacy Hour (Barber thinks there is a good deal of fun to be had in its sixty minutes).

The issue is rather what sense of value animates a conception of literacy in which we are told everything about *how* (and indeed *when*), but in which there is a great gap where we might expect to find a sense of quite what sort of thing literacy is, and what it is *for*. The Standards and Effectiveness Unit's Web page tells us that 'Literacy unites the important skills of reading and writing. It also involves speaking and listening. . . . Good oral work enhances pupils' understanding of language in both oral and written forms and of the way language can be used to communicate. It is also an important part of the process through which pupils read and compose texts'. So literacy is all about reading and writing, and of course the 'skills' of them; and other forms of expression are valuable in that they contribute to the reading and composing of texts. But what is the point of reading and writing, of this reading and composing of texts? The Web page's next paragraph explains: 'Thus the Framework covers the statutory requirements for reading and writing in the National Curriculum for English and contributes substantially to the development of Speaking and Listening. It is also relevant to teaching across the whole of the National Curriculum'. Tempting to conclude, then, that the purpose of the literacy strategy is to feed the system of which it is itself a part. Recall again Barber's sentence, quoted above: 'The key to the strategy is that teachers master the skills involved in it'. The whole, it seems, is justified in terms of its parts; beyond that, reference is made to statutory requirements. Where we look for justification in terms of significant values there is silence.

This is, of course, not wholly surprising in an educational world where discussion of ends and values appears increasingly to be a cause of embarrassment, relegated to the margins of education and beyond into oblivion. The European White Paper 'Teaching and Learning: Towards the Learning Society' (1995) reports that 'Everyone is convinced of the need for change, the proof being the demise of the major ideological disputes on the objectives of education'. Here the possibility of reflecting on ends or 'objectives' at all is consigned to the dustbin of history (cf. the section on p. 24, entitled 'The end of debate on educational principles'). We note elsewhere (Fragment I) the contempt expressed for those who want to hold 'a values debate and discuss the "ends" of education'. What can those of us who insist on the importance of such discussion make of the ends of the new literacy initiatives? Bethan Marshall (1998) writes of these initiatives that 'the bleak spectre of utilitarianism hangs over our schools like a pall'. This does not seem quite right (Barber, above, describes it as 'ludicrous', which does not seem right either). A thorough-going and unashamedly utilitarian conception of literacy would justify reading and writing in terms of their usefulness to the individual in filling in forms and acquiring and keeping employment, and their usefulness through this to the nation's economy. But we are not offered this justification, even if sometimes it can seem to be implicit. The charge of utilitarianism and Marshall's complaint that 'Gradgrind has the upper hand and the Government is on his side' does not go to the heart of what is wrong here even though it captures something of the dour spirit of the new literacy.

The Lyotardian critique of education, and of so much else in our 'postmodern condition', is now familiar. Lyotard writes that the obsession with 'efficiency' and 'effectiveness', which he memorably named 'performativity', has subsumed all other questions, including questions of what we should be trying to achieve. 'In matters of social justice and of scientific truth alike, the legitimation of . . . power is based on its optimising the system's performance – efficiency' (Lyotard 1984: xxiv). Performativity eclipses deliberation about ends.[1] This too seems true in part of the current approach to literacy. Yet it does not quite catch the way that the absorption in *technique* has become total, such that one senses it has the power to override even considerations of 'the system's performance'.

In his lectures *On the Future of Our Educational Institutions* (trans. Kennedy 1909), Nietzsche expresses concerns in some ways similar to those we are exploring here. Schools, he writes, are not truly cultural, that is educational, institutions 'so long as they do not regard the immediate and practical discipline of speaking and writing as their most holy duty, so long as they treat the mother-tongue as if it were only a necessary evil or a dead body' (p. 55). Such respect for language as pupils acquire through the study of Greek and Latin 'hangs in the air': they are delighted to throw it off 'like a theoretical burden' as soon as they return to their mother-tongue (p. 63). But it is only through 'self-discipline in one's mother-tongue' that we reach 'sound aesthetic judgement' (p. 59), for 'Culture begins . . . with the correct movement of the language' (ibid.). The mother-tongue is not to be taught 'as if it were a dead language' in which 'the living body of the language is sacrificed for the sake of anatomical study' (p. 50).

This is precisely where culture begins – namely, in understanding how to treat the quick as something vital, and it is here too that the mission of the cultured teacher begins: in suppressing the urgent claims of 'historical interests' wherever it is above all necessary to *do* properly and not merely to *know* properly.

(Ibid.)

Nietzsche's concern, here and elsewhere, is that what should be a matter of engagement and commitment, of doing and not merely knowing, 'understanding how to treat the quick as something vital' (above), has become reduced to the conventional, to acquiescence in established beliefs. What should be suffused with value is evacuated of it. In perhaps his most often quoted characterisation of nihilism, in *The Will to Power* (section 2), Nietzsche writes that 'The highest values have devalued themselves. There is no goal. There is no answer to the question, "why?".' As we have seen, things are even worse than that, for in what passes for educational thinking in our time matters are framed so as to by-pass 'why?' questions altogether, or those who insist on asking them are cast as suspect, or such questions have become redundant, the vast majority of people having no doubt come to see that they are outmoded.

This is the state that Nietzsche attacks as *nihilism*, and this seems to us the most accurate criticism of the new view of literacy. It is coloured by utilitarianism, certainly, and by the prevailing 'performativity', but above all it is devoid of value, nihilistic. Literacy is to be acquired and books are to be read not because (say) our ability to construct meaning empowers and inspires us but because literacy can be broken down into skills and skills, as we know, must be listed and taken on board. This, in our nihilistic age, is what they are for, with no sense of what wider ends they serve. Statutory requirements are there to tell us to get on with it in double-quick time.

A fuller account would show that the very language in which the requirements of the new literacy are set is itself frequently *illiterate*: stumbling, mechanical, ill-expressed, lacking the capacity to enliven or inspire. To read it is to be confronted with a notion of literacy that suggests its joys are the tranquil satisfactions of operating a bureaucratic system. This is of course the literacy of those who make lists (perhaps it should be renamed 'listeracy'), to whom the magic electricity of reading is something dangerous to be earthed; to whom the mysterious and complex presents the challenge of reducing it to simple and manageable units. Once the zealots of the new literacy can break reading down into a matter of orchestrating a full range of reading cues (phonic, graphic, syntactic, contextual), knowing grapheme/phoneme correspondences, tracking the text in the right order, page by page, left to right, top to bottom; pointing while reading/telling a story – then their task is done. Literacy is taken apart and spread out for inspection, like the engine of a car dismantled and displayed on the garage floor. *This is not to say that these things may not be valuable to learn.* The point is crucial. It may well be useful (and interesting) to know grapheme/phoneme correspondences. But to say this is very different from foregrounding these skills, as skills, in a conception of literacy. It is the difference between (the comparison, if sensitive, nevertheless presses itself) being able to locate your partner's clitoris and imagining that such an ability is *the* prerequisite of a rich sexual relationship.

The technicist and essentially nihilistic conception of literacy contrasts with the conception made manifest in much of the extraordinary children's literature of the last thirty years or so: particularly those books in which the reader is engaged as constructor of meaning beyond the words on the page, as the bringer of value into the void. (Meaning, like virtue, has to be *our* invention, Nietzsche tells us: *A*: section 11.) There are famous examples. In *Rosie's Walk* (Hutchins 1968) Rosie the hen walks from her henhouse, around the farmyard and back to her roost. The words on the page report her itinerary: she walked 'around the pond . . . past the mill . . . under the behives'. The child reading the book, however, sees to her joy that the pictures tell a different story. A fox is pursuing the hen. But things don't go well for the fox: he treads on a rake which strikes him on the nose, a sack of flour falls on him from the mill, he knocks over the hives and is pursued by the bees. Rosie the hen marches on, sublimely oblivious to all this (although the artist has given her a knowing look: not so oblivious, perhaps, as she first seems). Why do the words on the page not report all this, and what is the relation between the words and the pictures? May it be that the words are related to the pictures by something like affectionate irony, as when mother says of the bedroom the child has tidied: 'I see the good fairy has been busy here'?

There are no cast-iron and ready-made meanings to be found in *Rosie's Walk*, in the way there would be if the picture showed Rosie walking past the pond while the words declared 'Rosie walked past the pond'. Meaning and value are not presented here as something to which the reader must *submit* but as something in whose active and necessary construction the reader is *engaged*. Watch the child's face as she reads these pages: the surprise, incredulity, understanding – and then a look of complicity as she joins in the game. The sense that she is involved in a kind of dialogue with the text is unmistakable.[2] Of course you can call this a matter of orchestrating graphic and contextual reading cues if you like, but that seems a perverse way of putting it, an act of violence to what is going on here. The language of sensitive and attuned response has been replaced by the language appropriate to a manual. (The sexual analogy suggests itself again.)

In a rather similar discussion of *Rosie's Walk* to our own, Margaret Meek (1994) comments that there is a 'need to attend to what the author is not saying – the beginning of an experience that leads to Jane Austen'. What is true for the child's reading is true too for the adult's. In a remarkably interesting article entitled 'Education, Education, Education: or, What has Jane Austen to teach Tony Blunkett?' Maskell (1999) discusses the different reactions of the members of the Bennet family (*Pride and Prejudice*, Chapter 13) to Mr Collins' letter apologising for being the heir to the entailed Bennet estate. Their task is to judge the letter and its writer: this is especially important since he has hinted at his willingness to make amends for his good fortune by marrying one of the Bennet daughters. Clues to his character must be found in the letter. His values and meaning cannot simply be read off from it, since they may be obscure to Mr Collins himself. Mary, the most bookish of the Bennet daughters, subjects the letter to a purely technical reading: 'In point of composition, his letter does not seem defective. The idea of the olive branch is perhaps not wholly new, yet I think it is well expressed'. Her phoneme/grapheme correspondences are in fine working order, but there is something not fully literate about Mary's literacy. Elizabeth, by contrast, has, as Maskell notes, a 'hunger for meaning'. She brings her own sense of value to the letter and its writer, and judges them against it:

> Elizabeth was chiefly struck with his extraordinary deference for Lady Catherine, and his kind intention of christening, marrying, and burying his parishioners whenever it were required.
> 'He must be an oddity, I think,' said she. 'I cannot make him out. – There is something very pompous in his stile. – And what can he mean by apologising for being next in the entail? – We cannot suppose he would help it, if he could. – Can he be a sensible man, sir?'

Here is a reader who reads, as Maskell puts it, 'not just studiously but with pleasure; and while that is so, there is hope, even for our education system. For the pleasure stories and poems give us is bound up with the degree and varieties of assent they draw from us. Our pleasure depends on our assent, or, we might say, is one form it takes' (p. 173). Literacy requires the reader's assent or affirmation, and is not just a matter of skills.

The sense of a gap at the heart of education is, it appears, becoming widespread. Michael Barber writes (*Times Educational Supplement*, 12 February 1999):

> At a number of conferences recently, teachers have asked me about 'the big picture' given that media coverage of the government's education programme inevitably focuses on individual proposals. This is my answer.

Before we come to the answer we should pause to note that blame for focusing on individual proposals rather than 'the big picture' is attributed to the media, and that the structure of the sentence implies that teachers wholly accept this. Barber's answer is couched in terms of raising standards (but standards of what, Nietzsche will ask?); of 'commitment to consistent, real growth in educational expenditure';[3] 'firm foundations' (foundations of what?); 'promotion of a model of improvement' (improvement in what?).

> All of these should improve the capacity of the system to deliver higher educational standards. They will contribute to the creation of a world-class education service. An education system second to none is, of course, not an end in itself. It is a key element of achieving the government's goals of a more productive economy, a more cohesive society, a more successful democracy and more fulfilled individuals.

With these words Barber's article ends. One does not question the commitment to social cohesion, democracy and personal fulfilment. The question is whether the prevailing nihilism in government thinking about education is to any extent dispelled by the occurrence of these few bare phrases at the end of such an article, or confirmed by it.

Notes

1 Much more of this in Blake *et al.*, *Thinking Again: Education after Postmodernism* (1998).
2 We have offered a somewhat similar discussion of literacy in our earlier book: ibid., ch. 4.
3 'This expansion belongs to the most beloved of the dogmas of modern political economy. As much knowledge and education as possible. . . . In the quarter now under consideration culture would be defined as that point of vantage which enables one to "keep in the van of one's age", from which one can see all the easiest and best roads to wealth, and with which one controls all the means of communication between men and nations' (Nietzsche, *On the Future of Our Educational Institutions*, op. cit. p. 36).

Chapter 7

Apollo and Dionysos

> Everything that we now call culture, education and civilization will one day appear before that infallible judge, Dionysus.
>
> (*BT*: 95)

In *The Birth of Tragedy*, his first revaluation of all values, Nietzsche draws a distinction between the Dionysian forces of Ancient Greek tragedy and the Apollonian form and clarity of Socratic dialectic. The former is characterised by surging energy unleashed in anarchic ways, impulse alike to creativity and destruction; the latter by the ordering of logical thought and faith in reason. With the advent of Socrates – or to be more precise, of a certain 'Socratism' that has been his legacy – the possibility of bearing witness in the manner of tragedy is seriously eroded, and the lives we live become thinner as a result. There is an optimism to the arguments and counter-arguments of the dialectic that progressively invades tragedy and forces 'its death-leap into bourgeois theatre' (ibid.: 69). Excessive faith in the progress of reasoned enquiry undermines myth and cuts human beings off from sublime recognition of the irreconcilability of tragic forces. Looking back on *The Birth of Tragedy* seventeen years later, Nietzsche identifies the book's two principal new insights: the force of the Dionysian phenomenon, the sole root of the whole of Hellenic art; and the understanding of Socrates' rationality as the agent of Hellenic decadence and disintegration. '"Rationality" at any price as a dangerous force, as a force undermining life!' (*EH*, 'The Birth of Tragedy': section 1). It became increasingly his conviction that, while the Dionysian and Apollonian forces must be seen as inseparable, it is the suppression of the Dionysian that now most impoverishes us. This is the background to the nihilism of the age.

The forms that nihilism takes in contemporary educational policy and practice, of the kind that we identified in Part 1 of this book, now need to be seen in the light of this relationship between the Dionysian and the Apollonian. Just as the excessive influence of the Apollonian led to the degeneration of tragedy into what Nietzsche calls bourgeois theatre, so we argue has a similar theatricisation occurred in education: standards and values have now become flickering shades of what they might be. Practice has become contrived and self-conscious, staged and presented as the object of accountability's gaze. The psychology of the child must be understood in terms of developmental learning stages (for which, of course, there are appropriate tests). The very words 'learning' and 'education' are now uttered with thespian *gravitas*. Education, education, education and education. Education and heavy breathing.

Yet such artificial respiration can only inflate the deadened forms of our cultural life. Without a horizon of myth, Nietzsche argues, 'all culture loses its healthy and natural creative power' (*BT*: 109). Modern procedural reasoning dissipates content and devalues context, laying the way for abstraction:

> Myth alone rescues all the powers of the imagination and the Apolline dream from their aimless wanderings. The images of myth must be the daemonic guardians, omnipresent and unnoticed, which protect the growth of the young mind, and guide man's interpretation of his life and struggles. The state itself has no unwritten laws more powerful than the mythical foundation that guarantees its connection with religion and its growth out of mythical representations. Let us now, by way of comparison, imagine abstract man, without the guidance of myth – abstract education, abstract morality, abstract justice, the abstract state; let us imagine the lawless wandering, unchecked by native myth, of the artistic imagination; let us imagine a culture without a secure and sacred primal site, condemned to exhaust every possibility and feed wretchedly on all other cultures – there we have our present age, the product of that Socratism bent on the destruction of myth. And here stands man, stripped of myth, eternally starving, in the midst of all the past ages, digging and scrabbling for roots, even if he must dig for them in the most remote antiquities. What is indicated by the great historical need of unsatisfied modern culture, clutching about for countless other cultures, with its consuming desire for knowledge, if not the loss of myth, the loss of the mythical home, the mythical womb? Let us consider whether the feverish and sinister agitation of this culture is anything other than a starving man's greedy grasping for food – and who would wish to give further nourishment to a culture such as this, unsatisfied by everything it devours, which transforms the most

powerful, wholesome nourishment that it devours into 'history and criticism'?

(Ibid.: 109–10)

These phrases point to a development that reaches its apotheosis in education today. The dominance of procedural reasoning and performativity is symptomatic of a thinning of our ethical lives. Instrumental reason and managerialism, as it were, stage-manage what have become the rituals of presentation, communication, assessment and accounting. The ideal product of such an education is a being with a portfolio of transferable skills, a being with a set of masks to put on, appropriately listed in a record of achievement and instantly recognisable to employers; and there is plenty of demand today for people with presentation skills. The optimism of the beliefs that for every problem there is an appropriate technical solution, that human knowledge accumulates without limit, that understanding is possible only where things are fully available to scrutiny has as a correlate a kind of plundering and display of other cultures – as theme parks and the heritage industry suggest, as the burgeoning of the virtual world reveals. Multiculturalism is thematised as a series of spectacles, foreign travel a collection of packaged experiences. Modern epistemology *grasps* knowledge, containing it in the concept, so that the knowledge economy can then turn it into a commodity and can trade. Criticism is the business of the student's crib, of book reviews in the Sunday papers and of late night television arts magazines. The plundering and display divert attention from the vacuousness of the culture in which such ideas thrive, a vacuousness for which psychotherapy and New Age spirituality are scant compensation.

The nihilism of the educational practices sketched here has, of course, been our concern throughout this book. In this chapter we consider it in the light of its degenerate theatricisation. But our ultimate purpose is to indicate the kind of revitalised educational practice that the renewal of the Dionysian might provide. Shortly we shall consider more directly some of the forms of nihilism against which Nietzsche develops this distinction. In the course of our account, however, let a drama unfold . . .

'. . . to jump clean-hoofed on to a whole new track . . .'

Some time around 1970 the playwright Peter Shaffer heard from a friend the true story of an alarming crime. The friend knew only one horrible detail, but the mention of this was enough to arouse in Shaffer an intense fascination. A seventeen-year-old stable boy had blinded six horses with a metal spike. A few months later the friend died. Shaffer was left with a desire to interpret the event 'in some entirely personal way . . . to create a mental world in which the deed could be made comprehensible' (Shaffer 1976: 201). Equus *is the play that resulted.*

The central character of the play is the overworked child psychiatrist, Martin Dysart. His wise and understanding friend, the magistrate Hesther Salomon, persuades him that he should take on this extra case as he is the only person who will be able to help. His colleagues, Bennett and Thoroughgood, for all their cool and exact professionalism, will be 'revolted, and immovably English'. Martin Dysart is the boy's last chance. Dysart reluctantly agrees, though he expects very little: 'One more dented little face. One more adolescent freak. The usual unusual' (ibid.: 213). But their encounter is not so easily circumscribed.

The play depicts the boy's obsessive and perverse relationship with the horses, a relationship that encompasses sexual intensity and a kind of religious fervour, the cult of Equus. We witness the boy's obsession through some extraordinary staging, with scenes cross cut and Dysart's consultations providing a window onto events in the stables, with his soliloquies offering a window onto his own anguish. The horses themselves are an extraordinary creation – the human, chestnut-tracksuited bodies of the actors are headed by stylised wire horse-head masks that combine a strange beauty with menace; the raised wired 'hooves' clomp disturbingly on the wooden floor of the stage. The staging itself, a railed square of wood set on a circle of wood, suggests a boxing ring with, roundabout, the benches on which the actors sit when they are not taking part in scenes. They provide also the listening and observation post for Dysart when he is out of the square, his viewpoint that of the main audience. The actors, who are on stage throughout, are witnesses, stage assistants and chorus. At times they provide a choric effect of humming, thumping and stamping that denotes the presence of Equus the God.

A possible psychology of the boy's extraordinary obsession is sketched in the characters of the boy's parents. His mother, the repressed Dora, tells her son Bible stories and warns of the Devil's work, but promises him that one day, if God wills, he will meet the right girl and marry: his task, she tells him, is to prepare himself for the most important happening of his life, and after that, if he is lucky, he may know a higher love still. His father Frank is an old-style Socialist, earnest with self-improvement and disapproval of television (which he forbids his son to watch), and regarding religion as 'the opium of the people'. He worries over his son's 'mooning over religious pictures' ('real kinky ones, if you receive my meaning'), and one day this family rift over religion ('our only real problem in this house' (ibid.: 226)) opens wide: he destroys the much cherished picture that hangs over Alan's bed, a sadomasochistic picture of Christ on the way to Calvary. Distraught for days, the boy is only comforted when the reproduction is replaced with a

photograph of a horse – taken, unusually, head-on, with the head all eyes.
Dysart is fascinated by the way that whatever has happened with the
horses is at the core of this boy's being: the appalling cruelty is not to be
separated from a kind of reverence for the unspeakable otherness of the
horse, from his sense of the eyes as watching and judging, from his desire for
union, centaur-like, with that hugely powerful magnificent animal.
Yet the horse's elemental strength is also presented as reined and bridled.
Haunted by the huge head, Dysart tells the audience:

> *The thing is, I'm desperate. You see, I'm wearing that horse's head*
> *myself. That's the feeling. All reined up in old language and old*
> *assumptions, straining to jump clean-hoofed on to a whole new track of*
> *being I only suspect is there. I can't see it, because my educated,*
> *average head is being held at the wrong angle. I can't jump because the*
> *bit forbids it, and my own basic force – my horse-power, if you like – is*
> *too little. The only thing I know for sure is this: a horse's head is finally*
> *unknowable to me.*

(Ibid.: 210)

Dysart's doubts have been piling up for years. The extremity of the case
makes them active.

Psychology of the redeemer

Dysart's business is the saving of children from their disturbance and
the recuperation of mental health. He works towards a kind of
redemption, a redemption through the revisiting of the past in order
to purge it through explanation and analysis. His response and
approach are not, it is clear, quite that of his routinely professional
colleagues. He is troubled and this humanises him. The cure that is
sought, it is clear, is not only the boy's. This is the process we are
presented with in this play. What are the patterns of redemption to
which the thought of the Dionysian responds?

All healthy morality, Nietzsche affirms, is dominated by an
instinct for life. He recurrently condemns the search for redemption
as the symptom of a kind of nihilism. In a certain Platonism this is
seen in the disparagement of the world of appearance in favour of
the higher reality of a world of forms. Nietzsche's greater contempt
is reserved, however, for Christianity which, in its pervasive denial of
life, takes this other-worldliness to new lengths ('One does not say
"nothingness": one says "the Beyond"; or "God"; or "*true* life"; or
Nirvana, redemption, blessedness . . .' (*A*: 130, section 7)).
Christianity, which is treated with a profound hostile silence in *The
Birth of Tragedy*, is regarded as nihilistic, as a negation of all aesthetic
values. Christianity is neither Dionysian nor Apollonian.

Modern liberal agnosticism, whose debased conception of happiness and ideal of good adjustment renew Nietzsche's contempt, is little better. Who has found happiness? 'Modern man perhaps? – "I know not which way to turn; I am everything that knows not which way to turn" – sighs modern man. . . . It was from this modernity that we were ill – from lazy peace, from cowardly compromise, from the whole virtuous uncleanliness of modern Yes and No' (A: section 1). This modern liberalism persists in some of its forms in subordinating life to some ideal – of rational autonomy, say, or post-reflective desire satisfaction, an ideal of morality, an ideal of happiness. But it is absurd, Nietzsche says, to hand over one's nature to some purpose or other, when one is necessary, one is part of fate, one is part of the whole:

> That no one is any longer made accountable, that the kind of being manifested cannot be traced back to a *causa prima*, that the world is a unity neither as sensorium nor as 'spirit', *this alone is the great liberation* – thus alone is the innocence of becoming restored. . .
>
> (*TI*, 'The Four Great Errors': 65, section 8)

It deflects the sense of one's life away from the fate within which one finds oneself, in the finding of which values inhere, promising a freedom and fulfilment that depends on a negation of that life as it is, that depends on myths of origin, myths of end. The idealist is in cowardly flight in the face of values. So too then there can be no turn back to a kind of Romanticism, an aestheticisation of the real. The modern concern with authenticity is apt to be worn on the sleeve, with the ironic outcome that 'in our idolization of the natural and the real we have arrived at the opposite pole from our idealism – the realm of the waxwork museums' (*BT*: 38). Dutiful concern and Gaia sensitivity become too easily poses and masks.

Contemporary psychology in many of its forms is redolent of these problems, while psychotherapy is especially implicated. Nietzsche comments:

> *Psychological explanation*: These tendencies of thought orientate a certain kind of psychological explanation: 'To trace something unknown back to something known is alleviating, soothing, gratifying and gives moreover a feeling of power. Danger, disquiet, anxiety attend the unknown – the first instinct is to eliminate these distressing states. First principle: any explanation is better than none.
>
> (*TI*, 'The Four Great Errors': 62, section 5)

The explanation recuperates the something unknown by locating it in a causal framework. Unspeakable cruelty and horror, elemental fear, passionate worship, affirmation, intoxication and ecstasy. How is this to be understood? How far does drama rein this in? It is tragedy that should make it possible for us to bear witness to this, and to the heroic affirmation of life even in the midst of pain and suffering. But in the Aristotelian conception of catharsis, the 'pathological discharge' (*BT*: 107), this recuperative tendency is seen once again. What is suggested then is resolution, and this negates the terrible. The power of Greek tragedy depends on the way that these antithetical tendencies are held in a kind of balance together. But this is not a simple opposition, closer perhaps to the relation between form and force. Its degeneration in the plays of Euripides indicates what is at stake:

> Thus the Euripidean tragedy is at once cool and fiery, capable both of freezing and of burning. It is incapable of achieving the Apolline effect of the epic, and has also made the greatest possible break with the Dionysiac elements, and now, in order to have any effect at all, it needs new stimuli which can no longer be found within either of these aesthetic impulses, neither the Apolline nor the Dionysiac. These stimuli are cool, paradoxical *thoughts* rather than Apolline contemplations, fiery emotions rather than Dionysiac ecstasies – and these thoughts and emotions are highly realistic counterfeits, by no means immersed in the ether of art.
>
> (*BT*: 61–2)

It is the artificial inflationary nature of the stimuli that should be noticed here, and their dangerous plausibility. Art dies with these counterfeits. The plausibility of Euripides' drama depends, of course, on a certain theatricality. His weakness is compared to 'the phenomenon of aesthetic Socratism, the chief law of which is, more or less: "to be beautiful everything must first be intelligible" – a parallel to the Socratic dictum: "only the one who knows is virtuous"' (*BT*: 62). We shall, in Chapter 12, take issue with this dictum: we shall take ignorance seriously. Again the tendency we resist is of a hasty move towards explanation and the suppression of the unknown.

Nietzsche connects the Apollonian especially with the visual, the art characterised by beauteous forms and representation – typically the art of the sculptor:

Apollinian intoxication alerts above all the eye, so that it acquires power of vision. The painter, the sculptor, the epic poet are visionaries *par excellence*. In the Dionysian state on the other hand, the entire emotional system is alerted and intensified: so that it discharges all its powers of representation, imitation, transfiguration, transmutation, every kind of mimicry and play-acting, conjointly.

> (*TI*, 'Expeditions of an Untimely Man': 84, section 10)

The true tragic artist affirms all that is questionable and unknown, celebrating a fearlessness in the face of the terrible, bravery and composure in the face of the enemy and great hardship, a refusal to turn away from what is repellent. The Dionysian is then

a formula of *supreme affirmation* born out of fullness, of superfluity, an affirmation without reservation even of suffering, even of guilt, even of all that is strange and questionable in existence. . . . This ultimate, joyfullest, boundlessly exuberant Yes to life is not only the highest insight, it is also the *profoundest*, the insight most strictly confirmed and maintained by truth and knowledge. . . . To grasp this requires *courage*, and, as a condition of this, a superfluity of *strength*: for precisely as far as courage *may* dare to go forward, precisely by this measure of strength does one approach truth.

> (*EH*, 'The Birth of Tragedy': 50, section 2)

This is a celebration of virtues of courage and strength, and the readiness for pain and suffering, virtues that bring with them tonic emotions joyously embracing the energy of life. In the face of tragedy the warlike in our souls celebrates its Saturnalias (*TI*, 'Expeditions of an Untimely Man': 93, section 24).

But Dysart's work of redemption, the pattern of analysis he must weave for his patients, is aimed at the recuperation of mental equilibrium. This is not achieved without sacrifice in which things are clearly identified and put in order.

'. . . just like a seamstress following a pattern . . .'

On the day he meets Alan Strang, Dysart has a very explicit dream, his disturbance at which is only partly masked by his feeble self-mockery as he recounts it to the audience. He is a chief priest in Homeric Greece. Wearing a wide gold mask, noble and bearded, he stands in front of a thick stone holding a sharp knife. He is playing his part in the immensely important ritual sacrifice of some 500 boys and girls, on which depends the fate of the crops or of a military expedition. Two enormously strong, absolutely tireless assistant priests, also masked, stand on either side of him. Each child steps forward and is thrown on to the stone. And then,

> *with a surgical skill which amazes me, I fit in the knife and slice elegantly down to the navel, just like a seamstress following a pattern. I part the flaps, sever the inner tubes, yank them out and throw them hot and steaming on to the floor. The other two then study the pattern that they make, as if they were reading hieroglyphics. It's obvious to me that I'm tops as chief priest. It's this unique talent for carving that has got me where I am.*
>
> *(Shaffer 1976: 216)*

But, Dysart goes on, the only thing is that the mask has begun to slip, and he is feeling distinctly nauseous. With each victim it is getting worse. But he knows that if his assistants so much as catch a glimpse of his distress, of his growing doubt that his smelly and repetitive work is doing any good at all, he will be the next to be thrown over the stone. But the mask does slip, the priests turn and look, and they take the knife out of his hand . . .

False coinage

There are Christian variants of the sacrifice:

> *Cure for the depressed.* – Paul himself was of the opinion that a sacrifice was needed if God's profound displeasure at the commission of sins was to be removed: and since then Christians have never ceased to discharge their dissatisfaction with themselves on to *sacrifice* – whether this sacrifice be the 'world' or 'history' or 'reason' or the joy or peace of other people – something *good* has to die for *their* sin (even if only in effigy)!
>
> *(D, Book I: section 94)*

Christianity, a religion of thou shalt not, 'desires to dominate beasts of prey; its means for doing so is to make them sick – weakening is the Christian recipe for taming, for "civilization"' (*A*: 144, section 22). The debilitation is the result of a decadence whose psychology is to be understood in terms of *ressentiment*. Indeed morality is the product of teachers and leaders whose hidden intention is to avenge themselves on life. So too, we can say, the mental stability that psychotherapy seeks is achieved through a process of tranquilisation (How to Manage Stress) in which what is remarkable is negated. The values of such professionals are inimical to life. Unmasking morality is unmasking the value of all values that are or have been believed in (*EH*: 103, sections 7, 8).

The Dionysian encompassing of space, the access to opposites, means that redemption by some other is consistently opposed, and the affirmation of transitoriness, of creation and destruction, radically rejects the concept being in favour of becoming (*EH*, 'The Birth of Tragedy': 51, section 3). Being is stability, object of knowledge and control; becoming is the dynamic, the flow of energy and force.

Dysart's weak points expose him, and these are weak points around which different webs can be spun. But they enable a kind of insight to dawn.

'. . . Advanced neurotics can be dazzling at that game . . .'

> *Brilliant! Absolutely brilliant! The boy's on the run, so he gets defensive. What am I, then? . . . Wicked little bastard – he knew exactly what questions to try. He'd actually marched himself round the hospital, making inquiries about my wife. Wicked and – of course, perceptive. Ever since I made that crack about carving up children, he's been aware of me in an absolutely specific way. Of course, there's nothing novel in that. Advanced neurotics can be dazzling at that game. They aim unswervingly at your area of maximum vulnerability. . . . Which I suppose is as good a way as any of describing Margaret.*
>
> (Shaffer 1976: 252)

Dysart explains to Hesther how he had once been attracted to the kind of inaccessible briskness of his dentist-wife Margaret, just as she no doubt had liked what was then his own antiseptic proficiency. After marriage, brisk had been the disappointment and briskly had they turned to their separate surgeries and childless lives. Now she sits by the fire knitting 'things for orphans in a home she helps with'; he opposite turning the pages of books on Ancient Greece. Occasionally he 'trails a scent of [his] enthusiasm across her path' (ibid.: 253) only to be told that really Agamemnon and that lot were nothing but a bunch of ruffians. All his wife has ever taken from 'that whole vast culture of the Mediterranean' are four bottles of Chianti to be made into table lamps and two china condiment donkeys. Expert in extraction and reduction, she has become 'the Shrink's Shrink'. He goes on:

> *I wish there was one person in my life I could show. One instinctive, absolutely unbrisk person I could take to Greece, and stand in front of certain shrines and sacred streams and say 'Look! Life is only comprehensible through a thousand local Gods. And not just the old*

dead ones with names like Zeus – no, but living Geniuses of Place and Person! And not just Greece but modern England! Spirits of certain trees, certain curves of brick wall, certain chip shops, if you like, and slate roofs – just as of certain frowns in people and slouches' . . . I'd say to them – 'Worship as many as you can see – and more will appear!' . . . If I had a son, I bet you he'd come out exactly like his mother. Utterly worshipless.

(Ibid.: 254)

Affirmation

The great despisers, Nietzsche says, are the great reverers. The brisk and shrinking are the nihilists. The instinct for life requires a joyful and trusting fatalism: only what is separate and individual can be rejected; in the totality everything is affirmed and this is its redemption, a saying yes to life. This is a joyousness that Dysart only glimpses. Nietzsche calls himself the last disciple of Dionysos, teacher of eternal recurrence: *'To redeem the past* and to transform every "It was" into an "I wanted it thus!" – that alone would I call *redemption'* (*EH*, 'Thus Spake Zarathustra': 80, section 8).

And the only sacrifice that befits this affirmation is the sacrifice of the highest types. One does not save oneself, one expends oneself. Through such a sacrifice the will to life rejoices in its inexhaustibility – that is the essence of the Dionysian (*TI*, 'What I Owe to the Ancients': 121, section 5). When we look at the relationship between morality, which, Nietzsche implies, the Germans represent, and *esprit*, the province, of course, of the French, we find a German anxiety that *esprit* will put out the eyes of morality, fascinated as the moralists are, in spite of themselves, by the spectacle (the dread of the little bird before the rattlesnake (*D*: section 193)). For it is the eyes that scrutinise and judge, that put human kind on the stage of representation.

How then can Dysart represent himself now? Whose is the gaze to which he must submit?

'. . . Such wild returns . . .'

Dysart cannot get away from the thought that that boy has known a passion more ferocious than anything he has ever felt in any second of his life. The boy's haunting stare, he tells Hesther, presents him insistently with an Accusation: 'At least I have galloped! When did you?' He is, believe it or not, jealous of Alan Strang! Look, he says, how he, Martin Dysart, goes on about the smug woman who is his wife, while saying nothing of the finicky, critical husband that he himself is. What worship has he ever known?

Real worship! Without worship you shrink, it's as brutal as that . . .
I shrank my own life . . . I settled for being pallid and provincial, out
of my own eternal timidity. The old story of bluster, and do bugger-all
. . . I tell everyone Margaret's the puritan, I'm the pagan. Some
pagan! Such wild returns I make to the womb of civilization.

(*Ibid.: 254*)

His annual three weeks in the Peloponnese is, of course, carefully planned
and fully booked in advance, properly covered, no doubt, with holiday
insurance, sensibly equipped, we can assume, with travel sickness pills,
Factor 15 sun protection, and UVF Raybans. Back home he sits looking at
pages of centaurs trampling the soil of Argos, and watching the woman
opposite whom he hasn't kissed in years. Then, in the morning, 'I put away
my books on the cultural shelf, close up the Kodachrome snaps of Mount
Olympus, touch my reproduction statue of Dionysos for luck – and go off to
hospital to treat him for insanity' (ibid.: 275).

Later, it is to Alan that he says that he would quite like never in his life to
see this room again. When Alan asks where he would go, he talks of
somewhere, perhaps secret – a great sea he loves, where the Gods used to
bathe. 'What Gods?' Alan asks.

– The old ones. Before they died.
– Gods don't die.
– Yes, they do.

(*Ibid.: 279*)

Dissimulation

With the spotlight turning on to him, Dysart is burdened by self-
analysis, his need to interrogate and account for himself. Is it the
petty frustrations of his life or the weight of the avaricious controlling ego that now trouble him so? Does he seek greater self-
knowledge or Dionysian release from the 'fetters of individuality'
(*BT*: 99)? Nietzsche speaks of the 'wretched bell-jar of human
individuality' from which one hears cries of delight and woe from a
'wild space of the world's night'; he considers the wonderful lure of
the pastoral metaphysical dance (ibid.: 101). Is it a kind of
anonymity that Dysart needs?

It is important to realise that the nihilism that arises with the loss
of the Dionysian can extend throughout our thought: the danger is
at the heart of the way that we think and speak. Lyotard, in the
most Nietzschean of his books, helps to show something of what is
at stake here: 'We must first grasp this: signs are not only terms,
stages, set in relation and made explicit in a trail of conquest; they

can also be, indissociably, singular and vain intensities in exodus' (Lyotard 1993: 50).[1] Signs can be associated with pre-existing systems, and they can be taken as stimuli to further action and creation, non-cognitive, non-structural. This suggests then not the sublime witnessing of the rare event but rather a potential intensity of the commonplace, the concealment of intensity in all signs. While power relates to the ego, a kind of passivity is required for the releasing of force. We can exercise power, but force flows through us when we are enthralled by intense feelings and desires. Force is lightning to be conducted, flows of water to break through.

There is tension between these two aspects of the sign, recuperation as meaning and singularity of affect (the material sign). With the emphasis on the former (on the way the sign is intelligible on grids of what it is not), nihilism can be seen to extend. The differential structure involves identification through the *not-this*. And this negativity is replicated in the drawing of borders that define insides and outsides, where what is outside can then be held up for scrutiny and judgement, made to identify itself, to become theatre. A politics of identity and an ethics of control are surreptitiously bolstered by these shifts:

> It is this exteriorization of the not-this that will give rise to theatricization: the outside 'will have to' *be conquered*, the concept 'will will' its own extension, to master what it had left at the gates of its territory. . . . What anguish in these limits, in these devaluations followed by exclusions! How they are loved, these exteriorities! Hence voyages, ethnology, psychiatry, pediatrics, pedagogy, the love of the excluded: enter beautiful Negresses, charming Indians, enigmatic Orientals, dreamers, children, enter my work and the spaces of my concepts. All this is theatre; it is the white innocence of the West in expansion, base cannibalistic imperialism.
>
> (Ibid.: 14)

Lyotard's concern is with the way that recuperation of meaning – the redemption of the sign – with reference to structures of difference has the cost of directing attention away from, and hence reducing, its affective dynamic singularity. It is the differential system that brings the sign under control and stabilises it. This is an extension of power (*pouvoir*) of a kind appropriate to rational control, say, but a stifling of force (*puissance*). It is a reinforcement of subjectivity, but its effect is to stifle intensity. The 'theoreticians' (this time the structuralists and semioticians), the moralists and accountants require a cooling of intensity with containment and representation. This makes possible the spectatorial stance of a conceptual thought no less than the louche gaze of the voyeur. It puts the spotlight on representation and analysis. Theatre comes with the concept, Lyotard says (ibid.: 25), and thinking moves into the boxing ring of dialectics. This is the space too for psychoanalysis. Lyotard's response is clear:

> The demand for clarity must be strongly denounced; it requires the power of he who loves, or who speaks, over his intensities. It demands: have power, define the intense. No, we must receive this demand in terror; flee from it, that's all we can do. . . . Hence no clarity: sometimes it works, sometimes not. What you demand of us, theoreticians, is that we constitute ourselves as identities, and responsible ones at that! But if we are sure of anything, it is that this operation (of exclusion) is a sham, that no-one produces incandescences and that they belong to no-one, that they have effects but not causes.
>
> (Ibid.: 258)

The overemphasis on the structural aspects of the sign is evident not only in theoretical analysis but in our deference to the pure positions that our forms of discourse are apt to erect:

> Must our fear of sign-systems, and therefore, our investment in them, be still so immense that we search for these pure positions (from the heights of which we would not fail to give everyone everywhere lessons, and it will be a sinister para-noiacs' revolution, once again)!
>
> (Ibid.: 262)

But against the kinds of responses that the parenthesis suggests, Lyotard ponders the possibility of a different kind of action, one that would release the rich affective aspects of the sign in Joycean affirmation:

> What would be interesting would be to stay put, but quietly seize every chance to function as good intensity-conducting bodies. No need for declarations, manifestos, organizations, provocations, no need for *exemplary actions*. Set dissimulation to work on behalf of intensities. Invulnerable conspiracy, headless, homeless, with neither programme nor project, deploying a thousand cancerous tensors in the bodies of signs. We invent nothing, that's it, yes, yes, yes, yes.
>
> (Ibid.)

The kind of affirmation sought here is not to be found in anarchy or rebellion. These good intensities require rather dissimulation's more subtle operation. It is a patient working at the borders that is required then, not a denial of their existence. This is not a wholesale rejection of autonomy and reason. But it demands sensitivity to the inherent perversity of power:

> [D]espots need their fools: their justification, the court's representative of what it excludes. Just like doctors and their patients, politicians and their workers. No pretence at madness, just a *search* for it. But let's be careful here . . . Madness is not a good, and we detest those who cry: Long live madness! Madness is not the conquest of the individual singularity. It is what is intolerable in intensity. To pursue madness would be to become, to make of one's body, to make of language, a good conductor of the intolerable.
>
> (Ibid.: 260)

Strange contortions of reason and power! Nihilism turns force into power, however (ibid.: 118). And it lays the way for the return of the ego.

'. . . Do you think feelings like this can be simply re-attached? . . .'

One night Alan is enticed by the stable-girl, Jill, to go with her to see a blue film. As they sit in the cinema and watch, Alan turns to find to his horror that the man furtively finding a seat at the back is none other than his father. He sees Alan at the front and, suddenly the responsible father, comes down to their row of seats and makes Alan leave the cinema. The three of them wait in mortified silence at the bus-stop. Eventually Frank explains that he had been at the cinema on business – a contract to print posters for forthcoming attractions – and had come into the auditorium simply out of curiosity to see what film they were showing. Now that he knows the kind of place it is he will not only refuse the work but will write to the council to complain. With some reluctance he leaves Alan to see 'the young lady' home.

Jill and Alan have no illusions as to why his father was at the film, but, after the initial shock and with Jill's reassurance and prompting, this releases in Alan a kind of sympathy for him and a dawning awareness of his father's passionless life: 'Poor old sod! . . . I mean, what else has he got? . . . He's got mum, of course, but well – she – she – she – . . . She doesn't give him anything' (Shaffer 1976: 288).

Jill takes him to a place she knows, a place she keeps as a surprise, but Alan finds himself in the stables. He is frightened that they will be watched by the horses and, even though they are all in their stalls, insists that she locks the door to the barn. Pressed by Dysart, he describes the room with growing horror: 'Large room. Straw everywhere. Some tools. . . A hoof pick! . . .' (ibid.: 292) They undress, lie down in the straw, and kiss, but the horses are restless behind the door, the hooves smashing on the wood of the stalls. Dysart questions again and again, and eventually the boy blurts out: 'Every time I kissed her – He was in the way. . . When I touched I felt Him. . . When I shut my eyes, I saw Him at once. . . Then I couldn't even kiss her. . . He was there. Through the door. The door was shut, but he was there! . . . He'd seen everything' (ibid.: 294–6). Alan craves forgiveness, hugs himself in pain, but cannot escape the horse's gaze, while Dysart, masterful now, finds the words to say what the boy is trying to say: 'Lie with anyone and I will see? . . . Forever and ever you will fail! You will see ME – and you will FAIL! The Lord thy God is a Jealous God. He sees you. He sees you forever and ever, Alan. He sees you! . . . He sees you!' (ibid.: 297)

Dysart comforts him, reassures him, the crisis now past. With this finally he can make him well. Yet, as the boy sleeps, he says:

> *I'm lying to you, Alan. He won't really go that easily. Just clop away from you like a nice old nag. Oh, no! When Equus leaves – if he leaves at all – it will be with your intestines in his teeth. And I don't stock replacements. . . . If you knew anything, you'd get up this minute and run from me fast as you could.*
>
> *(Ibid.: 299)*

But he must, Hesther presses him, take away the boy's pain, and that surely should be enough. Dysart knows that he can deliver him from madness, knows that he can make him acceptable again. But do you think feelings can be simply re-attached, stuck on to other objects we select? He may make this boy a dutiful citizen, loyal husband, believer in an abstract and unifying God, but this achievement will probably in the process turn him into a ghost. This is exactly what he will do:

> *I'll heal the rash on his body. I'll erase the welts cut into his mind by flying manes. When that's done, I'll set him on a nice mini-scooter and send him puttering off into the Normal world where animals are treated properly: made extinct, or put into servitude, or tethered all their lives in dim light, just to feed it! I'll give him the good Normal world where we're tethered beside them – blinking our nights away in a non-stop drench of cathode-ray over our shrivelling heads!*
>
> *(Ibid.: 299–300)*

Alan will be restored to a Normal life, in which there will be little pain or passion, and it will only be the occasional 50p bet that will make him even think of horses – they will become nothing more to him than the bearers of little profits and little losses. The Normal, remember, exacts its sacrifices, and he, Dysart, is its high priest. But,

> The Normal is the smile in a child's eyes – all right. It is also the dead stare in a million adults. It both sustains and kills – like a God. It is the Ordinary made beautiful; it is also the Average made lethal. The Normal is the indispensable, murderous God of Health, and I am his Priest. My tools are very delicate. My compassion is honest. I have honestly assisted children in this room. I have talked away terrors and relieved many agonies. But also – beyond question – I have cut from them parts of individuality repugnant to this God, in both his aspects. Parts sacred to rarer and more wonderful Gods. And at what length . . . Sacrifices to Zeus took at the most, surely, sixty seconds each. Sacrifices to the Normal can take as long as sixty months.
>
> *(Ibid.: 257)*

Now for Dysart with the mask fallen, the voice of Equus out of the cave never stops:

> 'Why Me? . . . Why Me? . . . Account for Me! . . .' All right – I surrender! I say it! . . . In an ultimate sense I cannot know what I do in this place – yet I do ultimate things. Essentially I cannot know what I do – yet I do essential things. Irreversible, terminal things. I stand in the dark with a pick in my hand, striking at heads! . . . I need – more desperately than my children need me – a way of seeing in the dark. What way is this? . . . What dark is this? I cannot call it ordained of God: I can't get that far. I will however pay it so much homage. There is now, in my mouth, this sharp chain. And it never comes out.
>
> *(Ibid.: 300–1)*

The choric effect

It is, says Nietzsche, a fraternal bond that symbolises the relation between the Apollonian and the Dionysian in tragedy. Dionysos speaks the language of Apollo, but finally Apollo speaks the language of Dionysos. It is the Dionysian that must predominate in the end: the sharp metal chain in the mouth, humming and thumping out of the cave, standing in the dark with a pick in the hand before the infallible judge. The Chorus, suggested here in the strange effect of the Equus noise, is the non-individuated expression of the upsurge of Dionysian force and effusion of unconscious will. The Chorus shares the sufferings of Dionysos and heralds a truth from the very heart of the world, and this is the 'origin of that fantastic, apparently repellent figure of the wise and inspired satyr, which is also the "simple man" in contrast to the god: the image of nature and nature's strongest impulses . . .' (*BT*: 44). In its earliest beginnings tragedy is, first and foremost, this choral conduit of Dionysian force. This does not end up resolving doubts or answering questions. Dysart reaches towards Dionysos but in the end wants to see in the dark. He wants to be more in touch with himself. However extraodinary the events he now confronts, and that the boy causes him to confront in himself, he wants an account and he wants to understand. Still the autonomous human subject, he dreams of extending the little drama of his Greek trips – self-knowledge (and a better relationship with his wife in the process) and a better theatre for his consultations. But . . . is this fair? For all the bathos of his self-deprecating humour, does he perhaps have some greater sense of intensity, the intensity occasioned by this exceptional horror? He still works for the God of Health but now knows that he is striking at heads in the dark.

So we must not expect some *answer* from the past. The modern play cannot hope to revive Greek tragedy. It only half-escapes the problem that to plunder the Greeks is to bring back Elgin Marbles or Attic souvenirs. And besides there is nothing 'originary' about the Greeks. It is not that 'Being' has withdrawn from us. Nothing becomes clearer, says Nietzsche, day by day than that the nature of the Greeks and of antiquity is hardly accessible at all, that the facility with which the Greeks are spoken of must arise either from frivolity or from thoughtless arrogance (*D*: section 195). Nothing has 'withdrawn', Lyotard insists, we have not 'forgotten' anything: Heraclitus is no more originary than Janis Joplin (Lyotard 1993: 257). That way melancholy and nostalgia lie. Don't expect then some fruitful issue from a healthy balance of forces (a less frigid wife and a higher sperm count). That would be bourgeois theatre. The health we seek is strength in the face of difficulty. If we explain Dionysos we surely get it wrong.

We need some sense of intensity that is not vulnerable to theatricisation in this way. We need some sense of the dynamism and totality that is suggested recurrently by dance. If it is in singing and dancing that we express ourselves as members of a higher community (*BT*: 17–18), the forms of our dancing may also show something of the manner of the dissimulation we engage in to foster rich affects:

A dance includes suspense, as music includes silence. And the important thing not being whether it is 'well composed' (it must, however, be well composed), but that in the event of this semiotic perfection there is tension. That the structure be merely something that 'covers' the affect, in the sense that it acts as a cover: that is its secret and almost its dissimulation. This is why we must dearly love the semioticians, the structuralists, our enemies, they are our accomplices, in their light lies our obscurity.

(Lyotard 1993: 52)

It must, please note, be well composed. There is no suggestion here that anything goes. It is dissimulation that harbours difference within identity, passion within reason, chance even within structured composition. It suggests a way for our thought and action, and so possibilities for our teaching and learning.

Conducting intensity

But this burdensome self that wants to understand is a self that's still there and it stands in the way. Consider my kind of idealism, sometimes my negativity:

> My regrets: 'If only I had done this . . . If only I could do that . . . If only I wasn't like this . . . If only that hadn't happened.'
> My future: 'Everything will be all right once I have . . . I wish this was over and done with . . . I can't wait to get out of here . . . It's all part of my career plan. . . It will all make sense in the long run.'
> Advice about my work: 'When you are working, think this and not that. When you are writing, this and not that. For any idea there is its opposite. Do this and not that. Be clear about your aims and then plan your objectives in their light. Understand what you are doing in terms of an ideal that you are reaching towards.'
> My identity, my morality: 'I wouldn't do what *she* did . . . *We* don't behave like that, like them.'

Ressentiment runs through these, feeling turned back on itself. But if these are my problems and not yours, let's contrast them with that exuberance you have sometimes felt.

As a child you played outside on a summer's evening and they said 'Come on in it's time for bed', but you didn't notice, you didn't hear, you just wanted it to go on. On a beach you made sandcastles and watched the tide come in. You didn't notice the sun burning your back or the sand in your hair or the cries of the gulls, and they said 'Come and get dressed, it's time to go.' You play a game – *Monopoly*, let's say. Give out the money, set out pieces, throw dice. To begin with it's slow. But then you land on Bond Street, buy more streets, collect money, buy more streets, build green houses, red hotels. The others consolidate on orange Vine Street, cheap mauve Whitechapel, posh Mayfair and blue Park Lane. And then somewhere in the middle there is a time when things are balanced delicately, where the game has suddenly picked up speed: can you buy more now or must you conserve your money to pay your rents and fines, money in case you get sent to jail? And now, absorbed in the game, you are concentrating, and the ludicrous time it takes seems like nothing. Your gamble pays off and gradually it becomes clear: you bankrupt your opponents, progressively taking rent, and buying them up . . . But then the speed has slipped away and as you go through the motions, the game comes listlessly to its end. Speed happens somewhere in the middle, in the absorption in the play.[2]

Reading a novel, you find that first you must discipline yourself to come back to its pages, to get slowly into the story, but then again it suddenly takes off and you are caught up in the plot: you want to know what will happen next. And on it goes with you absorbed, not wanting it to end. And then as the story is progressively resolved, you see what is happening and the rhythm slows. Speed happens somewhere in the absorption in the middle.

As a student you sat staring out of the window, slowly getting your brain into gear. You set targets: read this much by 11.00, then coffee, then this much, then lunch with a friend. You read or you wrote and at first it was slow: your mind wandered and you had to keep pulling yourself back. Ten pages, you counted, to the end of the chapter, and looked at the clock. But then something you read, an example, an idea, perhaps just a phrase, something you read caught your imagination and your interest turned away from those planned distracters and petty rewards, and suddenly without knowing it you were running with the text. Perhaps sometimes you were, as it were, dancing with it, as your thoughts came and went and wove in and out around the words tumbling down the page. When at last you were suddenly disturbed, you were surprised at how much time had suddenly gone by.

So also now you write and you struggle with a blank page, with sketching out a few notes and drafting a plan. You rewrite,

rearranging the items, discarding this and adding that. And
you cannot imagine that this is ever going to come together.
But later in the midst of a paragraph ideas come to you and
somehow take over and the words come together faster than
you can type, and you sit upright in your chair and alert and
focused even though it is getting late and you should be tired.
In fact you are far less tired than you would be if you sat on the
sofa to 'relax'. Writing, you become lost in the ideas. What you
are writing picks up speed. But you must in due course bring
this to a close, break the spell, cast your eye over the whole,
cutting-and-pasting and rearranging, developing your argument and closing gaps, making sure you show that you are
addressing the question, explaining the approach, drawing
your conclusions, and checking the items in your bibliography,
detailing your methodology. And then, of course, though you
may be well pleased with what you've done, then really the spell
has gone.

We must not be in the grip of reason or in full self-possession. We
must be absorbed in the game. 'To understand, to be intelligent,'
Lyotard says, 'is not our overriding passion. We hope rather to be
set in motion. Consequently our passion would sooner be the dance
. . .' (Lyotard 1993: 51). Because what can be controlled here (and
certainly it can be controlled) is like the control that we have when
we set up the rules for a game. We cannot legislate for the kind of
exuberance that arises in the course of the game. We cannot plan
the event's irruption.

Make the classes you teach then flows of intensity that are both
energising and responsive. Let thinking dance. Let there be
affirmation without negation. Not the dialectic of this and not the
other, but more the continuous surface of the Moebius strip. (Take a
strip of paper and twist through 180 degrees, then carefully stick
the ends together so that you have a continuous strip, then follow
with your finger around this loop and you will see that it has no
back. This is a surface with no other, neither recto nor verso,
affirmation without negation. Escher's waterfall feeding its own
source.)

But beware the numerous false dancers here (ibid.: 51): enthusiastic facilitators and earnest enablers, transferrers of skills and
critical thinkers, motivators and school improvers, progressives in
various guises, beware find-the-learning-style-that-suits-you-best,
the onanism of learning-to-learn. Beware ICT-will-transform-
education (though, of course, we passionately hope it will). Beware:
as-a-teacher-you-must-plan-your-lessons, you must state clearly the

aim of the lesson, specify the learning outcomes, list the resources you will use, describe the method you will use, you must keep the class moving so that the children's attention doesn't wander, you must not stray from your plan, and so, with this careful planning, and with the inspection that ensures you are fully accountable, what is taught and what is learned become channelled to predetermined ends. These are highly realistic counterfeits of education.

'But how,' they will say, 'will you know what you are doing? How can you be sure that this will work?' And then will 'Screw the system!' be your response? Is that how you'll dedicate your life and work? You will then set yourself up in rebellion, defining yourself negatively by what you despise. No! You should work within the system, but work carefully at its weak points. Lyotard calls this flight and conspiracy, but its purpose is not to overthrow, rather to unsettle settled discourse and too firmly established centres of power. To work at these by releasing the energies at their borders. Anything else is negative from the start.

Near the end of *Libinal Economy* Lyotard writes:

> Keats said that the poet is a chameleon, and Hofmannsthal that he had no ego, but this is not enough, it is not just the poets who should have this romantic privilege, already attributed to them and to the gods by Plato; let everything go, become conductors of hot and cold, of sweet and sour, the dull and the shrill, theorems and screams, let it make its way over you, without ever *knowing* whether it will work or not, whether it will result in an unheard-of, unseen, untasted, unthought, unexperience, effect, or not.
>
> (Ibid.: 258–9)

Notes

1 For detailed discussions of Lyotard's libidinal philosophy and apedagogy, to which this chapter is greatly indebted, see James Williams 2000a, 2000b.

2 We owe the example to discussions with Gordon Bearn. For a rich evocation of similar ideas see his outstanding essay 'Pointlessness and the university of beauty' (Bearn 2000).

FRAGMENT VI

'Few can seriously doubt that learning has come of age': so begins an article by Peter Honey (*People Management*, October 1998). Learning has 'moved centre stage'. We are in an era of constant change and uncertainty, in which learning is the way to stay in employment now that 'jobs for life' have disappeared. But what *kind* of learning do we need for this new age, or – to put it in Honey's terms – if learning has come of age, what does it look like, in its new maturity? Honey and his colleagues have written a 'Declaration on Learning', reproduced in the same article, as 'a basis for dialogue and discussion'. Who could be against dialogue and discussion? 'If something in the declaration makes you wince, that's good. Use it as an irritant and express your opinion'. All that is bad is good. We contain all contradictions, for we are skilled facilitators of learning. We affirm everything (and thus of course nothing). We are wholly non-judgemental; we ourselves are value-free.

The opening sentence: 'Learning is the most powerful, engaging, rewarding and enjoyable aspect of our personal and collective experience'. Here is élan, vitality indeed. Such a life could be loved unconditionally. The lifelong learner would gladly embrace the eternal recurrence of such a life: is it not so? In Nietzsche's words (*EH*: 10), 'My formula for greatness in a human being is *amor fati*: that one wants nothing to be different, not forward, not backward, not in all eternity'. In Honey's words: 'The ability to learn about learning and become masters of the learning process is the critical issue for the next century'. (Masters of the learning process: Masters of the Universe, as a current television series calls the management consultants. *Übermenschen* indeed.)

The Greeks declared otherwise, holding that we learn through suffering: τῷ πάθει μάθος, *pathemata mathemata*.

However, learning has now come of age. Being of age, and now thoroughly grown-up, the nature and benefits of learning can be listed in bullet-points. 'The effectiveness of how people learn can be improved . . . when self-managed, learning becomes more effective . . . learning to learn is the key to effective learning'.

If this were the case then there would be no need for learning declarations.

Chapter 8

Beyond pain and pleasure
Affirmative ethics and integrity

The discipline of suffering, of *great* suffering – do you not know
that it is *this* discipline alone which has created every elevation of
mankind hitherto? That tension of the soul in misfortune which
cultivates its strength, its terror at the sight of great destruction, its
inventiveness and bravery in undergoing, enduring, interpreting,
exploiting suffering, and whatever of depth, mystery, mask, spirit
cunning greatness has been bestowed upon it – has it not been
bestowed through suffering, through the discipline of great
suffering? In man, *creature* and *creator* are united: in man there is
matter, fragment, excess, clay, mud, madness, chaos; but in man
there is also creator, sculptor, the hardness of the hammer, the
divine spectator and the seventh day – do you understand this
antithesis? And that *your* pity is for the 'creature in man' for that
which has to be formed, broken, forged, torn, burned, annealed,
refined – that which has to *suffer* and *should* suffer?

(*BGE*: section 225)

The importance of the good life

Nietzsche's response to nihilism was characterised in Chapter 5 as
taking a certain sort of responsibility for what we say about the
world and for accepting that we cannot lean on something else for
the values that we hold. As there are no objective values, as all
values are the creation of human beings, they typically serve the
needs of their creators. This creation should, however, not be
understood as a kind of subjectivism, as if the subject could create
values *ex nihilo*, could impose or project values on to the world.
Nietzsche's general antipathy toward what he calls moral values is
aimed at those ways of life that deny life. He wants to overcome the
reaction of those who seek compensation in an imaginary revenge.
Failing to take responsibility characterises what he calls 'the herd'
and this threatens the very possibility of individuality in the present
age. In our opinion his position is often reproached unjustly for

being merely negative. In this chapter we will deal with a number of key ideas that present the positive aspects of his position. After the naturalistic and vitalistic elements in his work have been considered, the idea of *amor fati* as the highest expression of human flourishing is developed. Finally it is argued that the recent reading of Nietzsche by Altieri may dispel some potential possible points of criticism and prove fruitful in educational contexts.

The distinction recently made by Leiter (1997) between theory critics and morality critics may be helpful in understanding Nietzsche's positive morality. Where the former (he mentions Baier, Larmore, Taylor) think that our particular moral assessments and common-sense moral principles are not the sort of thing about which we can or should have a theory in some precise and technical sense, the latter (he mentions Slote, Stocker, Wolf, Williams) criticise moral theory because of its moral commitments (the substantive content of the morality endorsed or the weight assigned in practical reasoning to moral demands). Authors such as Williams, Leiter argues, seem to be objecting not that the best moral theory requires obligation to regulate life, but rather that, once moral obligation is allowed to structure ethical thought, it has a natural tendency to rule out all other considerations. Yet where is the evidence, he asks, that real people treat moral obligations as inescapable and that they accept the idea that only an obligation can beat an obligation? Nietzsche sides with this 'importance of the good life' against 'the encroaching demands of the moral life'. He finds universality objectionable because he holds that 'the demand of one morality for all is detrimental for the higher men' (*BGE*: section 228). His hostility to normative theorising grows out of his naturalism and *amor fati*, which lead him to be deeply sceptical about the utility of propounding normative theories about what we ought to do. The value of life itself cannot be estimated, not because it is without value but rather because its essential nature itself determines the ultimate standard of value, because it itself in its highest form of development is the ultimate value. Though Nietzsche does not hold that there is no objective basis for the assessment of particular moral claims and purported moral principles, what he rejects is the complete autonomy of moral principles. His fundamental innovation lies therefore in the naturalisation of morality.

It may be the case, as Leiter argues, that Nietzsche's repeated denunciations of morality might lead us to conclude that, in some measure, the stance he takes against morality is overstated. But his paradigmatic worry still concerns us: that a nascent creative genius will come to take the norm so seriously that he will fail to realise his genius:

Rather than tolerate (even welcome) suffering, he will seek relief from hardship and devote himself to the pursuit of pleasure; rather than practice what Nietzsche calls 'severe self-love' and attend to himself in the ways requisite for productive creative work, he will embrace the ideology of altruism and reject 'self-love' as improper; rather than learn how to look down on himself, to desire to overcome his present self and become something better, he will embrace the prevailing rhetoric of equality – captured nicely in the pop psychology slogan 'I'm OK, you're OK' – and thus never learn to feel the contempt for self that might lead one to strive for something more. It is not, then, that Nietzsche thinks people *practise* too much altruism – after all, it is Nietzsche who notes that egoistic actions 'have hitherto been by far the most frequent actions' (*Dawn* [*Daybreak*], 148) – but rather that they *believe* too much in the value of altruism, equality, happiness and the other norms of morality in the pejorative sense.

(Leiter 1997: 281)

It is the prevalence of this ideology (not of actions associated with it) that worries Nietzsche. For even if there is not much altruism or equality in the world, there is almost universal endorsement of the value of altruism and equality by those who are its worst enemies in practice – the politicians whose hypocrisy Nietzsche derides. For Nietzsche morality does not consist of principles but of practices. As Solomon argues: 'It is *doing* not willing that is of moral significance, an expression of character rather than a display of practical reason' (Solomon 1986: 80).

Nietzsche rejects neither the Enlightenment nor the classical tradition per se. He finds it psychologically impossible or, at least, socially naive to imagine that one can extract oneself thoroughly from one's genealogy – though he does not wholeheartedly endorse either of these traditions and clearly rejects the version of morality that has as its instrument the universalisable principles formalised by Kant. Yet Nietzsche's favourite image for his time is the 'twilight of the idols' – that is to say, the dominant values and sustaining ideals of modernity as a whole. The image signifies an advanced stage of decay that can express itself only in a self-destructive retreat, an epoch in which modernity attains its debilitating self-consciousness. His thinking does not operate in the manner of emotivism, ethical or meta-ethical; instead it arouses a self-conscious awareness of the connectedness of our feelings and judgements. And though Nietzsche '. . . preaches self-creation and freedom from convention as the highest ideals, he thinks that these rare achievements require not less but more discipline in the social context in which they occur' (Richardson 1997: 31). It is, according to Richardson, out of an improved philosophical community and method that, he hopes, the (very) few creators will come: 'Genuine philosophers, however, are commanders and legislators: they say, "thus it shall be!"' (*BGE*: section 211). A revaluation of values is all that is possible. Unlike the philosophers of the future, whom Nietzsche identifies as legislators of new values, he can do no more than challenge and perhaps reverse the reigning values of his age. As outlined in Chapter 5, this revaluation of all values does not (and could not) involve the creation *ex nihilo* of new values. As Conway argues:

> Nietzsche apparently believes that 'new' values arise either from an originary act of creation or from a reversal of existing values. The former, 'active' mode of evaluation is available only to healthy peoples and ages, whereas the latter, 'reactive' mode of evaluation characteristically falls to decadents, invalids, slaves and anyone else who cannot afford the luxury of spontaneous self-expression.
>
> (Conway 1997: 182)

Nietzsche gives a helpful picture, Williams suggests (1993), of a 'naturalistic' moral psychology, according to which our view of moral capacities should be consistent with, even perhaps in the spirit of, our understanding of human beings as part of nature. He leads us towards a realistic rather than an essentialist moral psychology: not the application of an already defined scientific programme, but rather an informed interpretation of some human experiences and activities in relation to others. Williams interprets Nietzsche's doubts about action as doubts not about the very idea of anyone's doing anything, but rather about a morally significant interpretation of action in terms of the will (understood as something 'simple' and as a peculiar, imperative, kind of cause). 'Willing' has to be conceived as a complex of sensations and thinking, and as an effect of command. We can thus be helped to see that the integrity of action, the agent's genuine presence in it, can be preserved without this picture of the will. The kind of psychological power Nietzsche affirms is not a raw 'given' but something that has passed through the sublimative and rational process of transfiguration and self-overcoming: the 'is' becomes 'ought' only if it undergoes an intensive elaboration and trans-formation.

Vitalism and decadence

The genuine source of thinking and of all human endeavours is for Nietzsche located in the invisible, unconscious drives and impulses that animate all of animal activity. He understands human physiology to be continuous with human psychology and insists that all psychology has become stuck in moral prejudices and fears, that it has not dared to descend into the depths (cf. *BGE*: section 23). Decadence is defined as an organic disorder that involves 'the degeneration of the instincts' (*TI*, 'Expeditions of an Untimely Man': section 41), and elsewhere as 'instinctively to choose what is harmful to oneself' (*TI*, 'Expeditions of an Untimely Man': section 35). He characterises decadence as a corruption or clash of the instincts on which individuals and people customarily and un-reflectively rely to guide their everyday behaviour. Conscious intentions, volitions and actions are for him derivative manifestations of a more basic, vital core of animal agency:

> Man, like every living being, thinks continually without knowing it; the thinking that rises to *consciousness* is only the smallest part of all of this – the most superficial and worst part – for only this conscious thinking *takes the form of words, which is to say signs of communication,* and this fact uncovers the origin of consciousness.

(*GS*: section 54)

Decadence is predicated of the invisible, instinctual body, the sub-system of drives and impulses that propagates the native vitality of the animal organism. Its ultimate source and necessity is located in the sickness of the 'bad conscience', which during its long moral history has obliged human kind to exhaust its native vitality in the struggle to refuse the incessant demands of their natural, instinctual heritage. It has renounced its animal instincts and natural inclinations such that a life-affirming instinctual nature has become inseparable from a tormenting bad conscience. In order to gain peace and security from civil society, humans must forfeit the natural state associated with the instantaneous discharge of their primal drives and impulses (cf. *GM*, II: section 16). The clash of instincts is the inevitable result of the artificial mode of internal regulation required by civilisation and imposed by consciousness, which is itself mainly superfluous (cf. *GS*: section 354). Lacking the structural organisation and integrity provided by a single, dominant instinctual system, decadent souls cannot distinguish friend from foe, kin from stranger, virtue from vice, treasure from trash, or triumph from collapse: they instinctively prefer that which leads to dissolution, that which hastens the end (cf. *TI*, 'Expeditions of an Untimely Man': section 39).

> The wish to preserve oneself is the symptom of a condition of distress, of a limitation of the really fundamental instinct of life which aims at *the expansion of power* and, wishing for that, frequently risks and sacrifices self-preservation. . . . The struggle for existence is only an *exception*, a temporary restriction of the will to life. The great and small struggle always revolves around superiority, around growth and expansion, around power – in accordance with the will to power which is the will of life.
>
> (*GS*: section 349)

The soul is thus conceived as the human animal organism that in its most primal, uncomplicated, and rudimentary form functions as a pure, amoral engine of the will to power. What philosophers have traditionally called morality largely amounts to a confused attempt to impose order on to the chaotic drives and impulses of the soul.

Nietzsche distinguishes *Trieb* from *Instinkt*: unconscious drives and impulses compose the circulatory network of the soul; the instincts constitute the patterns of regulation that govern the internal operations of this network. The drives and impulses remain 'invisible', but the instincts admit of indirect empirical observation by virtue of the traces they manifest in detectable, public patterns of behaviour (see Conway 1997). Decadence as the loss or dis-integration of the instincts does not mean that the underlying drives have somehow decomposed, but that their previous configuration has been compromised; it pertains to the systems of internal organisation that regulate the discharge of the drives and impulses. According to Nietzsche it is not possible to restore the drives and impulses to their original or raw form; his aim is rather to perfect the process of acculturation whereby the drives and impulses become fully civilised. In the late 1880s particularly he evinces an ever-strengthening commitment to a form of (amoral) vitalism and regularly insists that one's prospects for flourishing, for attaining nobility and greatness, depend in complicated ways on the quantity and quality of the native vitality that one's soul reserves and expends. Affect, energy, force, health, life, power, strength, vitality and will all carry a strongly positive connotation. The exemplary human being (the genius) is portrayed as a swollen river that spontaneously floods the surrounding countryside. It is in this mode of amoral human flourishing that the *noble* soul is situated.

Vitalism not only expands the scope of the critique of sub-jectivity exposing the ego and the will as metaphysical fictions, it also challenges the very notion of individual agency: individual subjects are not causal agents but passive conduits of the will to power. The metaphysical will is nothing more than a phantom, invented for the purpose of punishment (cf. *TI*, 'The Four Great Errors': section 7). Willing refers to the complex phenomenal state that attends the organisation of the drives. There are strong and weak wills: health is understood as an integration of the will and decadence as a weakness of the will, a failure of the instincts to maintain the specific organisation of drives and impulses needed to sustain a threshold level of affective engagement which occasions the enhanced feeling of power associated with willing. But there is no being behind doing; the doer is merely a fiction added to the deed; the deed is everything (cf. *GM*, I: 13). The disintegration of the will makes the soul increasingly unable to propagate and discharge its native vitality and thus decadence manifests itself as a volitional crisis which prevents individuals from acting in their own best interests. Everything that heightens the feeling of power in man is defined as good, and the feel-ing that power is growing is identified as happiness (cf. *A*: section 2):

> Life itself is *essentially* appropriation, injury, overpowering of the strange and weaker, suppression, severity, imposition of one's own forms, incorporation and, at the least and mildest, exploitation. . . . 'Exploitation' does not pertain to a corrupt or imperfect and primitive society: it pertains to the *essence* of the living thing as a fundamental organic function, it is a consequence of the intrinsic will to power which is precisely the will of life.
>
> (*BGE*: section 259)

The kind of power Nietzsche has in mind is not simply the power of self-discipline or self-control but the power to rule and dominate others, lust for power as the driving force of life: in all what we do there must therefore be an egoistic drive. He repudiates the notion that the most basic human instinct is that of self-preservation; there is much that life esteems more highly than life itself, more highly than pain and pleasure. Life involves domination, and so, as he argues in the *Genealogy of Morals*, that domination itself is not intrinsically wrong. Treating every will as equal to every other will would be a principle hostile to life. Such a way to organise society involves an imposition of forms that is often described as 'a work of art', yet in the imposing of their own forms and values on their subjects such political artist-creators are conduits of forces beyond themselves. Thus, for instance, Nietzsche's objection is directed at the socialist vision of a future classless society, in which social domination arising from economic exploitation will be eliminated, because this, he says, essentially involves a rejection of the will to power, the fundamental principle of life. Nietzsche does not demand the destruction of tradition; he demands rather the destruction of any tradition that has become incapable of making possible the founding of a new tradition, hence of being a ground for culture. Any tradition that does not provide such grounds for growth, any tradition that does not embody critique, is not worthy of the name. In his eyes society is devoid of substantial solidarity where individuals assert their rights over any communal rights and where society is organised according to (nihilistic) mechanical principles in economy, legislation and bureaucracy.

In its most primordial state the will to power is boundless, indifferent, amoral. But life remains bounded by a horizon of anthropocentric preferences and values. Life requires us to legislate, to design, to register preferences, to deviate from nature and to regulate the economy of life (cf. *BGE*: section 9). It is not the expression of violence that Nietzsche celebrates but rather the relationship between conflict and creativity. It is his conviction that human beings are essentially unequal and that any attempt to equalise these differences will necessarily have pernicious effects on the health of individuals and on the culture at large. Though he is the philosopher of power *par excellence*, it is dangerous to misappropriate Nietzsche as a champion of individual agency, for the power he discloses is neither native to nor commanded by individual subjects. Nietzsche is not a radical voluntarist who offers a plan for restoring decadent souls to a more robust standard of vitality. Human flourishing is a remote and attenuated expression of one's physiological destiny (cf. *EH*, 'Why I Am so Wise': section 6). Individuals thus cannot be held responsible either for their respective endowments of vital forces or for the economic laws that they invariably obey. Nietzsche's stance in *Beyond Good and Evil* is not simply antagonistic to particular kinds of asceticism. All morality that accepts the metaphysical apparatus of will, responsibility, blame and guilt are rejected. His conception of the model of agency operating here is in part derived from contradistinction to the vitalism he endorses.

Exemplary human beings do not deserve our moral approbation, but are to be admired for their expression of vitality, a species of aesthetic evaluation indeed. He warns us:

This seems to me to be one of my most essential steps and advances: I have learned to distinguish the cause of acting from the cause of acting in a particular way, in a particular direction, with a particular goal. The first kind of cause is a quantum of dammed-up energy that is waiting to be used up somehow, for something, while the second kind is, compared to this energy, something quite insignificant, for the most part a little accident in accordance with which this quantum 'discharges' itself in one particular way – a match versus a ton of powder. Among these little accidents and 'matches' I include so-called 'purposes' as well as the even much more so-called 'vocations'. They are relatively random, arbitrary, almost indifferent in relation to the tremendous quantum of energy that presses, as I have said, to be used up somehow. The usual view is different. People are accustomed to consider the goal (purposes, vocations, etc.) as the *driving force*, in keeping with a very ancient error; but it is merely *the directing* force – one has mistaken the helmsman for the steam. And not even always the helmsman, the directing force.

Is the 'goal', the 'purpose' not often enough a beautifying pretext, a self-deception of vanity after the event that does not want to acknowledge that the ship is *following* the current into which it has entered accidentally? that it 'wills' to go that way *because it – must*? that it has a direction, to be sure, but – no helmsman at all?

(*GS*: section 360)

(Some) individuals enjoy some influence over the specific expression of their native vitality. But the condition of their souls, as well as the capacity of expendable resources at their disposal, are largely a matter of their unalterable destiny. Only under certain conditions can they determine the qualitative disposition of the quanta of force they involuntarily propagate, and influence the ship's initial course and ultimate destination.

The greatest danger for Nietzsche, Swanton claims (1998), is the contagious display of the sickness and associated mediocrity of society. This arises out of the cauldron of unsatisfied hatred, itself a rage at impotence, and spawns a variety of sick forms of will to power: envy, self-lacerating asceticism, altruism in which self-interest wilts away. The vengeful self-protective values of the impotent, perversely obsessed with results, express mediocrity; vigorous desires and attitudes do not.

For Nietzsche, in the end all great things bring about their own destruction: only in a self-destructive retreat from, and betrayal of, its founding ideals and values can an age express itself. A decadent age moves inexorably towards the exhaustion of its vital sources, and it is a self-deception on the part of philosophers and moralists to believe they are somehow extricating themselves from decadence when they are merely waging war against it. All expressions of strength and vitality must eventually decay. To this Nietzsche himself is no exception. His advanced decadence is the inescapable destiny of late modernity.

Amor fati, resentment and integrity

Eternal recurrence expresses a love of life as it is, in its painful, amoral immanence. It is an acceptance of how one is, and of one's desires. It is to look things in the face. It is to live with oneself on the terms that one has willed. The good life is where one wants the wants that one has, but to want all one's wants does not constitute the good life. It conveys a parsimonious naturalism that contrasts with the proliferating spectres that have haunted philosophy, and it promotes a respect for the earth as a singular, closed system for which humankind is solely and uniquely responsible. It champions the perfection of the human soul and sanctions the project of self-overcoming. It invites the highest humans to advance to full maturity. An unflinching *amor fati* is enshrined as the highest expression of human flourishing.

Nietzsche wished to love and to affirm, but also to judge. Judgement without love is for him but another word for *ressentiment*; without judgement love is reduced to pity. One cannot judge lovingly without the capacity for love of one's own life. Loving one's life involves a yearning and struggling for perfection that necessarily involves contempt for how one now is; it involves aversion from all that inhibits growth and development. The self must be affirmed as a whole: one must love oneself, the plurality one is, enough to want to see the drama of life played out. And love of others follows the same formula: plurality is to be cultivated and embraced (cf. Thiele 1991). Above pity, love marks an active, engaged relationship because it delights in the overcoming of suffering; it promotes involvement in, not avoidance of, struggle. For Nietzsche love is the greatest of life's affirmative forces, but it is always accompanied by the greatest dangers: in its decadent forms love is perverted into self-indulgent commiseration and infatuation, the self-delusory projection of ideals as achievable rather than always still to be realised. Love as the passion for perfection must remain sceptical, for it to escape decadence, of its necessarily imperfect object. Thus one creates a world worthy of affirmation: a partnership of actuality and aspiration, Thiele suggests (1991: 93), in which the potential to transform being is produced by the feeling of power one receives through the illusion of a perfected world. To love is to negate and to affirm: through endless change and growth one seeks to become what can be accepted as it is. The struggle is to become a person who can truly love herself. Only through the strength gained by constant self-overcoming does one find the power necessary to embrace destiny. *Amor fati* is therefore not fatalism, nor a providential distribution of meaning and justice: rather it is what befalls us.

> The latter [fatalism] takes hold of a person as the wind of a leaf: the forces of nature, of history, of chance, are simply too great to be affected or combated. Resignation yields rest and comfort. *Amor fati* is a struggle with these forces. Fate is not merely what happens to one, but what happens as a result of one's active involvement with life. The love of fate is the love of this involvement and of its outcome.
>
> (Thiele 1991: 94)

The lover of fate makes everything that comes his way a cause for celebration; temporary defeats are welcomes as preparations for greater victories. Living the present must be its own reward.

Conventional moral values are born, in Nietzsche's view, out of the peculiar condition he calls *ressentiment*, and this encompasses three central phenomena: the distinction between good and evil, the feeling of moral guilt, and the ascetic ideal. It is not the value judgements themselves that he focuses upon, but the psychological state of the agent who makes these value judgements. *Ressentiment* is objectionable because it undermines the integrity of the self, an integrity that is, Reginster claims (1997), internal to the perspective of the agent who pursues his needs, desires, or interests. *Ressentiment* is a state of repressed vengefulness that arises out of the combination of the desire to lead the kind of life that one deems valuable, the inability so to do because of weakness or impotence, and the refusal to give up the original pretensions. Revaluation in the spirit of *ressentiment* cannot be the work of slaves, as they do not create values. Because (political) power matters to the man of *ressentiment*, indignation and (moral) resentment are by no means the first reactions to his defeat: shame and self-contempt are.

It is worth noting that there is a difference between this and Nietzsche's attitude towards truth as perspectivism – a claim that does not deny the possibility of truth as such, but that undermines the plausibility of a metaphysical concept of truth the logic of which leaves no room for the possibility of competing, equally veridical perspectives and interpretations. 'The truth', he holds, has no unconditional value. Self-deception is not a 'lack of knowledge', but a lack of acknowledgement of what one knows, what one holds to most truly. Integrity, in the broad sense, is associated with a kind of wholeness, autonomy and sense of responsibility; in the narrow sense, with such qualities as honesty, truthfulness and intellectual conscience. The creation of values is the agent's self-affirmation. It expresses her own view of what sort of life is worth living. According to Reginster (1997), Nietzsche appears to believe that an agent genuinely endorses a desire only if he acknowledges the other desires that conflict with the one he chooses. Thus, it becomes clear where the problem lies. Without integrity in the narrow sense a person cannot regard her values as genuinely her own creation, and in consequence she lacks integrity in the broad sense. She lacks, that is, nobility: 'While the noble man lives for himself in trust and openness . . . the man of *ressentiment* is neither upright nor naïve in his dealings with others, nor is he honest and open with himself. His soul squints . . .' (*GM*, I: section 10). Here, the adoption of new values is motivated by the desires they condemn. Thus, the man of *ressentiment* is left suspended between the impossibility of enjoying the satisfaction of desires he does not really have, and the impossibility of enjoying the satisfaction of desires he has but cannot embrace.

According to Conway (1998), an *Übermensch* is anyone who in virtue of a surpassing endowment of vitality and creative energy stands closest to reality as it is, in its painful, amoral immanence. In any particular culture or epoch a person of this kind functions in such a way as to bind the people or community as closely to the real world as their native vitality will allow; and this ensures the possibility of a continual expansion of the range of human perfectibility. Nietzsche apparently models the *Übermensch* on Emerson's ideas of the potentialities for perfection resident within the human soul (the Oversoul). It is in these terms that he refers to any higher human being whose 'private' pursuit of self-perfection occasions an enhancement of the species as a whole. This is a pursuit embodying a justification of humankind grounded in its reality rather than in some abstract ideal. A healthy political regime is one that produces individuals of this type. The individualism Nietzsche suggests is therefore neither the atomistic individualism of libertarianism nor that of liberal humanism. He speaks of the essential unity of the world of flux, the interrelationships that constitute existence, and the individual as dynamic multiplicity. No stable self or single identity, the individual's uniqueness lies in the ordering of internal impulses. In *Human, All-too-Human* (I: 57; II: 76) he argues that morally a human being is not an individual (*individuum*) but a multiple (*dividuum*), that there is no unity but rather dividedness in individuality. The acknowledgement of this inner dividedness takes courage and strength. It marks the amount of truth a spirit can dare and endure. Nietzsche promotes the individualism of the highest human types while recognising that values are initially established by peoples. The aesthetic justification of human existence is located in the continued advancement of the species as a whole.

In *Untimely Meditations*, Nietzsche states that only he who has attached his heart to Great Men is consecrated to culture. Human communities are founded on any number of principles and pretexts, but culture originates only in the love excited by, and bestowed upon, a great human being. And the multiple aspects of such a being, so Conway argues (in Kemal *et al.* 1998), are those of philosopher, artist and saint. Love is thus identified not only as the impetus to self-overcoming but also as the constitutive and unifying principle of culture. Great human beings introduce others to the next selves they might become; thus only those individuals who are touched by the madness of *eros* dare to enter the circle of culture described by the self-overcomings of a representative exemplar. Only *eros* too furnishes the psychological motivation to overcome oneself, to place one's soul at mortal risk in the pursuit of self-perfection. In the course of their self-overcoming, great individuals produce in themselves the beauty that alone arouses erotic attachment. As artist, producers of surpassing beauty, exemplary human beings fulfil their social role as lawgivers. Self-overcoming presupposes suffering: genuine *Erziehung* is therefore both painful and dangerous, eliciting and provoking the uncharted plasticities of the human soul. Only engulfed in the madness of *eros* would human beings ever attempt to overcome or transcend their natural limitations (see Chapter 11).

The importance that Nietzsche attaches to intellectual integrity for the philosopher cannot be overstated, but he also compares him to the player of a game:

> . . . and today if one hears anyone commended for living 'wisely' or like a 'philosopher', it means hardly more than 'prudently and apart'. Wisdom: that seems to the rabble to be a kind of flight, an artifice and means for getting oneself out of a dangerous game; but the genuine philosopher – as he seems to *us*, my friends? – lives 'unphilosophically' and 'unwisely,' above all *imprudently*, and bears the burden and the duty of a hundred attempts and temptations of life – he risks *himself* constantly, he plays *the* dangerous game.
>
> (*BGE*: section 205)

And the product of philosophy is one's life, not just one's books. He expects his new philosophers to put their knowledge into practice concretely, to live by that knowledge.

Nietzsche's moral critical position has thus to be conceived in terms of the living of a particular kind of life which is experimental in the living and thus as free as the spirit is. For Nietzsche an ethical law can only be a law if legislated for oneself; it is from this that it derives its function and recognisable worth for the individual. A free spirit has her own laws. She wants to follow these on her own grounds and from her own strengths. Whether others do the same is neither here nor there; she cannot rely on others for the validity of the laws that she, a sovereign individual, accepts as her own; she has to find justification herself. The Nietzschean subject can be seen as the person who determines the particular good for herself in a way that captures the individuating role of personal commitments through a form of narrative reasoning. What makes a project, relationship, or ideal part of the good life for someone is that maintaining the commitment to it makes recognisable sense to the subject herself; she takes responsibility for what she has done (or could have done) in the past. In finding a richer and more compelling articulation of the point of one's affective-conative responses, one articulates a personal vision. As an expressive act, articulation can be thought of as revealing the particular evaluative colour that the world has for someone. Such articulation may even be understood as a form of inter-subjective practical reasoning. Expressing to you my own conception of the good life means that I articulate what underlies your existing moral intuitions or perhaps that I move you by my description to the point of making it your own. That these things are not indifferent to matters of power (and desire) is evident, but this is emphatically not to say that reason has no place at all.

There is, however, a major proviso that needs to be expressed here, and that has been expressed recently by, for example, Nussbaum (1994). Nietzsche's rather abstract and romantic praise of solitude and asceticism, fails, so it seems, to grasp the simple truth that a hungry person cannot think well. The person who lacks shelter, health and the basic necessities of life is not likely to become a great philosopher or artist. Nietzsche in short is a bourgeois, and it takes a bourgeois to value the commitment to such a life of hardship (to savour the characteristic commitments of poverty, humility, chastity). It is Nietzsche's bourgeois values that find a way into his philosophy:

> The solitude Nietzsche describes is comfortable bourgeois solitude, whatever its pains and loneliness. . . . And because

Nietzsche does not grasp the simple fact that if our abilities are physical abilities they have physical necessary conditions, he does not understand what the democratic and socialist movements of his day were all about.

(Nussbaum 1994: 158)

There is another way of seeing things, Nussbaum claims: there is a strength of a specifically human sort in the willingness to acknowledge some truths about one's situation – one's mortality, finitude, need for food and drink and shelter and friendship, the limits and vulnerabilities of one's body – a strength in the willingness to form attachments that can go wrong in a way that opens one's whole life up to the changes of the world, for good and for ill. But Nussbaum's detachment of Nietzsche from such views trades on a popular interpretation of Nietzsche's Overman that sees the will to power in an exceptionally crude way. It is his very grasp of the matters that Nussbaum raises that enables him to think as he does. It is not clear that the strength Nussbaum speaks of is not Nietzschean after all.

Nietzsche seems to suggest that we tend to lead double lives, with all the hypocrisy and self-deception that that implies. We demand of people that they behave decently, that they cultivate the herd virtues of modesty, humility, fairness, pity, etc. But if everyone did behave always and only like that (see Chapter 11), as the moral law seems to require, a lot that makes life interesting and valuable would simply disappear. Art and its glories are always at the forefront of Nietzsche's mind – the paradigm of human achievement; and in art there is an absolute lack of democracy, a ruthless elitism. He often says that he wants people to be artists of life, to make their lives works of art. An aesthetics of existence as conceived by Foucault can be one of the means through which we improve the quality and generosity of our connectedness to others. For Foucault normative questions cannot be adjudicated rationally. The aesthetic can be of some help here, however, as Bennett has argued (1996). The first reason for this is that insofar as moral agents and their principles are likened to works of art – to sculptures, carvings, pottery, to things worked and reworked in ways never free from the mark or force of prior embodiments, intentions are accidents – their constructed character comes to the fore. The second reason is that insofar as art is thought to call for a special mode of perception – that is, an attention to things as sensuous ensembles (scenes, songs, stories, dances) – artistic representation may reveal with special force the structural or networked character of the ethical.

A recent reformulation: Altieri's expressivist ethics

Within this structure, the role that others must play has recently been taken up in the Nietzschean position adopted by Charles Altieri (1994). The question he contemplates concerns the embeddedness of the subject in the inter-subjective level, that at the same time leaves enough room for the possibility of distancing oneself from that level and from oneself. There are two dialectical relationships: a relationship between the self and others, and a relationship between the self and the subject.

The ethical theory Altieri is arguing for will pay particular attention to the ways in which concerns for ethical identities hold implications for the pursuit of moral values. It will produce a thicker 'psychological' account of those implications than is common in analytical ethics. And finally, it will argue that we can define self-reflexive moral judgements in terms of how the first person engages with others from whom she seeks to read her sense of identity, and it will show, through this dialogical model, why the agent might want to submit herself to impartial third-person criteria for assessing her actions and even her projects. Thus, Altieri constructs a path from expressionist psychology to related notions of ethical value that afford agents a coherent and substantial structure for representing their own interests in caring about those values and in following the dictates that this care will produce. He does admit that ultimately ethical reasoning is a circular process, as our interests and our arguments, even our arguments about the need to take impartial attitudes towards specific interests, are deeply implicated in one another. But, as he goes on to say,

> What obligates us derives from what we take as somehow fulfilling us, and what allows us to seek understanding from others also binds us to the ways of structuring our concerns so that they participate in a common framework.
>
> (Altieri 1994: 156)

In developing his theory he relies on two meta-ethical principles: we need to cast our reflections in terms of whether agents' actions can win judgements that they are good – that they merit happiness – and we need to specify how agents can become candidates for such judgements. Submission to such judgements involves fear, but it also invites us to relate to idealised figures. While he accepts that positive reaction from others does equate to justice, he claims that the possibilities introduced by ideals of merit provide a model of motivation that can bring back into ethics consideration of the forces shaping the self and its desires, reuniting the ethical with a complex of positive impulses and interests basic to fully civilised lives.

Subjective agency is characterised in such a way that we can understand agents as responding to concerns about merit without thereby being seduced into psychological dependency or slavishness: one is not hanging on their every word. Altieri follows Wittgenstein when he writes that what people accept as justification is shown by how they think and live. They expect this, and are surprised at that, but the chain of reasons has an end. We are advised to be content in the recognition that we are on a track allowing us either to rest or to go on; that we need not be weighed down by confusion and contradiction. On the basis of the asymmetry between first- and third-person stances, Altieri treats actions as if their intelligibility depended on the reasons that agents might give for them. Because explanation in terms of causes does not seem as feasible, reasons define the force of agency. In this way Altieri gives a kind of substance to subjectivity. But he also wants to avoid existential relativism. This he does by accepting that ethical decisions stand out against a background of dispositions, habits, practices and social expectations; that they require a more complex model of self-constitution than we find in existentialism or even in poststructural idealisations of singularity (cf. Altieri 1994: 161). Taking responsibility for meanings is different from choosing meanings: one moves among meanings, perhaps through different spheres of argument, and thereby tries to reconfigure one's relation to actions and contexts. In effect what one does is to define oneself contingently by placing oneself anew within a world suffused with meanings. Here the intelligibility of the reasons for an action comes to an end within the parameters of a community's social structures, its 'grammars'. This is not a matter of doing something in a wholly new way but of doing something different.

To be sure, there will be within this process of reconfiguring one's relation to actions and contexts temporary phases and masks that are adopted. In the popular film *Educating Rita*, for example, the eponymous central character, a working-class mature student, changes as a person as she passes through the stages of her university course. Initially she is overawed by her lecturers and by the articulate younger students who seem to know exactly what to do and how to behave, and whose accent and idiom are different from hers. She quickly learns their 'sophisticated' ways and adopts their vocabulary and tastes in what amounts to a kind of pose. Later, the hollowness of this becomes apparent to her, and she advances to a

higher stage: she now relates more genuinely and more independently to the literature she studies on her course, and is more at
one with her own life. She is more autonomous and more authentic.
But the terms for this, indeed its very possibility, are given by the
contingent grammars of the social structures through which she
finds herself.

This perhaps helps to clarify Altieri's position and the extent to
which this is relativist. He is ready to accept that insofar as the good
depends on how agents are understood in terms of particular
grammars, rather than on universal principles, there will be social
groups for whom a person's reasons do not count, groups whose
moral priorities may even be incomprehensible.

Ethical theory should try to characterise what might be a
common thread in individual situations and to provide some sense
of how agents might make the best use of their powers to develop
and exchange ethical concerns. Altieri shows that his account of
expressivist desires can represent conative drives so that they do not
require specific acts of self-ownership at every moment but instead
find satisfaction in working towards long-term projects and stability
within the practices they engage. The following lengthy quotation
makes clear where he stands:

> What makes an act expressively 'mine' then is not quite consent
> (nor any reference to some attribute of 'me' that one finds
> objectively in it) but a more general willingness to, or need to,
> have myself represented by it. And what makes it moral is my
> willingness to, or need to, have that identity judged not merely
> as a state to be responded to but as one to be assessed in terms
> of whether in pursuing it as I do I become worthy to be happy.
> The scope and depth of any particular appeal to moral identity
> depends on how much of one's life one wants or needs any
> particular gesture to carry. Or, to put the same point another
> way, the scope projected for any one act of identification
> depends on how many other identifications one wants or needs
> to subsume within it or give purposive roles through it. To
> complete the identification, then, one must adapt oneself to
> complex social expectations which derive in part from promises
> or commitments we make to specific others, and in part from the
> many cultural grammars for assessment that we learn in adapting
> ourselves to the multiple practices folded into contemporary life.
> (Altieri 1994: 204)

Altieri sees the person in the process of negotiating for an identity
with an audience imagined as a tribunal whose understanding, if

not whose approval, is necessary for the agent's being confirmed in the substance that the expressive activity seeks. Though the audience can be almost entirely imaginary, to grasp the various roles it plays it is better to envision it as representative of an actual community. He concentrates on how the second-person function contributes to the identification process and thus treats the conferring of identity as a dialogical process responsive to cultural grammars but capable of modifying those grammars to accommodate specific expressive traits. Thus one invokes modes of judgement that not only bring to bear the necessary knowledge and sympathy to assess actions, but also the flexibility to take into account the transformations that the agent might work on the vocabulary shared with the audience. That flexibility also gives, Altieri argues, a useful way to imagine how agents internalise social norms not as rigid rules or conventions to be manipulated, but as aspects of dialogues by which we both try to invoke approval and work towards personalised identifications with the cultural structures framing our investments. The 'you' serves both as the constraint that holds one to obligations and as the source of idealisation that pulls the agent towards certain versions of its and its audience's 'best selves'.

In intimate relations, the way that we perform the action and – even more important – the way that the action reveals and extends certain qualities in relationships become the central concerns. It is not so much that we owe particular considerations to others (as if they had rights to make claims upon us) as that we want certain pleasures for them and certain identities – as lovers, friends or parents – for ourselves. In this sphere of agent-relative relations we treat the terms of justification less as an accord with principle than as an attunement to the distinctness we hope to feel and that, we trust, characterises our close relationships. Here obligation proves almost entirely a sense of duty to oneself, a sense of how one can represent oneself to oneself as worthy of certain predicates in the eyes of those with whom one is engaged. Here we monitor ourselves to ask whether or not we are living in accord with what we project as not simply a good life but the best possible way of maintaining those relationships. This ethics of attunement is content with analogues of the beautiful in which the way one experiences oneself in a range of specific harmonies with others becomes an end in itself. Parallel to Kant's position on aesthetic judgement, Altieri argues that in moral theory the agent pursues a sociality fundamental to her own self-enjoyment. The agent does not want universal agreement for its own sake but seeks a mode of assessment that will allow her to maintain in the eyes of others – and hence in her own self-representations – the identity of one who bases judgements on internalising shareable models of assessment. Such an agent must follow third-person procedures. But by positing a second-person basis (for accepting such conditions) she ensures both that her relation to those procedures takes on considerable flexibility, and that the procedures need not be grounded in terms of some independent principle. She thus remains responsible to specific determinations of ends, but she also encounters those determinations within complex discursive frameworks and clear expectations about the actions that must follow.

Personal identity is thus connected to accepting certain social procedures not as imposed but as necessary for certain realisations of ourselves. Indeed, what makes a judgement binding is not the coercive power of the judge but the commitment of the agent. The sense of responsibility that Altieri is proposing redistributes the relation between the passive and the active in a way that is basic to responsiveness. Expressivist theory argues that one cannot distribute responsibility without a strong sense of what commitments agents make themselves responsible for. Thus responsibility is defined in terms of consent to the practical consequences deriving from acting in accord with identities we invest in:

> What counts as consequences cannot be fixed abstractly. Instead the relevant consequences one accepts are determined by correlating a construction of a particular situation, an agent's specific version of some identity, the culture's grammatical expectations about that identity, and the pressures that exemplars of that and related identities bring to bear on how we both define the situation and develop paths of action.
>
> (Altieri 1994: 220)

Understanding the role of demands on oneself crucially depends on the possibilities of developing an account of self-respect that involves valuing oneself. To position oneself with regard to something is to find one's own worth in terms of how one conducts oneself with respect to it. Helm (1996) argues that although one normally identifies with something by virtue of a harmony between one's judgements and one's will, one's emotions and one's desires, in cases of fragmentation one's judgements and one's emotions can be largely separate sources of one's identity, and hence of meaning in one's life. It is seldom possible for a person to undo years of character formation, and consequent identification with its content, simply by making a judgement (or even many judgements) because those judgements have not been incorporated into her character:

she needs to live differently. A divided identity that finds its energy in different conflicts might be thought to survive in a Nietzschean way, but it meets the demand for consistency and integrity in a cowardly fashion because it is deaf to the voice of its own emotions and judgement. Perhaps Altieri can be seen as giving us a Nietzschean model that connects, on the one hand, the inner conflictual life, and on the other, the life in which we respond to the demands of reality.

If education can be conceived (at minimum) in terms of a relationship between one individual person and another, particularity, care, integrity and trust are of the utmost importance: so also is authenticity. Of course, an agent cannot articulate a project concerning who she wants to be without a context of inter-subjectivity. Such a project must constitute a particularly illuminating example of what can be done in a certain social predicament. Authentic identity presupposes a moment of recognition on the part of another. It can thus mean pursuing a project in which a willed uniqueness is expressed, as well as the wish for others to recognise this unique person who we want to become. The agent must be willing to take the risk that her intended identity will not be recognised. Recalling the inter-subjective origin of identity, the need for recognition and the inter-subjective nature of reflective judgement should dispel the impression that authenticity is yet another restatement of the philosophy of the autonomous subject. If the educator is characterised by her willingness to stand for something and simultaneously willing to care for someone, then the philosophy of authenticity, thus conceived, should also help the educator out of the problems that the Enlightenment project and some of its critics have left her with. Here, what we take as a kind of fulfilment, conceived also to a certain extent in a naturalistic way, binds us to the ways of structuring our concerns so that others can participate in a 'common' framework.

KING ALFRED'S COLLEGE
LIBRARY

Part 3

Raising standards

Chapter 9

Solitude, silence, listening

Learning solitude – O you poor devils in the great cities of world politics, you gifted young men, tormented by ambition who consider it your duty to pass some comment on everything that happens – and there is always something happening! Who when they raise the dust in this way think they are the chariot of history! Who, because they are always on the alert, always on the lookout for the moment when they can put their word in, lose all genuine productivity! However much they may desire to do great work, the profound speechlessness of pregnancy never comes to them! The event of the day drives them before it like chaff, while they think they are driving the event – poor devils! – If one wants to represent a hero on the stage one must not think of making one of the chorus, indeed one must not even know how to make one of the chorus.

(*D*: section 177)

On education – I have gradually seen the light as to the most universal deficiency in our kind of cultivation and education: no one learns, no one strives after, no one teaches – *the endurance of solitude*.

(*D*: section 443)

Talk radio, cable TV, mobile phones, teleshopping, pagers, CNN, Internet chat, MTV – these have been late developments in a century of unprecedented change in communications, a change accelerated also by the dramatic growth in road, rail, sea and air transport. Of the many startling social transformations that occurred in the twentieth century perhaps the most important, the one on which so many others depended, was this development of communications. The diversity of ways in which people interact, the frequency of their contact with others, the spectacular diminution of distance, and the saving of time all altered fundamentally the rhythm of life – for most people in the developed world, at least. The growth of the mass media fundamentally altered modes of entertainment, dissemination of news, and political life. Such changes have not come about without their effects on ways in which individuals come to understand their own speaking and listening, writing and reading. As a new site of our anxieties, the prominence of mass communication has been mimicked on the personal scale: new technology has become a medium of self-conscious communication, just as the 'C' has slipped so stylishly into 'IT'.

The science of communications has grown as an academic discipline, linked variously with media studies and journalism or with more specifically technical fields. The technical slant has been evident where, in schools and colleges, language education has given way on some courses to the development of communication skills. This has been motivated partly by a desire to give credibility to the development of language and partly by a commitment to vocational education – a disillusionment with the value to such learners of liberal studies and a wholesale commitment to the vocational and the functional.

The theorisation of communication in the wake of these changes has been characterised by a presumption in favour of the functional. Thus, in a now familiar and seemingly innocuous formulation, communication is understood schematically as follows: Transmitter > encodes thought in > message > decoded by > Receiver. A further schema, with additional arrows, illustrates the way that feedback functions.

One concept that recurs in such theorisations is that of coding. The role of coding in such different means of communication as, say, morse code and word-processing comes to be seen as an essential of communication, and so to be applied to less technologically mediated types of language use. It is then that we understand not only what we have to say in terms of thoughts that have to be coded into words, but also ourselves as beings who must, paradoxically perhaps through the messages we give out, make ourselves visible or present to others. That this is neither against common sense nor new is seen clearly in Aristotle's famous formulation in *De Interpretatione*: the thoughts I have are converted into words and passed on through speech; speech is converted into writing when those I address are not present to me.

The conception of communication that we have purports to a kind of objective neutrality, a hard factualness. But it is nevertheless rich with ethical implications, and with personal anxieties, in which the metaphor of touch is symptomatic. Am I keeping in touch with my friends, for example? Am I in touch with the news? Do I make myself understood? Are people hearing me? Is my relationship faltering because of a failure to communicate or express myself well? And, commercially and politically: is our message being communicated effectively? It goes without saying that such concerns are to the fore in recent theorisations of teaching too. The metaphor of touch betokens the commitment to presentation, a conception of the real steeped in the metaphysics of presence.

The political dimensions of this have been deepened in recent years with the recognition that information is power: we live in the information society and work in the knowledge economy. Clearly this is not just a matter of crude political fact – that control of the mass media is of critical importance for an oppressive regime. It is also the quasi-commercial fact that access to databanks is a key to the establishment and extension of large markets. Conversely, the skills of information access become regarded as part of the essential grammar of modern life, the lack of which is progressively linked with social exclusion. As the British Minister for Technology and Education, Michael Wills, describes the plight of the excluded:

> There is now a real danger that the information revolution is putting up new walls further barring them from the fruits of progress. If the digital divide is not tackled, it will entrench existing exclusion for generations. Familiarity with information and communication technologies is the indispensable grammar of modern life. Those not empowered by it are disenfranchised: job prospects and security depend on it. Access to these technologies are [sic] a key tool for lifelong learning.
>
> (DfEE Web page)

There is, it should be added in relation to fears about unemployment, an increasing number of jobs where the ability to communicate is of the essence. Call-centres and tele-sales employ people with a good telephone manner in non-stop talk, in the regime of a strategic approach to customer service and employment conditions of some duress.

Of course, there are very visible manifestations of the information overload that is popularly thought to be a feature of the societies we live in. The fact that the mass media broadcast twenty-fours hours a day and on multiple channels, the fact that music can be reproduced cheaply and be made available everywhere, mean that for many people it is normal to exist against a background of noise.

In this media-saturated world people are tuned in to hear the latest thing, talk radio, cable TV chat shows, endless news and comment, radio phone-ins. . . . They must always be watching or listening to what is being said ('Haven't you heard . . .?'); otherwise they are out of touch. ('If you have a touch-tone telephone, press hash now.') And, of course, people must always be available on their mobile phones, or slavishly attentive to incoming e-mail.

It is in this context that a kind of sociability and apparent openness is promoted, and this again is understood in terms of the nomenclature of skills – as interpersonal or social, communication or entrepreneurial. If these are seen as virtuous, the inclinations to isolate oneself or to remain silent are regarded less as vices than as weaknesses, as tendencies to be overcome on the path to confidence and self-awareness. As a popular principle of psychic health, we should be in touch with ourselves, and we should communicate with others.

The emphasis upon communication contrasts with an older notion of literacy, especially in the instrumental way in which reading and writing are regarded. New technology manifestly makes those in the vanguard of this change sanguine about their role, and there is little doubt of the effects of this on education. As a lecturer in multimedia and Internet applications and a designer of learning tools for schools and universities, Iain Arnison, explains: 'My attitude is: why do we need to be taught mental arithmetic when we have calculators? Why do we need to read text when computers can read it for us? Why do we need to write when the latest dictation software can take down our words as we speak?' (*The Guardian*, 29 February 2000). How far – the rhetorical questions labour the point – can that earlier notion of literacy be appropriate at a time when new media in some respects supersede or transmogrify reliance on the written word?

Of course, new communicational media promote their own characteristic kinds of listening, with the sense of a kind of public responsibility. The listening that is common extends to the political and commercial world where customer service and consumer research, now as never before, are critical to success, where a company's production becomes ever more finely tailored to customer desires, albeit desires that are subtly reinforced, if not created, by that research. We have the listening bank and the listening party. We have opinion polls and focus groups, and check-out machines in supermarkets that profile us on the evidence of our purchases and entice us with cut-price coupons for precisely what we most desire. For all this ostensible sensitivity to difference, however, there is a subtle normalisation here, one that promises the solace of inclusion, redemption through belonging. And participation may be more subtly coercive than we can easily admit.[1]

Modern communications mean that wherever you are, you can stay in touch, and, as we have seen, there is an ethical expectation on you to do so. Wherever you are, you can make your purchases, but you should also be expressing yourself, participating and exercising your rights. As the net of globalised communication extends across and around the world, Jean-François Lyotard's vision is of an endless suburbia, a megalopolis, stretching across the earth:

> If the *Urbs* becomes the *Orbs* and if the zone becomes a whole city, then the megalopolis has no outside. And consequently, no inside. Nature is under cosmological, geological, meteorological, touristic and ecological control. Under control or in reserve, reserved . . . You no longer *enter* into the megalopolis. It is no longer a city that needs to be rebegun. The former 'outside' provinces, Africa, Asia, are part of it, mixed in with indigenous Westerners in a variety of ways. Everything is foreign, and nothing is . . .
>
> The last bolt in the wild propagation of the megalopolis will be sprung loose when one's 'real' presence at work becomes superfluous. The body as producer is already an archaism, as are the time clock and the means of transportation. Telecommunication and teleproduction have no need of well-built cities. The megalopolis girds the planet from Singapore to Los Angeles to Milan. Wholly a zone between nothing and nothing, it is separate from lived durations and distances. And every habitat becomes a habitation where life consists in sending and receiving messages.
>
> (Lyotard 1997: 21–2)

The dystopia Lyotard presents here has been reached through the quest for freedom – freedom of a kind. And it is true that this is the realisation of a certain vision of desire satisfaction. This is the freedom to exercise choices, to assert oneself, to exercise one's rights, to communicate. Ironically though this turns out to be less the extension of freedom than its curtailment. Sending and receiving messages one is plugged into the system in such a way as to subdue one's responses, to stifle the silent, secret part of the self. The freedom of the megolopolis, its communication, is a kind of passive nihilism.

Lyotard's account links the preoccupation with presentation with a kind of aestheticisation of all aspects of life, with all the negativity that this ugly suffix suggests – *aesthesis* leading to *anaesthesis*. This is ultimately deadening. In what follows we will consider these benumbing effects more specifically in terms of communication. In Corradi Fiumara's *The Other Side of Language* this is seen as the result of a failure to listen. The emptiness of things keeps itself hidden, especially where attention is commandeered by bombardment with messages.

Benumbment

On the face of it the deluge of information that we now receive demands our attention: if we do not listen we fall out of touch. With every day the creation of new channels of communication more cheaply available, we live, it is said, increasingly in an attention economy. Commercial and political success depends increasingly on gaining and holding people's attention against formidable opposition. How do we listen in these circumstances?

We listen perhaps in order to pick up information. That way we know what is going on. We listen to a point of view and match it with our own. More often perhaps we tune in to the mood of a conversation – the repartee of a television chat show or a casual conversation over coffee with our colleagues. But all of these are forms of debased listening. We are adding information as to a ledger. We align ourselves with or oppose ourselves to a speaker. We share in comfortable phatic communion. Even where we engage in robust debate, we proceed through a dialectics of propositions – identifying a weakness, rebutting an argument – in such a way as either to overcome the other or to shore up our own point of view. Of course, someone will be quick to point out, this is not done in the name of winning the argument but in pursuit of the truth. But the fact that truth is conceived in terms of an argument that might be won limits the scope of what might come into view. All this then belongs to a debased form of listening in which we are linguistically overwhelmed even where, through our rational articulations (our cogent formal arguments, say), we seem most to be in control. As Corradi Fiumara puts this:

> The interactive modes that are commonly envisaged, in fact, are either that of 'listening' and falling victim to a possessive and exclusivist discourse that binds the 'hearer', or alternatively, 'listening' in order to be able to rebut by a more powerful offensive logic that fragments the expression of the 'speaker' and thus produces assent to one's theoretical system; an ongoing search for 'rational' agreement, for 'producing' consensus.
>
> (Corradi Fiumara 1990: 83–4)

Much of Corradi Fiumara's account of benumbment is concerned with specifically the kind of paralysis that has concerned philosophers such as Wittgenstein. But it is clear that this is also symptomatic of the contemporary world more generally. The saturation of our world with messages is something we cannot simply avoid; too quick a philosophical response becomes party to this more general benumbment. As we have seen, this noise-saturated environment is not without its ethical claims on us, demanding attention to the latest, whether this is a matter of new entertainment or the responsible call to greater awareness of current affairs. It imposes metaphysical presuppositions also: what is real is what can be presented in this way; what cannot be presented must fade from view.

This general benumbment is such as cannot tolerate silence; it needs the reassuring pulse of music or background chatter. It is evident in more or less automatic verbal sequences, in the engagement of others in 'friendly' conversation (and thus, wittingly or unwittingly, escapes or neutralises difficult or dynamic dialogical situations). It saturates discursive space only to annul it (ibid.: 103). It is evident in the therapeutic inclination to annul the space between people in a kind of communicative sociability, to chat and make people feel at home. The orientation towards communication, rather than towards listening, tends to frame language in terms that favour '"simple" mechanisms that divide and extinguish, whereas listening requires a laborious attitude more consistent with problems of integration and living' (ibid.: 93) The orientation towards discourse offers a greater sense of cognitive security and far fewer demands.

The possibilities of listening here depend in some degree on the recovery of that richer sense of *logos* that has been obscured in the Western philosophical tradition and in our daily lives:

> The whole question hinges on the capacity of 'letting-lie-together-before' and of freeing our thinking from its 'constitutive' compulsion to submit to a *lysis* – analyse – scrutinise, delve into, explore, exhaust, probe the famous 'object of knowledge' of our research tradition. The notion of integration thus becomes linked to a general idea of coexistence which is more ecological than logical in that it requires 'belonging' to our *logos*; it is concerned with domestic issues because there are no more foreign affairs.
>
> (Ibid.: 16)

It is Heidegger's thought that Corradi Fiumara plainly echoes here and which she blends with that of Wittgenstein throughout the book. 'Letting-lie-together-before' as an aspect of *logos* needs to be understood in terms of hearing as much as saying, though it is hearing that our philosophical tradition continually occludes; and it is to be understood in terms of a preserving and gathering rather than as a simple sign system devoid of reality but functionally matchable against it. If not, our thinking is set on a path of ordering and explaining, detached from any propensity to receive and listen.

In this context, silence is seen never to be a mere absence but as serving a number of purposes. It can have a creative function providing the listening space where the other can speak, a waiting (way of being) in which conversation can take place; it can be a non-verbal sign indicating a variety of things according to context, from assent to total refusal. Indicative of a depth of thought, it points towards the possibility of a 'non-polemical cultural style' (ibid.: 111). The mechanisms of a conventional noisy language constantly threaten the possibility of communicating well. Corradi Fiumara quotes the words of M.F. Sciacca:

> To communicate is to enter the other, while watching ourselves carefully, to enter without usurping . . . To usurp the other is to annul him, to prevent him from returning the gift; it is the refusal to accept his discrete word; it is to violate his inner home without allowing him to enter ours, it is the arrogance of someone who believes himself to be an entirely fecundating force and refuses to receive. The univocal gift, without reciprocity . . . is not communication, but violation.
>
> (Ibid.: 112)

The authentic attitude of thinking is not merely a putting of questions; rather it is a listening to the promise of what is put in question. It is not an acquisition of data but an openness to questions that may arise in ways that we cannot foresee, an openness that should bring with it a kind of reverence for the granting of such questions in this way.

Socrates is perhaps too much associated – because this is how he has been used by some later philosophers – with those assiduous processes of reasoning that work through an argument to its logical conclusion. Certainly such a figure is identifiable in the dialogues, but in some respects the familiarity of this figure is a product of too easy a reading, one that passes over the more puzzling aspects of the dialogues and the unresolved nature of some of the discussions, one moreover, that tends to ignore the dramatic staging of the various encounters (where they have just come from, the physical surroundings, the mood and humour). It is as one of these less easy aspects that Socrates' *daemon* appears. The *daemon* is a kind of inner voice, a voice, it is clear, to which Socrates feels a duty to attend. Like the voice of conscience, it calls to him when he is likely to go astray, and calls not with the heteronomy of an alien voice but in such a way that this silent listening makes what he does all the more his own. For such a voice to be heard there must be a suspension of attention to those more clamorous voices, to that noise, that typify our more habitual being with others, especially where this has the character of conformism. In Heidegger's terms, this suggests the possibility of an authenticity in which we free ourselves from our subjugation to the They-self (*Das Man*). We cannot do this without the kind of relation to *logos* that is indicated here, where waiting and silence are more characteristic of the patient attention that is required than that more frenetic attention that is courted by daily noise.

The perfect circle

> I have my own stern claims and perfect circle. It denies the name of duty to many offices that are called duties. But if I can discharge its debts it enables me to dispense with the popular code. If anyone imagines that this law is lax, let him keep its commandment one day.
>
> (Emerson 1982: 193)

We have seen how the picture of communication with which this chapter started is incompatible with the orientation elaborated above in terms of listening, how silence and stillness may be the antithesis of tranquillised passivity. In *The Birth of Tragedy* Nietzsche speaks of 'the Dionysiac receptivity of the listener' (p. 100). Given the upsurge of energy that the Dionysiac represents, it is clear that this listening cannot be thought of as 'merely' passive and therefore sterile. It is a mistaken conception of communication where speech is seen as an active pole with listening as its passive counterpart. Similarly, the tranquillising sociability that is commonly promoted through schooling and more broadly through the mass media is to be viewed with suspicion. Authenticity requires an ability to stand alone in order to resist the normalising influences of the crowd – and the better to attune oneself to the Dionysiac flux of creation and destruction. How far education develops the disposition to listen will depend on the kind of cultural life that we have, on the conditions that we fashion for ourselves to live in.

Corradi Fiumara sees a confluence of thought in Heidegger and Wittgenstein especially in respect of the orientation towards listening that is required. In *Conditions Handsome and Unhandsome: the Constitution of Emersonian Perfectionism*, Stanley Cavell argues that such ideas are anticipated in the writings of Emerson, in a line of thought that can be seen as passing through Nietzsche. Nietzsche was influenced, in his early and late writings especially, by his reading of Emerson, for whom the relationship between solitude and education is always critical. It is without doubt a kind of life-affirmation that we identify in what follows, one whose style suggests sometimes the combativeness that is commonly associated with Nietzsche, but sometimes a more cheerful leisureliness and attunement to things, a readiness to converse, that is, in something like the non-polemical style adumbrated above. How far can the receptivity that Nietzsche advocates be reconciled with a style in which the ability to listen and to pay proper attention, to behave in ways that are apparently passive, is of the essence? How far does Emerson provide a bridge between what might be thought to be divergent orientations?

Cavell understands Emersonian Perfectionism in terms of a loose set of features, all related to an outlook or dimension of thought preoccupied with a kind of cultural conversion. Its most salient features are seen in a pattern whereby, through friendship and education,

> each self is drawn on a journey of ascent . . . to a further state of that self, where . . . the higher is determined not by natural talent but by seeking to know what you are made of and cultivating the thing you are meant to do; it is a transformation of the self which finds expression in . . . the imagination of a transformation of society into . . . something like an aristocracy where . . . what is best for society is a model for and is modelled on what is best for the individual soul. . .
>
> (Cavell 1990: 7)

What is aspired to is typically understood in terms of a new reality – the good society, the good city. It involves thinking how our world should be constituted, what words we can find for it, what practices should give it substance, what standards sustain it.[2] Perfectionism, Cavell suggests, is not a competing moral theory but rather a dimension of any moral thinking; where, as is not uncommon, the moral life is assumed to be primarily a matter of moral reasoning and perhaps amenable to compartmentalisation, there is an imperviousness to its insights. The tone of moral urgency, elevated by the self-consciously religious timbre of the prose, expresses the fact that morality is not a (limited) part of ourselves but more like something that runs through all that we do.

There is an understandable resistance to such ideas because of the false or debased perfectionisms that confront us in the shape of new-age therapies, marketing ploys, staff development for aspiring managers – love yourself, be what you can be. In contrast:

> Emersonian Perfectionism requires that we become ashamed in a particular way of ourselves, of our present stance, and . . . the Emersonian Nietzsche requires, as a sign of consecration to the next self, that we hate ourselves, as it were impersonally (bored with ourselves might be enough to say); and that in the television promise to be all you can be, the offer is to *tell* you what all you can be, most importantly, a mercenary.
>
> (Cavell 1990: 16)

A further reason for doubt about perfectionism comes in the shape of a suspicion of perfectionism's proximity to utopian delusion and grotesque totalitarianism. Yet, in spite of appearances, Emerson offers, Cavell argues, the only means for democracy to sustain its truth to itself, its necessary voice within. The aversion from conformism is at the same time a response that values, that seeks to uncover a possibility, against conformism, of what that society might be. It provides the possibility of movement towards a democracy that, as Derrida might put this, is always still to come.[3] Emerson is the friend to democracy precisely in his willingness to take issue with it. Democracy survives best where it keeps alive the question of what democracy is:

> in a democracy embodying good enough justice, the conversation over how good its justice is must take place and must also not have a victor, that this is not because agreement can or should always be reached, but because disagreement, and separateness of position, is to be allowed its satisfactions, reached and expressed in particular ways . . . Responsibility remains a task of responsiveness.
>
> (Cavell 1990: 24–5)

And the microcosm of this is being prepared to be challenged by the other, by the friend or the challenging text.

A crucial point here is that perfectionism, unlike ideas of the realisable perfectability of human kind such as Leninism or National Socialism or Skinnerian behaviourism,[4] or for that matter the vapid satisfactions of the megalopolis, is motivated by a vision of wholeness that, it knows, can never be actualised. Hence it involves the recognition of our partial nature, of our essential incompleteness, and this engenders at once a poignant sense of our lack and an elevation by something that is ahead of us, beyond our grasp, and, if not ineffable, at least defiant of any tidy literal formulation. Emerson writes: 'We live in succession, in division, in parts, in particles. Meantime within man is the soul of the whole; the wise silence; the universal beauty, to which every part and particle is equally related; the eternal ONE' (Emerson 1982: 207). Utopian vision here functions as something non-real but visionary, and having such leverage on our real world as to enable the raising of standards in its pursuit. Such standards enable us to live a life that is more fully realised.

Emerson anticipates the complaints he provokes, how his concern with what constitutes real standards will not be appreciated: 'The populace think that your rejection of popular standards is a rejection of all standard, and mere antinomialism; and the bold sensualist will use the name of philosophy to gild his crimes' (ibid.:193). Cavell tracks Emerson's play in 'Self-Reliance' on inflections of standing and understanding in relation to standing for and in relation to standards:

> 'Standing for humanity', radiating in various directions as *representing* humanity and as *bearing* it (as bearing the pain of it) links across the essay with its recurrent notation of postures and of gaits (leaning and skulking among them – postures of shame) of which *standing* or uprightness, is the correction or conversion that Emerson seeks, his representative prose. This opens into Emerson's description of our being drawn by the true man, as being 'constrained to his standard'.
>
> (Cavell 1990: 58)

The moral law within us is the mark of the human. As man does not merely obey instinct but can judge himself, he lives in two worlds, and hence must adopt two *standpoints*. Standards are raised under which we should live, as giving form to the economy of our home, our world. Of great literature Emerson says: 'In every work of genius we recognise our own rejected thoughts; they come back to us with a certain alienated majesty' (Emerson 1982: 176).

It is important to realise that for Emerson the pursuit of this vision is not to be understood programmatically in terms of a foreseeable linear continuum towards the good. On the contrary our relation to this vision, indeed our upholding of standards, is jeopardised where the delusion that it is so, causes us to subside into a dull or complacent conformity. The stroke, Emerson says, is followed by the recoil. Our best efforts must take the form of this contrariness. Emerson's prose is sprung with a movement between earnest assertiveness and seemingly casual lightness of tone that constantly wrong-foots the reader.

The journey that the self makes towards a next state of the self is made possible by the provision of exemplary next selves, of lives that represent other and enhanced possibilities for ourselves. There is here the sense of the self as both attained and unattained, as in partial compliance with its idea of itself, and hence a sense of its distance from itself – the space for self-consciousness and for the call of duty. The friend does service by presenting back to me another possibility of myself, a more exacting one, that otherwise flickers in my vision and may escape me entirely. The pages of Emerson's text, he suggests, can function as a friend does in setting up before us for our silent contemplation and response an *other* – a way of thinking in which we find some of our own thoughts but in such a way that they are challenged. Any idea I have of myself as a whole is essentially only provisional: the soul is 'an immensity not possessed and that cannot be possessed' (ibid.: 208). Imagining that I can construct myself incrementally, in a progressive acquisition of experience and skills, blinds me to this reality. 'Our life is an apprenticeship to the truth that around every circle another can be drawn; that there is no end in nature, but every end is a beginning; that there is always another dawn risen on midnoon, and under every deep a lower deep opens' (ibid.: 225).

Indeed, there is a kind of blasphemy in any attempt to approach such deeps directly, and idolatry in the unswerving pursuit of fixed ends. The quality of our lives will not depend on any search for final answers in terms either of the identification of secure foundations or of the delineation of any realisable *telos*. Rather it will depend on the kinds of words we find to describe our situation and to construct the institutions of our society. Cavell's titles gesture clearly to what is at stake here. 'Emerson's Constitutional Amending' alludes to the ways in which the words we find become foundations for the social structures (the constitution and institutions, the set-ups) we have, how I find myself, how I am founded, in the words I have: finding as founding. *Conditions Handsome and Unhandsome* points to the seamlessness of the relation between our everyday practices of working and making and both the problematic construction of our higher institutions and our quasi-religious self-examination. Self-understanding is not to be achieved by narcissistic introspection any more than is religious enlightenment by the authoritative pronouncements of religious leaders. It is not in a debased search for ultimate answers or for assurances of salvation that revelation is to be found but rather in a turning back to our ordinary practices:

The only mode of obtaining an answer to these questions of the
senses is to forego all low curiosity, and accepting the tide of
being which floats us into the secret of nature, work and live,
work and live, and all unawares the advancing soul has built
and forged for itself a new condition, and the question and the
answer are one.

(Ibid.: 216)

Work and live, work and live – the degree to which our condition is
handsome depends on the quality of our handiwork. Heidegger, of
course, tells us that thinking is a handicraft; Emerson that 'The
secret of fortune is joy in our hands' (ibid.: 196). And both
emphasise the way that a thinking that is too quick to grab and
grasp stands in the way of our living better. Emerson takes – this is
the epigraph to Cavell's text – the 'evanescence and lubricity of all
objects, which lets them slip through our fingers then when we
clutch hardest, to be the most unhandsome part of our condition'
(Cavell 1990: 38). Emerson's own handiwork, his writing, is in the
hands of the reader.

The process and practice of reading has a special importance in
Emerson's thinking and in the conception of culture and education
that he promotes. Our habitual reading, he complains, is 'mendicant and sycophantic' (Emerson 1982: 186). In contrast: 'One must
be an inventor to read well . . . There is then creative reading as
well as creative writing. When the mind is braced by labour and
invention, the page of whatever book we read becomes luminous
with manifold allusion' (ibid.: 90). Not that we are to look in his text
for any final resolution of matters: 'I unsettle all things. No facts are
to me sacred: none are profane; I simply experiment, an endless
seeker with no Past at my back' (ibid.: 236). This is an openness and
responsibility that refuses to be deadened by the burden of memory
(by, say, the accumulation of data or dead texts). But the lists of
names that Emerson frequently cites, his predecessors and
intellectual benefactors, indicate that this is no denial of history but
rather a proper way of honouring his influences (see Cavell 1995:
23).

Emerson satirises the popular notion of a revelation as a telling
of fortunes, its religious questioning a picking at locks. Revelation,
in contrast, must be seen as 'the disclosure of the soul' (Emerson
1982: 215). The inward turn here, the modern sense of ourselves as
beings with inner depths, as Charles Taylor has put it, leads not
quite to the Kantian moral law within but rather to the sentiment of
duty, there in one's mind. When Emerson requires us to 'dispense
with the popular code' with its false sense of duty, this is replaced by

the exacting demands of something within me, something that the idea of conscience is too loose adequately to convey. It needs to be understood rather in terms of another possibility of myself that stands next to me as something that I might aspire to and attain, a wider circle around me, a representation such as a friend might make to me. Although in some sense this suggests an internal dialogue, its tentativeness and resistance to articulation mean that it is something other than dialectical. Solitude and silence are its favourable conditions: 'The action of the soul is oftener in that which is felt and left unsaid than in that which is said in any conversation' (ibid.: 212). One must insist on oneself and not imitate. As Emerson puts it: 'He must greatly listen to himself, withdrawing himself from all the accents of other men's devotion' (ibid.: 222).

It might be thought that Emerson speaks here along lines similar to those who advocate rational autonomy when he affirms that something like sovereignty must rest within the individual, but his suggestion that there must be something godlike (rather than regal) in the person who has cast off the common motives of humanity (ibid.: 194) suggests rather the presence of a kind of light that illumines that person's character. The religious tone is not incidental. In contrast to the deadening other-worldly concerns of conventional religion (the withdrawal of the soul), it is the jubilant soul that is capable of prayer in the contemplation of ordinary things. And although such prayer seems to require a kind of solitude, it betokens an energising and pantheistic force:

> More and more the surges of everlasting nature enter into me, and I become public and human in my regards and actions. So I come to live in thoughts and act with energies which are immortal. Thus revering the soul, and learning, as the ancient said, that 'its beauty is immense', man will come to see that the world is the perennial miracle which the soul worketh, and be less astonished at particular wonders . . .
>
> (Ibid.: 223)

It is not primarily tuition that we require to acknowledge this but the wisdom of intuition, in the 'calm hours' of which there is a sense of 'that deep force, the last fact behind which analysis cannot go, all things find their common origin' (ibid.: 187). The soul is not separated from things.

We have seen the way in which the friend is important in spurring the self on to something beyond itself. The constant danger of a cultural decline, with its reciprocal relationship with the con-

formity into which we are inclined to subside, means that education
has a similarly critical role. Emerson connects intuition with instinct
and spontaneity and it might be thought that this underwrites the
child-centred conception of education as growth that has been
opposed to an initiation into traditions of enquiry and understanding. One does not have to look far in Emerson's writings,
however, to see that the picture he presents is more qualified and
more complex, and that the inner voice is enabled through a
reading of the texts of the past.

The objects of Emerson's attack on conformism are found variously
in blind adherence to doctrine, in acquiescence to received opinion,
in deference to rank and title, in sycophancy in the face of power and
authority, and in the bigotry of do-gooders; such of course are the
ways of the herd. But these are not discrete vices: overcoming
conformism requires a deep reorientation of the self, perhaps a kind
of rebirth. For our nonconformism we may be 'whipped with the
world's displeasure', but it is the condition of our being fully human
('Whoso would be a man, must be a nonconformist' (ibid.: 178)). It
imposes on each of us a singular duty:

> What I must do is all that concerns me, not what the people
> think. This rule, equally arduous in actual and in intellectual
> life, may serve for the whole distinction between greatness and
> meanness. It is the harder because you will always find those
> who think they know what is your duty better than you know it.
> It is easy in the world to live after the world's opinion; it is easy
> in solitude to live after our own; but the great man is he who
> in the midst of the crowd keeps with perfect sweetness the
> independence of solitude.
>
> (Ibid.: 180–1)

Here then, beyond the escape from society that solitude affords,
there is a conjunction of 'perfect sweetness' with an inner solitude,
and this is what characterises a greatness of spirit. Greatness, it is
important to emphasise, is not to be achieved through isolation,
through physical solitude; it is characterised by the 'perfect
sweetness' that comes with an inner solitude.

Just as we should not seek an easy consistency with the opinion of
the crowd, so also we should not feel overly constrained by this
quality in our own opinions. This also can rob us of our self-trust on
the strength of 'reverence for our past act or word because the eyes
of others have no other data for computing our orbit than our past
acts, and we are loth to disappoint them' (ibid.: 182). What is
commonly taken as a virtue quickly becomes a dull compliance with
a formal principle that deadens the responsiveness on which insight

depends, and that panders to the ways in which others evaluate us. 'A foolish consistency is the hobgoblin of little minds' (ibid.: 183). Cultural degeneration is identified in education where there is a subjection to received wisdom and hallowed traditions and where dusty books are received uncritically. Scholars and authors often lack hallowing presence; they have knack and skill instead of inspiration, and their talent is an exaggerated faculty (ibid.: 218–19). With the spectatorial stance that is typically adopted, we subjugate nature to deadening systems of classification and so come to think of it only in those terms. We fail to see our own relation to nature, our self-constitution through our perceptions: 'One is seal and one is print' (ibid.: 87). The precept Know Thyself should be seen as the requirement to Study Nature. Books should inspire but they too can become dead in the hands of the bookworm. And the scholar who is shut away from the world pursuing a narrow specialism loses the broader engagement that education should bring. In the degenerate state the student is a victim of society. In the right state he is *Man Thinking*:

> Him Nature solicits with all her placid, all her monitory pictures; him the past instructs; him the future invites. Is not indeed every man a student, and do not all things exist for the student's behoof? And, finally, is not the scholar the only true master? But the oracle said, 'All things have two handles: beware of the wrong one.' In life, too often, the scholar errs with mankind and forfeits his privilege.
>
> (Ibid.: 85)

Thinking is not so much something the scholar does as something he is drawn by. (Heidegger speaks of us getting in the draught of thinking.)

If one form of erring from this has to do with conformism, another is seen in a restless flitting about from topic to topic. This is familiar enough where the attention of children, overwhelmed by distractions today, cannot rest quietly with any one object, but is also perhaps evident in advanced scholarship where, even – perhaps especially – in a narrow field of specialisation, the study reduces to the accumulation of a wealth of detail but without any more disturbing and more wide-reaching engagement. As emblem of this and of a range of cultural problems, Emerson elaborates on an idea that is symptomatic of pervasive cultural problems, and this he refers to as the 'superstition' of travelling, the fascination with superficial and constantly changing experience: 'The intellect is vagabond, and our system of education fosters restlessness' (ibid.: 198). Travel does not broaden the mind but titillates. In travel, the metaphysical pretensions of the spectatorial stance are mimicked in common experience. In contrast wisdom is more likely to be found through a kind of solitude and stillness: it is the scholar's explorations of the private and personal that reveal the universal.

It is a tenet of Emerson's account of education that genius is universally distributed. This is to be understood in terms of the possibility, indeed the necessity, of our finding within ourselves the sentiment of duty, and hence the possibility of an authentic life. We can, all of us, be touched by the pathos of our inadequacy to ourselves. If this were not the case, the interrelationship between goods for the individual and for society could not be sustained. Again in contrast to child-centred theory, this genius is not something that naturally evolves but rather a potential that remains dormant until it is given the chance of rebirth through education. At this point a clear connection with the account of listening provided by Corradi Fiumara can be seen. We have been metamorphosed into a thing and hence need rebirth and this, says Cavell, needs brooding over (see Cavell 1990: 45). Such brooding suggests a different, perhaps feminine style of thought and patient labour.

In the metaphor of midwifery in the Socratic dialogues, as Corradi Fiumara shows, there is reference to two functions: to the process of delivery and to the earlier and easily overlooked process of appropriate match-making. Without good match-making, where appropriate connections are made, there can be no good issue. In Plato's philosophical maieutics both are essential:

> In the absence of a real maieutics of listening and thought, the very amalgamations of thoughts among themselves become the work of mere panders. If the weddings of thoughts are considered to be more important than the actual birth of thinking, it is a fact that Plato insists on the *indivisibility* of the two philosophical attitudes, and stresses this conviction with a very precise double articulation.
>
> (Corradi Fiumara 1990: 147)

Perfection's obsession with education, Cavell says, expresses its focus on finding one's way rather than on getting oneself or another to take the way (Cavell 1990: xxxii). A manner of reading that failed to make appropriate connections, we might say, would be able to accumulate and replicate information, but it would remain educationally sterile. The thinking it issued would be sickly at best. When Emerson says that in reading we can either recognise something of ourselves in the text or fail to and so gain nothing new, there is the sense that the text must set up something next to me, adjacent to me, that I can move towards. This would be a maieutics of good connections.

There is a further depth to this maieutics also. 'For Dewey', Cavell suggests, 'the philosophical interpretation of experience was cause for taking up scientific measures against old dualisms, refusing separation. For Emerson the philosophical interpretation of experience makes it a cause for mourning, assigning to philosophy the work of accepting the separation of the world, as of a child' (ibid.: 40). With that rending separation of birth there is then an enduring sense of loss, and this perhaps is a condition of the authenticity of that difference to myself that I realise within the perfect circle. This would be a condition of my responsibility.

Culture cannot be something extra that I merely take up or acquire: '[T]he address to culture that Emerson and Nietzsche call for is not one of consuming it but of discovering it, its reality. To assert the good of consuming culture, in general, as it stands, would be for them as philistine as to question, in general, the good of producing it' (ibid.: 18). Instead my education requires a kind of rebirth. Discovering culture cannot be a matter of coming across something wholly new. I need to find or confront a response in me to the cultural objects and the language that have come down to me, the ways that I have been educated. It is only through such a process that a culture can live. I need to read. The encounter of reading is then akin to an encounter with a further self. It is a kind of edification. Heidegger connects building with dwelling and thinking. And are not Wittgenstein or his builders engaged in a kind of edification, as Thoreau surely is? Why is it that Wittgenstein makes his strange tribe *build*, near the beginning of that extraordinary book (*Philosophical Investigations*) that shows us the conditions of our living? In 'Fate' Emerson writes: 'Every spirit makes its house; but afterwards the house confines the spirit' (Emerson 1982: 365). Hence the profound importance of the language we use in the standards we create.

'My thought,' writes Cavell,

> is that a certain relation to words (as an allegory of my rela-
> tion to life) is inseparable from a certain moral-like relation to
> thinking, and that the morality and the thinking that are
> inseparable are of specific strains – the morality is neither
> teleological (basing itself on a conception of the good to be
> maximised in society) nor deontological (basing itself on
> an independent conception of the right), and the thinking
> is some as yet unknown distance from what we think of as
> reasoning.
>
> (Cavell 1990: 46)

It is not only our reading that is mendicant: our housekeeping, our arts, our occupations, our marriages, our religion which we have not chosen . . . With this we shun, Emerson claims, 'the rugged battle of fate, where strength is born' (Emerson 1982: 194). Our relation to the ordinary needs to be understood and appreciated in terms of the finitude of the human condition, a mode of 'inhabiting our investment in words, in the world' (Cavell 1990: 61).

The problem, the nihilistic problem that lurks at the edge of Emerson's text, is that nothing really matters to us. This is the nihilism that arises from reading a text that is not well connected, from an initiation into a culture, an education, where we do not recognise something of ourselves, where there is no friend-like relation that reflects back to ourselves a possible, well connected next self. It arises with our failure to take responsibility for the standards that we set up and live by, for the words that we use and the institutions that we build. It is not instruction but provocation that I must seek from another soul. Reading, reading Emerson, is an indication of how this might be found.

In Emerson's conception of genius as universal there is a connection with an idea of aristocracy that can be found in Nietzsche, along the lines that we have indicated in Chapter 4 (see especially p. 65) and at various points in this book. But, if there is this connection, it is clear that there are tensions also with other aspects of Nietzsche's thought. In what ways can the Dionysiac receptivity of the listener be reconciled with what is said here? The surges of everlasting nature and immortal energies of which Emerson speaks suggest a pantheistic flow of force that avoids the melancholy of lack that otherwise follows from the birth pangs of the personal (and therefore cultural) regeneration he seeks. It suggests the kind of libidinal energy that is so strongly present in the Nietzsche that Deleuze at least presents to us. Yet the dominant impression is of a maieutics of thought. The perfectionism of Emerson's thought is logically tied to a sense of lack, and the possibility of genius is tied to an education that only makes sense in the light of that lack.

Notes

1 'Perhaps "participation" in the dominant culture is more subtly coercive that we are prepared to admit . . .' (Corardi Fiumara 1990: 70).
2 'Perhaps [Socrates said] it is laid up as a pattern in heaven, where those who wish can see it and found it in their own hearts' (Plato 1955: 369).
3 See especially *The Other Heading* (Derrida 1992).
4 Contrast B.F. Skinner's *Walden Two* with Thoreau's *Walden*.

Chapter 10

The courage for immorality

> Whoever lacks the courage for immorality is suitable for anything, but not to be a moralist.
>
> Nietzsche, *The Will to Power*, 397

We report the following snatch of dialogue, overheard in a secondary school, between a girl of about fifteen years and a teacher.

'You know perfectly well that there are regulations about which shoes you may and may not wear, and those shoes are against the regulations!'

'I don't see why we have to have regulations about what shoes we can wear . . .'

'Then let me ask you a question: *what would happen if everyone wore shoes like that?*'

There was a pause, as if to signify that the pupil had been suitably stunned by this devastating question. Then, in a voice of icy politeness, a question in response that suggests this girl will go far: 'I don't know, Miss. What *would* happen if everyone wore shoes like mine?'

A further pause, suggesting a different order of stunnedness, ensued. Taking advantage of this, the girl left the classroom, where the conversation had taken place, in triumph. But she was pursued by the trump line, delivered in similar clipped tones of icy superiority, the voice rising towards the end in the certainty that the speaker had clinched the argument: 'Well if you don't know, I can't tell you!'

What are we to make of this? Perhaps the first thing to note is that this incident displays several of the characteristic features of morality at work in education. First, and most obviously, there is the *universality* of the prescription against which the pupil is held to have offended, a universality which can supposedly be perceived by reflecting on what the consequences would be if 'we all did that'. We return to this below. Second, there is the mismatch between the solemnity of the moral apparatus thus conjured up and the context – trivial if not bizarre – in which it is invoked. To put the point differently, it is not clear that these shoes are a *moral* issue at all; or if they are, presumably that can only be because the breach of dress regulations is held to be the first step down a slippery slope at whose foot lies general anarchy. Expressing it thus highlights the surreal air surrounding the incident. (Is it not surreal, does it not make us laugh? Nietzsche writes of 'the stupidity of moral indignation, which is in the philosopher an unfailing sign that he has lost his philosophical sense of humour': *BGE*, section 25.) Third, there is the smugness of the morally superior party in contrast with the guilt implicitly enjoined upon the offender. The moral superiority is occasioned by her guilt and increases it in turn, a vertiginous spiral of cause and effect that elevates the morally saved in proportion as it crushes the unredeemable sinner. In our example not only does the girl contravene the dress code: she is not privy to the mysterious web of moral meanings that holds such verities in place. She is an ethical outcast, a moral imbecile, who can only crawl away and puzzle over her fallen state until enlightenment, awareness of the true nature and extent of her culpability, dawns on her.

Now none of this is intended as a criticism of the particular teacher: which of us, in dealing with our own children or those of others, has not sometimes found ourselves uttering such absurdities? Furthermore, as heirs to the Kantian moral tradition that insists there are no moral *facts* we may feel that moral education has to proceed much of the time on the basis of waiting for the moral penny to drop: that if the child does not know then it is indeed true that we cannot *tell* her. *Instruction* is as inappropriate here as when someone trying to teach us mathematics begins by assuring us that $a+b=b+a$ (cf. Wittgenstein, *On Certainty*: section 113). As instinctive Kantians too we tend to hold that universalisability is the most significant feature of moral judgements: that the judgement that one should not lie, steal or wear non-regulation shoes applies to all relevant persons. You cannot claim exemption because you are *you*, contingently located in this unique bundle of DNA, carbon and water. And of course the Kantian will complain that the example chosen is trivial and unfair. No evidently *moral* issue arises here as it would if the teacher asked: 'what would happen if we *all* took money from our class-mates' purses?'

Having made all due acknowledgements and concession here, we nevertheless believe that some reflections on the Incident of the Shoes have power to disturb what may be called the received version of moral education, as well as elements of the moral philosophy that underpins it. These reflections, in the spirit of this book, are broadly Nietzschean, and argue that the commonly accepted picture of moral education is about as nihilistic – as empty of genuine value – as the most nihilistic, anarchic subverter of our educational institutions could wish it to be.

Nietzsche's radical challenge to us is to consider 'the value of our values'. What does it do for us, and for whom amongst us in particular, to have the 'peculiar institution' of morality, as it has been called, with the universalisability of judgements as its most characteristic and distinguishing feature?

> Under what conditions did man invent the value-judgements good and evil? *And what value do they themselves possess?* Are they a sign of indigence, of impoverishment, of the degeneration of life? Or do they rather reveal the plenitude, the strength, the will of life, its courage, confidence and future?
>
> (*GM*, 'Preface': section 3)

Nietzsche asks us to consider what kind of people would choose to live in this way; and his own famous answer is that it is people in the grasp of a slave morality. The Judaeo-Christian ethical tradition derives from those oppressed groups who made virtues of the harsh necessities they endured. Their humiliation became the virtue of humility; their suffering became patience. Unable to secure the riches that any sensible individual desires, they named distributive justice as among the chief moral goods; unable to become the equals of those who held power over them, they sought to bring the powerful down to their own level, and invented egalitarianism. At the heart of what we now think of as the moral dimension of life, therefore, lies *resentment*, the envious urge to ensure that no-one is putting one over on us, that our neighbour is not avoiding the taxes we have to pay or finding a way round the building regulations that obstruct our own favourite project; that the child at the next desk is not finishing her work by an easy route we have not discovered or, naturally, sporting the kind of footwear we have all been forbidden.

This kind of argument can easily be made to appear trite and naïve. Certainly we do not reveal the falsity of a thesis by demonstrating its origins. Newton's laws do not cease to hold if we discover Newton's research was motivated significantly by professional rivalry (which it appears to have been) or fuelled by opium (which it was not). And yet, for all that, the Nietzschean critique has the power to unsettle. It does this perhaps most successfully when it reveals the difference between what we have called the 'received version' of morality or moral education and other pictures of the moral life: the Aristotelian one, for instance, which foregrounds human excellences such as generosity and the capacity for friendship rather than the importance of not doing what is forbidden. At the very least Nietzsche's observations prompt us to consider whether what we have been told are the features of *any* moral system worthy of the name may not rather be those of the latest (several centuries) local (predominantly northern and western European) one. And from here it is no great step to wondering about the allegedly distinctive and supreme nature of morality. What is it, among all the qualities and perspectives that make human life more endurable – for example aversion to cruelty, concern for welfare, an instinct to care for others, compassion, love for humankind or for particular persons – that, supposedly, makes the Kantian moral perspective and the criterion of universalisability unique? 'How presumptuous it is', Solomon (1996: 203) writes, 'for morality to give itself "trump" status at the expense of any other "nonmoral" virtues such as heroism, wit, charm and devotion'.

Now let us consider the obvious (obvious, but still worth examining) point, that this perspective on morality has peculiar force in the context of formal education. We can begin at the end of the nineteenth century, with the opening paragraph of the first of the stories that make up Rudyard Kipling's *Stalky & Co.*:

> In summer all right-minded boys built huts in the furze-hill behind the College – little lairs whittled out of the heart of the prickly bushes, full of stumps, odd root-ends and spikes, but, since they were strictly forbidden, palaces of delight. And for the fifth summer in succession, Stalky, M'Turk and Beetle (this was before they reached the dignity of a study) had built like beavers a place of retreat and meditation, where they smoked.

In these stories boys do what is forbidden. They cheerfully break rules, steal and trespass. They are left to themselves a great deal, as Stalky observes (p. 134), and their 'bounds are pretty big'. The better kind of schoolmaster – notably the school's Head – treats this all as entirely natural, as an extended game in which punishments are inflicted where appropriate and the slate then wiped clean. Lesser masters pontificate:

Boys who crept – who sneaked – who lurked – out of bounds, even the generous bounds of the Natural History Society, which they had falsely joined as a cloak for their misdeeds – their vices – their villainies – their immoralities . . . such boys, scabrous boys, moral lepers . . .

(p. 27)

The story 'The Moral Reformers' makes particularly interesting reading. The school's Chaplain makes a social visit to Number Five study, the home of the book's young heroes. There is some talk about what a good thing it is that the school does not have married house-masters ('they have babies and teething and measles and all that sort of thing right bung *in* the school; and the masters' wives give tea-parties – tea-parties, Padre!', p. 132) or a clerical head-master. It is agreed that if the Head went off and got ordained 'the Coll. 'ud go to pieces in a year'. The purpose of the genial, pipe-smoking Chaplain's visit gradually emerges. There is a serious case of bullying in the school, and Stalky and his friends are to be the Padre's Tenth Legion and sort it out. Accordingly they trick the bullies into allowing themselves to be tied up, and then inflict on them a series of tortures which would do no discredit to Special Forces in any part of the modern world. As the Padre remarks, once all has come to its satisfactory conclusion and the bullies are traumatised and reformed, if he had used 'one half of the moral suasion' Stalky and his friends employed, he would now be 'languishing in Bideford jail'.

There is a good deal here to discomfort the modern liberal sensibility. Kipling depicts a world held in place by forces significantly different from those which contain the late twentieth-century pupil in what we think of as the civilised world. For Kipling's boys there is a code of honour, the ties of comradeship and clearly marked boundaries whose transgression invites barbarous sanctions. Within those boundaries there is a degree of freedom (and of freedom from surveillance: hence freedom of the imagination) hardly conceivable now. A sense of guilt, of the kind the moralising housemaster attempts to arouse, is seen as a low and contemptible emotion: one could almost say that the way the school is run is designed precisely to avoid it. But this can only be achieved by means – those savage assaults on the body, whether by teachers or fellow-pupils – from which the modern sensibility flinches. As it has become steadily less acceptable to inflict pain on children during the course of the century, so it has become necessary to hold the social world of the school in place by different kinds of sanctions. And so the modern child is monitored to a degree perhaps unparalleled in human history. By the process made familiar to us by Michel Foucault the child learns to monitor his own behaviour, to turn the gaze inward. A different set of values grows up to replace the anarchic, independent ones of the Victorian public school (for these Victorians were not as conformist as we sometimes like to believe): values centred on caution, moderation, striking a proper balance, looking over one's shoulder, and building a respectable *curriculum vitae*. Where Stalky spent a spare afternoon smoking a pipe and reading in his den among the furze on the cliffs beyond the school, his pleasure immensely heightened by the knowledge that the masters were wasting their time in vain attempts to discover him, Charlotte the modern sixth-former visits Alzheimer's patients in the local hospice or takes handicapped children to the swimming baths. Or so the personal statement written on her university application form would have us believe; and if such statements are not always veridical in the sense of mirroring reality, they are perhaps even truer in their reflection of the idealised self that has been internalised, inscribed on the soul as much as on the application form.

We may be inclined to shrug our shoulders and simply conclude that different eras require different values. Stalky, Beetle and M'Turk will become servants of the Empire, their work as soldiers in India or as District Officers in the Sudan requiring just the qualities of enterprise, ingenuity and loyalty to friends that their education has developed in them. A century later we demand other values: flexibility, perhaps, the affability which consists in the readiness to 'rub along' with all sorts and kinds of people, industriousness, the good sense of humour so prized in the lonely hearts advertisements. One would want still however, in our own time, to put in a good word for enterprise, ingenuity and loyalty to friends. It is easy to overestimate the extent to which values alter. It is perhaps the overestimation of the mutability of values that causes some to reach for what in morality does not change. If the (so to speak) front-line virtues change – *then* the courage to hold the line against the foe, *now* the dogged persistence that takes you into work day after day to stock the shelves or answer the telephone – we need something unchanging if the dangers of relativism are to be held at bay. That unchanging element is of course found in universalisability, the thin formal element supposed to run through any substantial morality whatsoever.

But the longing for such a necessary, even if thin and formal, element in morality is fuelled by more than just the reflection that substantive values change. It may seem that we now hold our values in a different way from the past. Consider how we esteem the readiness to slip easily between different personas: Charlotte's university reference, four years on, may declare approvingly that 'she is as much at home on the hockey field or with deprived children in the local school as she is in the seminar room'. In the modern idiom we incline to talk of all the moral dimensions of character as 'skills' (listening skills, caring skills, the skills of being a good parent . . .), eliding the difference between enduring qualities of self and temporary acquisitions. And have we not been told that the happy, healthy self wears many masks (cp. Gergen 1972)? Nietzsche helped us to understand the fragmentary nature of the self, but now this is commodified and sold back to us as how we *ought* to be. Our instinctive dissatisfaction with all this, together with the way that thicker moral languages offend the modern ear that is informed by such a rudimentary grasp of history and philosophy ('character' sounds too Victorian for words, 'values' look as if they are probably subjective, morality itself seems only a step away from moralising), causes us to fasten with relief on universalisability as that elusive moral *quiddam*, so etiolated and general as to be sure of causing no offence.

In criticism of universalisability one may take a number of lines. First, there is the well-known Nietzschean argument that it is just one more way in which the weak attempt to deny the powerful their characteristic virtues. Not all can be an eminent warrior or a captain of industry; therefore these cannot be virtues of any moral worth. They are no more an expression of morality than the samurai's propensity to try out his new sword on the chance passer-by, or the share-dealer's eagerness to make a quick killing in the stockmarket (we would all like to make a lot of money quickly, but what – we hear the desperate defender of the Kantian criterion ask – would it be like if everyone did that?). The virtues of the weak and powerless, on the other hand, may be held by all. All can be humble without infringing their neighbour's humility; we can all be endlessly forbearing with each other, moving in a warm mist of unconditional positive regard, acting on maxims which we have no difficulty at the same time willing to be universal laws. This, mysteriously, is supposed to take them through the moral prism, where all moral colours, if only they are universalisable, are revealed as the same white moral light.

Why should we not regard universalisability rather as just another piece of rhetoric, just one more expression of a kind of power, almost unparalleled in its capacity to engender guilt and bring about the behaviour that answers to the interest of the utterer? Our world is full of these strategies. Compare 'I know you better than to think you really mean that', said to someone who has made some mildly iconoclastic remark; or 'It would be irresponsible of me not to . . .', said by the manager intent on sacking part of the workforce in order (allegedly) to save the jobs of the rest. How easily moral discourse becomes a kind of cant through which we impose our will!

We get things right here, rather, when we make our judgements in the right *spirit*. Talk of something like the right spirit is logically necessary, because (the Wittgensteinian point) the rule itself cannot determine *how the rule is* applied. So the reflection that we ought to pay our income tax can be in a grudging spirit, in the manner of one who accepts ungraciously that we live in a world of reciprocal ties and mutual benefits, or affirmed in the confidence that this is a just and right way of proceeding. I can forebear from blocking my neighbour's drive knowing that I certainly would not like him to block mine, or in the pleasant knowledge that he would never do such a thing to me. Nietzsche writes that the spirit of morality is of the greatest importance:

> submission to morality can be slavish or vain or selfish or resigned or obtusely enthusiastic or thoughtless or an act of desperation, like submission to a prince: in itself it is nothing moral.
>
> (*D*: 97)

It can be all of those things or, of course, it can be less a submission than a glad acceptance that we live in a world where by and large people do not go around wilfully blocking each other's drive for the sake of momentary convenience, nor stealing the milk from each other's doorsteps. There is a great difference here between morality as a matter of not doing what you want to do because you know that in some sense it is wrong or forbidden ('oh – but I wouldn't like it if others did that to me') and morality as a matter of happily observing the habit of greasing the wheels that make our lives run better. Kant did much damage here with his insistence that to the extent that an action is done gladly, to that extent it does not contain truly moral motivation ('An action compelled by the instinct of life has in the joy of performing it the proof it is a *right* action: and that nihilist with Christian-dogmatic bowels understands joy as an *objection*', Nietzsche writes (*A*: section 11)) . The good person, we may feel, is rather the one who takes pleasure in doing good acts, as Aristotle believed. Here the goodness expresses the kind of person she (half-consciously, perhaps) allows herself to be. It is in this sense that Nietzsche's morality is correctly and uncontroversially describable as a morality of self-expression.

However, Nietzsche means more than this. For Nietzsche universalisability is part of the moral picture but only part of the moral picture, and the quality of that picture turns on what else is in it. A school, or a family, whose moral life consists of little else but reminding children of what it would be like if everyone did that is a very different place from one where the full range of the moral life is expressed and given its due. One of the beneficial effects of the new interest in environmental and animal ethics, for example, is that the limits of universalisability are quickly reached. The absurdity of trying to solve the difficult issues here by asking if we would like it if oysters ate us, or if the rainforest turned round and started chopping *us* down, is sufficiently obvious to force us to expand the range of our moral vocabulary. Similarly the moral quality of a life in which caring has a central place – as in the caring relationship between two gay men, one of whom is dying of AIDS – is self-evidently not to be captured by thinking of how we ourselves would want to be cared for, simply because the value of the caring is not only for the one cared for. In such ways as these our children may be beginning to live in a richer moral universe than those (us) who are their nominal teachers, formal or informal.

So the important question is just how rich and varied the moral world and moral vocabulary are that we introduce our children to. The signs, when we look at them, are discouraging. Recent writing about moral education seems more often than not to have been driven by moral panic: by the fear that children are doing things they should not be doing, such as taking drugs, sexually abusing other children or assaulting their teachers. The title and the general thrust of Graham Haydon's recent book *Values, Virtues and Violence: Education and the Public Understanding of Morality* (Haydon 1999) underscores this. The crucial issue becomes how children's activities are to be circumscribed for the general good; and while this is of wholly undeniable importance it leads to a moral climate and a kind of moral education rather different from one where the central question is taken to be how children's lives may be richer, more engaged, more triumphantly affirmative (and taken to be the central question perhaps because we are confident of our ability to stop or deter them from doing the things we want them to desist from doing rather than having to fall back on morality to do the job).

And quite what kind of moral education does that lead us to? We need look no further than the Office for Standards in Education (Ofsted) for the clue. When its inspectors, the guardians of all our standards in schooling, turn their microscopes on the moral and spiritual ethos of a school it is *awe and wonder* they look for. The children may be campaigning for better treatment of animals or the cancellation of Third World debt, they may have shamed their teachers into equal treatment of the sexes or exposed the hypocrisy of the visiting politician, but it is awe and wonder that are taken as the infallible sign of the moral health of the patient. Awe and wonder! As if the most important sign of a child's growing moral sense was this: that she has properly appreciated her own utter insignificance in the vast and portentous universe. Awe and wonder! Not the informed delight in the known and understood detail of things (flowers, car engines, constellations, microprocessors), but a sense of their necessary and proper incomprehensibility, of the rightful powerless and humility of the individual rather than her developing mastery and confidence *through* her wider engagement with the world. In *The Gay Science* ('this awesomely aweless book' as he calls it in the first section of the Preface to the second edition) Nietzsche asks whether our values are inspired by superabundance, the 'overflowing energy that is pregnant with future' (section 370) that he calls 'Dionysian'. If you find your energy overflowing, the merchants of awe and wonder tell the children, suppress it at once. We want no superabundance in *this* classroom. Take your lesson from the starry heavens above you: that will be your guide to the moral law within you. A suitable incomprehension is the thing, and when you are older we will teach you about Socrates who was the greatest Athenian because he alone know that he knew nothing. Know that your humble place: then we can begin. One is reminded of the drinker joining Alcoholics Anonymous, whose first step must be to accept that there is a Higher Power; one is reminded of the old-fashioned school where the first step is total humiliation, the head thrust into the lavatory bowl, hands not to be seen in pockets until the fourth year. Until you come as a supplicant we cannot begin with your education. Thus at all stages of their education learners are told to 'forget what they taught you' in the primary school, in the sixth form, or wherever. Knowledge is a dangerous energy and must first be drained off.

That is to characterise, perhaps to caricature a little, our moral climate of education, the company that universalisability keeps. If it is something of a caricature it is only too recognisable nonetheless. But we must not forget that the teachers and, in universities, the lecturers encounter a moral climate too. That, over much of the English-speaking world, has become a climate dominated by blame. Schools may be beacons of excellence, or they may be, in that most revealing of all phrases – revealing for what it tells us about our moral climate in education – named and shamed. All must go in fear of wearing the scarlet letter of failure, the mark that declares we have failed our inspection, have not met the Secretary of State's criteria, are not compliant with whatever standards prevail. Now a factory product can properly be said to be BS5750[1] (or whatever) compliant, without any sense that it has somehow had to lower itself to make the grade. But whatever has happened when a university committee, with only the smallest acknowledgement of the absurdity of the proceedings, can talk of candidates for promotion being 'senior lecturer compliant'? The words register the importance of obedience, of bending with the forces that demand to shape you.

Now we have allowed ourselves to find this language normal because we have been persuaded that as public servants we must be *accountable*. We are responsible for large sums of public money and must be prepared to show what we have done with it. We would not like to think we are *irresponsible*, of course; and perhaps something here plays upon our fantasies of standing arraigned in the court and proving ourselves before our peers (perhaps *acquittal* is the only sense of freedom we can any more grasp). To be accountable is to be thoroughly grown-up; to say that teachers or doctors must be accountable is like saying that managers must manage. It has, to the modern ear, the right sort of ring to it. You can declare that you are 'very publicly accountable' (a phrase from an application for professional promotion) as if you thereby established yourself as a contemporary Thomas More, unafraid and with nothing to hide.

Who can be against accountability or against its brother, transparency? Only, of course, those with nothing to hide (not theirs the untidy register, the planning not up to date, the aims and objectives that don't, in failing to match outcomes, bear scrutiny). Yet there is a certain moral climate in which accountability thrives, a certain moral company which this value keeps:

> Everywhere accountability is sought, it is the instinct for punishing and judging which seeks it. The doctrine of will (and accountable acts) has been invented essentially for the purpose of punishment, that is of finding guilty.
>
> (*TI*, 'The Four Great Errors': section 7)

Elsewhere Nietzsche writes that the emotions of vengefulness and resentment eagerly maintain the belief that the strong man is free to be weak and the bird of prey to be a lamb, 'for thus they gain the right to make the bird of prey *accountable* for being a bird of prey' (*GM*, 1.13). How long have you been a bird of prey? What are your aims and objectives, in being a sparrow-hawk? What evidence can you give us that customers are satisfied with what you provide? We may pretend that accountability is an opportunity to celebrate the successful teacher and bird of prey ('our mostly excellent teachers', as one recent UK Education Minister put it) and not simply to arraign the guilty, but no-one is deceived by such talk. Nietzsche asks just what kind of people would choose to live like this. The Nietzschean answer, perhaps, is that it is people who live without trust: whose fundamental anxiety is that people may be *getting away with things*. The teachers may be getting away with going home at four o'clock, the lecturers with having long holidays. Contracts and charters (students' charters, parents' charters) will tie them down to delivering specific services. Those who do not deliver will rightly be exposed (that naming and shaming again); parents will take their children elsewhere and the school will close, students will choose other modules where expectations are clearer and outcomes if not guaranteed then at least expressible in solid, that is bullet-pointed in terms of key skills, form.

Thus it comes about that we form our sense of morality, our values, on the basis of their being the opposite of what they are not. There are many dimensions to Nietzsche's concept of nihilism, mere acquiescence in traditional values and indifference to issues of value, to the question 'why?', being foremost among them. These days it seems the *reactiveness* of contemporary morality that consti-tutes its essential nihilism. A healthy morality – a noble morality, as Nietzsche calls it – develops from a triumphant affirmation of *itself*. The debased morality, which he calls slave morality, on the other hand,

> says no to an 'outsider', to an 'other', to a 'non-self', and *this* no is its creative act. The reversal of the evaluating gaze – this *necessary* orientation outwards rather than inwards to the self – belongs characteristically to *ressentiment*. In order to exist at all, slave morality from the outset always needs an opposing, outer world . . . its action is fundamentally reaction.
>
> (*GM*, 'First Essay': section 10)

For in our world, and particularly the world of education, we first (often with the necessary help of the tabloid newspapers) identify the 'outside', the 'other', and form our values in contradistinction. *They* are scroungers, parasites on the welfare state; they are conservative forces that stand in the way of change, teachers still entranced by the progressivism that has failed our children, bureaucrats who oppose modernisation. (Wonderfully, we are now encouraged to react against *reactionaries*. Clearly this process has not begun recently.) We may not know what we want to affirm, but we know what we want to deny and to be the opposite of. A morality constructed on this basis is nihilism; and if we say 'nihilism with a vengeance' then the phrase is peculiarly apt.

Let us repeat, and in the modern idiom *list*, three of the key elements of nihilism. They are:

* acquiescence in traditional values
* indifference to values or refusal to think about them
* forming values by reaction against their opposites

Consider how all three elements are present in the following paragraph from a daily newspaper. The government wishes to introduce performance-related pay for teachers; they and their representatives have complained that performance-related pay is destructive of collegiality and co-operation. The Prime Minister intervenes to remind us of the dominant values of our time:

> Mr Blair said: 'the vast majority of teachers do a wonderful job, but there are schools and education authorities that are not doing as well as they should'. The government could only justify higher pay if it was linked to performance. 'I cherish the notion of partnership and team-spirit. But I do believe that if we want to justify to the British taxpayer spending sums of money this big, we have to tie it in to raising standards' . . . Mr Blair said it was time to change his government's priorities. 'They used to be education, education, education. Perhaps now they should be education, education, education and education', he said.
>
> (*The Guardian*, 24 November 1999: 12)

The traditional values are there in the unquestioning acceptance of the notions of accountability and standards; the reactive conception of good teaching as the opposite of the incompetent teacher and the failing school or local education authority (the conception is not spelled out here but is present by implication); the refusal to consider the values of education beyond the simple criterion of better performance. If anyone has a problem with the value of 'education, education, education' that Tony Blair announced as his government's first priority then, by a rhetorical device, they can be browbeaten into submission both by reiteration of that priority and reduplication – the extra 'education' – of its substance.

We began by describing a real incident from a school: we end by describing another, witnessed by one of us on a train from Brighton to London. Four teenage girls, clearly not possessing a ticket to travel, were walking up through the train ahead of the ticket-collector who was checking passengers' documents. As he neared the front of the train they, carefully judging their moment, would alight at a station, run down the platform and board the train again at the rear. On the second round he pursued them, shouting that the next time they did this the train would not move from the station while they were still aboard. Still they ran down the platform and entered the carriage where one of us was sitting. Clearly they had played this game before, and were prepared to leave the carriage and run to another one ahead of the frustrated ticket-collector as often as he tried to accost them. But in this carriage one angry passenger (and not one of us, we are sorry to say) leapt to his feet and confronted the girls:

> 'Get off the train! Some of us are in a hurry, we have con-nections to make! *Get off the train!'*

Taken aback by his evident fury the girls scurried onto the platform and stayed there. As the train moved off, they ran alongside the carriage, pointing at the passenger who had expelled them, and chanting 'Wanker! wanker! wanker!' And as the train outstripped their ability to keep up with it, he called to them, in an assured and firm voice:

> 'Maybe, *but I'm on the train, and you're not'*.

We shall not analyse this incident, only noting of the morality implicit here its powerful affirmativeness and clear-headed sense of reality, in contrast to the manipulative evasiveness of the teacher in the first example. There smugness, here triumph; there guilt, here the straightforward consequences of the girls' actions for them. But in one respect the two incidents suggest to us an identical reflection about these high-spirited, if mischievous, teenagers: what would it be like if *nobody* did that?

It would be good to report that the second incident closed with the whole carriage cheering their fellow-passenger. But, whether out of the traditional English value of reserve, or simple indifference to these momentous things, the travellers all buried their heads in their newspapers or their books – including, in one case, *The Genealogy of Morals*, where the eye fell upon the following passage, in which Nietzsche writes of 'the possibility of one day being entitled to approach the problems of morality in high spirits':

But on the day when we say with full hearts: 'Onwards! our old morality is part of the *comedy* too!', on that day we will have discovered a new plot and potential for the Dionysian drama of the *'Fate of the Soul'* . . .

(*GM*, 'Preface': section 7)

Note

1 British Standard 5750 is the mark that the product has passed quality control.

FRAGMENT VII

The question of educational research. What use is educational research unless it tells us what to do (what is effective, what works)? We expect it to be relevant to the classroom. *Classroom teachers should therefore in the future maximise learning by use of the interactive whiteboard*, or whatever. We can see the point of that kind of research. The philosophers will not be excluded, for we do not want to seem lacking in moral values, and who knows when an ethical or spiritual (yes, we are sure there is a difference, but no time for that now) audit will not inform the league-tables?

'Learning must include dialogue about ethical and value issues' (Honey, see above, p. 124): you see? We will give you a place among the movers and shakers, we will let you listen to the grown-ups talk of globalisation, and human capital, and social inclusivity – in return we ask nothing more than appropriate lists of value issues . . .

In a speech made on 2 February 2000 to an ESRC seminar David Blunkett (according to the press release on the DfEE website) 'called upon social science researchers to join with policy-makers in breaking down the "seam of anti-intellectualism running through society". He also stressed the importance of sound, relevant and intelligible research'.

There shall be no more anti-intellectualism. Social scientists will do relevant research, joining government in the search for solutions. They will become an arm of the State. 'We shall cease mocking you as ivory-tower intellectuals. In return you will address yourselves to the questions we want answering: the ones that show us how to lever standards up'. That is what serious research is for.

At last, an end to the discourse of derision. A beginning to the *policy* of contempt.

Chapter 11

On having educative relationships with one's pupils

Introduction

Why do we want to be teachers? What is the peculiar fascination with educating children, conducting relationships with those who are not yet adults? Where can the satisfaction be, the lay person sometimes puzzles, in spending your time with people who are (as yet) your intellectual inferiors? It is intriguing also that the wisdom we have gathered, for ourselves, is something we actively wish to pass on. But it can seem at times, can it not, to be something wonderful that we can teach anything to anyone? The dawn of recognition on a human face, their stimulation by our thoughts, by how we make sense of life for ourselves – all this is fascinating and powerfully attractive. There is surely some narcissistic satisfaction here, someone might say, or some unsavoury enjoyment of power, perhaps simply comfort from the fact that our ability to elicit a response from the other helps us to feel that we are not alone. Yet in the context of schooling, at least, where the relationship of teacher to pupils is clearly more one-sided, the puzzlement remains, and the explanation may not be as tidy or comfortable as we might wish.

That there are dangers here is evident from the general concern today with codes of conduct, charters and student rights. This reflects the 'traditional' position in these matters (see Abinun 1977) to the effect that there are some important senses in which the teacher–pupil relationships ought to be impersonal, rather than personal or even interpersonal; and that the teacher–pupil relationship should be characterised by respect for persons and not, say, by love or sympathy. The resistance here is created not just as the result of homophobia and media sensationalism: there are genuine revelations of abusive behaviour, in the present and the past, that reflect the gravity of the danger and the peculiar violation of trust that is involved. And as a result, men who work in the caring and teaching professions, particularly those working with young children, are placed in a position of suspicion. People like to think that a teacher is 'up to something'. It is then more difficult to acknowledge, as Erica McWilliam (1996) argues, the fact that the infantilising and feminising representation of students can mask the ways in which they may be more powerful than the teacher. Similarly, this inhibition makes it difficult to recognise the coherence and value there may be to ideas of a 'seductive' pedagogy drawing its power from a sense of the inherent richness of the content of what is taught. (See, for example, the erotetic teaching advocated by James MacMillan and James Garrison (1988) or Richard Rorty's characterisation of study as 'erotic'.) Instead there is the inclination to connect any suggestion of the erotic with the cynical exchange of sexual for academic favours. It is no surprise that recent remarks Chris Woodhead, Her Majesty's Chief Inspector of Schools in England, to the effect that a pupil might benefit from her relationship with an adult teacher met with cries of outrage and clamorous media attention, confused and hypocritical though this may have been. Are we to accept then this voluble received opinion that a beneficial relationship of this kind is really impossible? Or should we at least attend to the question of whether something is obscuring the picture, something at odds perhaps with what we have been led to think that education ought to be – neutral, that is, of course, and detached?

Of course, people are commonly engaged in relationships with other human beings in diverse professional and other contexts. But educational contexts are in some respects quite different, characterised as they normally are by a high degree of personal involvement on the one hand and by their concentration on the learner on the other. What is it then that is distinctive about the particular kind of motivation that inspires educators? What, to put it more baldly, do they get out of these relationships? It goes without saying that several answers to this issue have been given: teachers are earning their living; parents are simply fulfilling their responsibilities. Sometimes people have spoken of a vocation in this context. We do not want to be critical of these answers. What we do want to do here is to focus on another aspect that for various reasons has been suppressed and sometimes even deliberately ignored. This requires returning to the beginnings of philosophy itself.

The essence of life: Eros[1] and the centrality of education and of philosophy

In Plato's *Symposium*, Socrates recounts the 'lesson' he was taught by Diotima:[2] that mortal man does all he can to attain immortality. By breeding he ensures that there will always be a younger generation to take the place of the old. Although we speak of a man as being the same so long as he continues to exist in the same form, we know that, with time, every bit of him is different, that every day he is becoming a new man – a matter that applies not only to his body but also to his soul. Every mortal seeks to reproduce himself since he cannot be, like the divine, unchanging throughout eternity. He can only leave behind new life to fill the vacancy that is left in his species by his own obsolescence. And the whole of creation is inspired by this love, this passion for immortality. This love is not only exemplified in the love of glory, the urge to win eternal mention in the deathless roll of fame, but it is there in every one of us, no matter what we do. Thus Diotima continues:

> 'Those whose procreancy is of the body turn to woman as the object of their love, and raise a family, in the blessed hope that by doing so they will keep their memory green, 'through time and through eternity'. But those whose procreancy is of the spirit rather than of the flesh – and they are not unknown, Socrates – conceive and bear the things of the spirit. And what are they? you ask. Wisdom and all her sister virtues; it is the office of every poet to beget them, and of every artist whom we may call creative.
>
> 'Now, by far the most important kind of wisdom', she went on, 'is that which governs the ordering of society, and which goes by the names of justice and moderation. And if any man is so closely allied to the divine as to be teeming with these virtues even in his youth, and if, when he comes to manhood, his first ambition is to be begetting, he too, you may be sure, will go about in search of the loveliness – and never of the ugliness – on which he may beget. And hence his procreant nature is attracted by a comely body rather than an ill-favoured one; and if, besides, he happens on a soul which is at once beautiful, distinguished, and agreeable, he is charmed to find so welcome an alliance; it will be easy for him to talk of virtue to such a listener, and to discuss what human goodness is and how the virtuous should live – in short, to undertake the other's education.
>
> 'And, so I believe, by constant association with so much beauty, and by thinking of his friend when he is present and when he is away, he will be delivered of the burden he has laboured under all these years; and what is more, he and his friend will help each other to rear the issue of their friendship – and so the bond between them will be more binding, and their

communion even more complete, than that which comes of bringing children up, because they have created something lovelier and less mortal than human seed'.

(*Symposium*: 43–4)

One of the purposes of the *Symposium* is to show that the most lofty manifestation of the 'Love' that binds the world consists in the longing for union with eternal and transcendent Beauty. The representation of Socrates as the person who has achieved that union is contrasted with that of the handsome, able and wealthy Alcibiades, who has dedicated himself to earthly pleasures and ambitions. Appetitive love (eros) in whatever form is, according to this dialogue, a reaching out of the soul towards a good for which it craves but upon which it has not yet laid hold: the desire for the everlasting possession of the Good. This passionate desire, serving the Form of Forms and the eternal and immutable 'Good', is first roused by Beauty. In its crudest form it is the desire for a beautiful person, since perpetuating one's genes (as the modern reductive gloss on this would have it) is all that lies within the body's power. A more exalted form of the longing for eternity, however, is man's aspiration to achieve undying renown by uniting himself with a kindred soul (to produce, that is, wise institutions and sound rules of life or – still higher – striving to enrich philosophy and science). The lover seeks to find a beloved to generate in his soul an everlasting offspring. The final objective lies far beyond these physical ends, however, in the form of the 'beatific vision'.

The nature of eros itself is that of a mean between two contraries (between the beautiful and the ugly, the good and the bad). It is neither a god nor a mortal but a great daemon mediating between the two; and it is a mean also between the wise and the unwise (as reflected in the very definition of a philosopher). While usually translated as 'love', eros is closely affiliated with desire – and this is a crucial distinction: while Love was praised and celebrated with Beauty and Truth as one of the highest cultural ideals, desire was seen as irrational and irresistible, an inevitable madness (divine and destructive), an amoral force, at worst a volatile and uncontrollable one. In view of these dangers then, as Elizabeth Ervin argues (1993), the integration of eros into Hellenic social and political institutions occurred for precautionary reasons as much as for celebratory ones.

The effects of eros cannot be fully understood apart from those of philosophy. This explains why there is a special place for philosophy, at least in the education of those young people who have the requisite affinity for the Forms. Indeed, for Plato, being told about the beautiful and knowing the beautiful for oneself is not the same thing. In love we passionately desire to possess the good. And so, if we love wisely, and are persistent in the pursuit, we may become wise. Our well-being depends on our wisdom in our love, and this is a wisdom beyond knowledge. Even if we had complete knowledge of the world moral questions would remain, and so it is an education beyond knowledge that we need. The fact that such an education has been the province of philosophers, the lovers of wisdom, explains the crucial relevance of philosophy for education.

Human nature requires education in order to reach its essence and this in turn creates the demand for philosophy. A closer look, however, reveals the much greater role of education: it may be seen as that which instils the very want, the very love, it proposes to satiate; it creates desire even as it offers the means for its gratification. This impulse is engraved in the erotic relations, so understood, between teachers and students. The relation between love and knowledge in classical Greek education is performed through a 'homoerotic' teacher–student 'economy', in which the teacher is invested with the authority to 'instil' desire in what is rightly called *paiderastia*. It is imperative to look beyond the connotations that this term has acquired in the twentieth century in order to understand what is at stake here. Though undeniably erotic in practice, the relationship in question was essentially educational in purpose; it represented a process through which older male citizens acted as 'civic mentors' to adolescent boys, providing them with guidance and support during their initiation into adult society. 'Eros' in its physical manifestation is to be understood in terms of the Greeks' ideal equation of perfect mind and perfect body, and their belief that physically beautiful boys were also endowed with gifts of wisdom and virtue. Since young men do not remain young men forever, and since one can assume that most Greek male adolescents aspired to civic activity within the polis, some sort of transformation had to take place, a rite of passage that generally occurred under the guidance and tutelage of an older male citizen in the practice of *paiderastia*. Although there has been some tendency to sanitise this picture, Ervin (1993) has argued that the practice denoted both disinterested affection and homoerotic physical relations between a man (around the age of 40) and a boy (13 to 20 years of age). In a pattern of mutually gratifying devotion and emulation the lover was responsible for developing the morals, values and ideals of the boy by transmitting the values of Greek culture, while the beloved was invested with significant powers of cultural procreativity, chosen according to the potential of his character. According to Ervin (1993: 86), the affectionate *paiderastia* relationship no doubt frequently manifested itself in sexual behaviour; it was neither entirely intellectual nor entirely sexual. It included ordeals of toil, humiliation and submission, for it was in subordinating his needs and desires to those of his elders that a boy learned to take his place in the power hierarchy of organised adult society. Though this may, Ervin claims, lead one to conclude that male homosexuality was more widespread than it actually was in ancient Attica, it is important to be clear about this particular kind of homoeroticism which served the purposes of friendship, learning, and moral and civic development more than anything else.

To unravel the different layers which are involved here, we will once more go back to the *Symposium*. Socrates felt himself responsible for what Alcibiades would do with his life. Having saved his life at the battle of Potidaea, Socrates experienced a life-long obligation to guide and love him, for before he could attempt to rule Athens Alcibiades would have to learn to take care of himself. Socrates decided that he could best achieve his educational goal by refusing to yield to the temptation which Alcibiades presented (the physical aspect of eros). Diotima explicitly mentions that Socrates was still chasing after handsome young men and other such beautiful things at the time she was instructing him – hence the deeper drama of the *Symposium*, as John Anton has argued (1974), with which Plato wants to confront his readers:

> Socrates is not a sophos-divine nor loved-and-not-loving; he is called a philosophos. What is expected of Socrates is to take the instruction seriously and test his ability to ascend the ladder of love. . . . If Socrates spurns Alcibiades it is not because he has taken the place of the divine, but because he tries to remain faithful to his philosophical eros as a paidagogos.
>
> (Anton 1974: 293)

This is, to say the least, rather ambiguous. The explicit physical attraction is downplayed by Plato in favour of the spiritual to the extent that it almost becomes instrumental, though not quite. As will become clear it serves a particular function in Plato's dialogue.

Indeed, not even the broken lives of students can legitimately call service to the Good into question. Though Socrates speaks truly when he says he loves Alcibiades, it is the particular focus of his desire that merits attention: he 'wants Alcibiades to know the truth but, more importantly, he wants him and others to come to the truth by themselves through critical reflection and thought' (Neiman 1995: 70–1). Wisdom must be struggled for and won only after a hard-fought battle; souls must turn toward wisdom for themselves. Following Gregory Vlastos, Alven Neiman draws attention to the complex nature of Socrates' irony in his claim to wisdom. Unlike simple cases of irony in which one asserts something to be the case but literally intends the opposite, what complex irony intends is more than simple negation: an understanding is intended beyond the conventional meanings of our words and beyond our final vocabulary. Socrates' claim to wisdom requires that he is known not to be wise in the conventional sense. His wisdom cannot be poured from one vessel to another. Truly to become Socrates' student may therefore imply the forsaking of appearance for Reality, the overcoming of uncertainty through union with Reality: 'It is to believe without irony in such Goods, and to allow the Ideal that such Goods exemplify to master us, to master our incomplete loves, and even our irony itself' (Neiman 1995: 71). This provides even some sort of a yardstick for judging our actual failures and for pointing us towards a better, 'truer', 'more Real' state. Diotima's instruction outlines a doctrine of correct *paiderastia* designed to regulate and enhance erotic relations between men and boys (physical desire and spiritual desire). The process of coming to know, as it is exemplified in the Platonic dialogues, is to be seen in such erotic terms.

Because of the desire for self-mastery and inner peace, affection stops short of physical fulfilment. Referring particularly to the *Phaedrus*, Martha Nussbaum concludes: 'Yet it is difficult to see how this is based on anything other than the sort of suspicion of the body and antipathy to intercourse that pervades Plato's works' (in Solomon and Higgins 1991: 327). The soul is regarded as the prisoner of the body. Intense pleasure (orgasm) welds the soul to the body. And then it may be impossible to detach and free oneself. Such pleasure then distorts one's sense of reality. The proper conclusion is that ordinary life, fulfilling as it is for the average man, cannot be his final aspiration, for that must be directed towards union with the eternal and transcendent. Whatever bears the mark of temporality, of matter or mortality (such as the human body), can only be of limited significance. Man's true self has to be sought beyond all of this. And because this is what must be longed for, there can in the end only be disdain, even contempt, for the *hic et nunc*.

The body of knowledge

Plato's framework is no longer ours, but his observations on human relationships repay our attention. That Diotima's advice has not been forgotten is clear in the writings of Roland Barthes. For him it is only by acknowledging desire in the very moment of denying it that the professor of Desire can teach the knowledge of love and love of knowledge, thus fulfilling the nurturing function essential to the learning process as a continuous affirmation of joyful wisdom (see Ungar 1982). But just as an examination of the relationship between the educator and the learner requires us to consider our contemporary frameworks in a new light, so it is necessary to reflect on a number of pertinent points.

Answering the questions raised at the outset of this chapter requires us to distinguish between the 'body of knowledge' and the involvement of the body of the person who is teaching or who is being taught. Paulo Freire and Henri Giroux (1989) argue that at its best the language of educational theory should embody a public philosophy dedicated to returning schools to their primary role as places of critical education in the service of creating a public sphere of citizens able to exercise power over their own lives and especially over the conditions of knowledge production and acquisition. Their position is opposed to a conception of educational theory and practice organised around a claim to authority that is primarily procedural and technical. Such a conception ignores its own partiality, it refuses to engage the ideological assumptions that underlie its vision of the future and appears unable to understand its own complicity with social relations that subjugate, infantilise and corrupt. About this language they point out that

> in its quest for control, certainty, and objectivity [it] cannot link leadership to notions of solidarity, community, or public life. It is a language that reduces administrators, teachers, and students to clerks and bad theorists, that removes schools from their most vital connections to public life, and that more often than not defines teaching in instrumental rather than enabling terms. It deskills teachers and disempowers students while purporting to empower them.
>
> (Freire and Giroux 1989: viii)

A critical pedagogy must therefore incorporate aspects of popular culture as a serious educational discourse into the school curriculum, and it must bring into the discourse of school policy and pedagogical planning the voices of those who have been marginalized and excluded. In engaging schools as cultural sites and recognizing that schools are about the lives and stories of particular people, it follows that they have to expand the possibilities for educating students so that they can be critical, rather than merely good, citizens. Freire and Giroux thus draw attention to the central connection of the content of what is learned to the education of the person for herself. Schools must recognize the multiple narratives and histories that make up pluralistic societies, and educators need to educate students into viewing schools as places that produce not only subjects but also subjectivities. Thus it is 'that learning is not merely about the acquisition of knowledge but also about the production of social practices which provide students with a sense of place, identity, worth, and value' (ibid.: ix). Though Freire and Giroux's commitments are clearly global, the reality they focus on is characterized by embeddedness, and this is something very different from what Plato is interested in.

In the same work, Giroux and Simon (1989) argue that while the production of meaning provides one important element in the production of subjectivity, it is not enough. It is also tied to emotional investments and the production of pleasure – both mutually constitutive of who students are, of the view they have of themselves, and of how they construct a particular version of their future (ibid.: 3–4). In their discussion of punk culture, for instance, they argue that it is the dialectic of affirmation, pleasure and difference that constitutes some of the basic elements of what Pierre Bourdieu calls 'the productive'. The focus is on the way in which cultural forms can be understood as mobilising desire. Pedagogy is not exclusively ensconced in the production of discourse, but rather constitutes also a moment in which the body learns, moves, desires and longs for affirmation. They say they are not trying to privilege the body or a politics of affective investments over discourse so much as that they 'are trying to emphasize their absence [the absence of the body or a politics of affective investments] in previous theorizing and the importance for a critical pedagogy' (ibid.: 16). They accept that the cultural forms that mobilise desire and affect (along with the struggles that take place over re/producing and investing desire, pleasure and corporeality) are constructed within power relations that are always ideological in nature, but they hold also that this production of an experience or form of investment cannot be understood merely as an ideological construction (re/presented and enjoyed through the lens of meaning rather than through the primacy of pleasure and affect). Affective investments have a real cultural hold. It is important thus to understand how the body becomes the subject of pleasure.

They illustrate this in their discussion of the movie *Dirty Dancing*. Giroux and Simon note that for women, bombarded with images and with information about how they should be and how they should feel, dance may offer an escape, a positive and vibrant sexual expressiveness: thus the importance of popular cultural forms (of working-class life) in constituting the identities which influence how we engage with new challenges and construct new experiences (new pleasures of the body). Interestingly, they close with a warning:

> Teachers engaged in a pedagogy which requires some articulation of knowledge and pleasure integral to student life walk a dangerous road. Too easily, perhaps, encouraging student voice can become a form of voyeurism or satisfy an ego-expansionism constituted on the pleasures of understanding those who appear as Other to us. So, we must be clear on the nature of the pedagogy we pursue. Popular culture and social difference can be taken up by educators either as a pleasurable form of knowledge/power which allows for more effective individualizing and administration of physical and moral regulation or such practices can be understood as the terrain on which we must meet our students in a critical and empowering pedagogical encounter.
>
> (Giroux and Simon 1989: 24–5)

A positive appreciation of 'the body' carries with it a danger in terms of subjectivisation. The relation has to be conceived in a sophisticated, subtle, perhaps in essence ambiguous, way in order to safeguard mobilising the desire needed to change particular power relations while at the same time seeing these basically as empowering.

Much interest in these themes is also found within feminist literature. Ursula Kelly (1997) argues that part of an explanation for the dearth of educational literature addressing eros and teaching may be found in the general resistance by educators to any acknowledgement of desire in teaching. Teachers have been positioned within the same discourses of desexualization to which students are subjected. Teachers are expected to deny eros – which is predominantly associated with the sexual – as part of the particular bourgeois ideology of moral order to which schools predominantly subscribe. Passion and teaching can be connected only if properly regulated and channelled. Kelly by contrast sees eros as an activating, arousing energy, not necessarily or only sexual, which quickens our sense of our own desires and reminds us of the constituency of our personal and collective pleasures (Kelly 1997: 128). She approvingly quotes bell hooks who argues that to understand the place of eros and eroticism in the classroom we must move beyond thinking of these forces solely in terms of the sexual, although that dimension need not be denied. Another inspiration for her is Roger Simon (1992). He contends that a pedagogy that is rooted in partiality, disruption and the recognition of the embodiment of knowledge requires an eros that does not subvert the desire to awake or incite a particular passion in those whom we teach, but rather finds its expression in the recognition of the particular dignity of others not as objects but as people with whom mutuality is possible. Kelly argues that the erotic character of pedagogy must, first and foremost, be recognised as a social and cultural practice of signification, historically specific and delimited by this specificity.

> The challenge posed by this erotic character of pedagogy is twofold: how to respect difference; and how to contend with the differentials of power that confront us in our pedagogies while, at the same time, insisting on the work of our pedagogical projects.
>
> (Kelly 1997: 131)

In referring to the work of Pagano, she makes a link between the individual and the societal levels. In that configuration students identify the teacher as the locus of desire and take on as their own the desires of the teacher, and it is in the teacher's likeness that students are recreated both to receive and to execute the passions of the one presumed to know. She draws attention to the fact that this dynamic, born as much out of the desires of the teacher as out of those of the student – as much a condition of countertransference as of transference – is a disturbing and dangerous one. This is particularly so for women and others whose position within the social order is constituted negatively and against whom the odds of attaining greater control over the process of signification are stacked. It is precisely because of the pitfalls of dependency and power that accompany transference/countertransference that demystification, diffusion and resistance are required.

> While pedagogy is always practised as a form of persuasion, a self-cautiousness should exist that attempts to counter inclinations that might usurp the dignity of desiring others with whom we engage on the grounds of (dis)pleasure and difference. . . . To maintain a respectful sense of the body (the subject) as the target of pedagogy and to tap the utopian inclinations of eros are real challenges for a radical pedagogy that commits to naming its desires.
>
> (Kelly 1997: 137)

Similarly McWilliam (1996) points to the embodied nature of pedagogical work, that is, 'an engagement some body has with other bodies in institutional spaces' (ibid.: 3). Thus, to her, the material body of the teacher seems a very significant factor in everyday textual constructions of effective and ineffective teaching. It is marked by specificities of class, gender, body shape, sexuality and ethnicity as well as by illness, aging, scars, make-up, facial hair and the like. Referring to Angel, she identifies the teacher's body as the site and sight of authoritative pedagogical display. And she quotes with approval the work of Madeleine Grumet who in her work on women and teaching insists upon a place for intimacy, 'for the legitimacy of the lived experience of women teachers, with all of its contradictions, in a new politics of educational knowledge that is inclusive of personal identity' (McWilliam 1996: 3). As the work of Michèle Le Doeuff on eighteenth-century models of pedagogy illustrates, this is not new. She notes the fact that individual women's acquisition of knowledge was often facilitated through their love for a man, a particular philosopher/teacher. Here pedagogy amounted to an erotico-theoretical transference:

> There has always been – at school, at university, in the pre-paratory courses for university, most often the latter in fact – a teacher around whom there has crystallized something analogous to the theoretico-amorous admiration of woman . . . This privileged teacher . . . the one who finally seduced you . . . captured your desire and turned it into a desire for [the subject discipline].
>
> (Le Doeuff cited in McWilliam 1996: 7)

McWilliam resists the narrowly instrumentalist view of women's erotic teaching in favour of the richer classical one. She argues that one of the ways to challenge the gendered – and hence abusive – cultural norms of great pedagogical works is to eroticize teaching within the theorisation of pedagogical work in the classroom, thus reclaiming a pedagogical tradition that offers us a real historical alternative for women. She approvingly quotes the words of Cryle:

> If we can (re)conceive of eroticism without being overwhelmed by the thematics of desire in its radically subjective forms, then we may be better placed to understand the discursive authority at work in transmitting received notions of refined pleasure.
>
> (Cryle cited in McWilliam 1996: 10)

McWilliam 'fleshes out' the notions of teacher desire and desir-ability by suggesting that a teacher's desire to teach is ambiguous and duplicitous in pedagogical events.

It is eros that dwells and moves in the matter of her students and her self. It is a corporeality that is experienced and rehearsed as student and teacher relate (with) each other. This idea both incorporates and transcends the notion of the erotic as our imaginative lives in sexual space. As a phenomenon of physiological in/tensity, it pervades bodies and circulates through bodies in pedagogical events. . . . The ambiguity of eros continues to render it troublesome as an intimate and disturbing physical and psychic pleasure experienced in pedagogical events . . .

(McWilliam 1997: 227)

For McWilliam powerful teaching is erotically stimulating. Thus, desire as teacher-centredness, or embodied self-interest, should not be dismissed as the antithesis of progressivism in educational work, nor as the first symptom of potentially abusive pedagogy. The yearning body of the teacher need not continue to be misconstrued as mere maleficence; its earthly materiality and sensuousness may well sustain the teacher who might otherwise join the ever-growing numbers of burned-out educational radicals. And what we do not need at all, she continues, are models of the good teacher as Virgin Mother or as clinician with a charisma bypass (McWilliam 1997: 228). She focuses on the embodiment of the pedagogical act and insists on knowledge and capability as carnal and visceral, inextricably linked with something more than the ir/rationality of the mind. Out of the refusal of effectiveness or emancipation,

facilitation transgresses and slips into seduction, motivation slips into desire, effect into eros; and all those metaphors about pedagogical bodies (bodies of knowledge or thought, the student body) become pregnant with meaning in ways that protrude and thereby disturb orthodox representation of the teacher–student relationship. Teachers teach some body, not just any body.

(McWilliam 1997: 229)

Demolishing the traditional stance: Nietzsche and Wittgenstein

We have argued that although the metaphysical framework of Plato is no longer ours, his observations on human relationships have important implications for our own lives. Of course, the dualism and metaphysical stance of his framework gradually had to give way, first to Thomism, after that to the Enlightenment, and finally to twentieth century philosophy characterised by pragmatism, language and context. An interpretation of the present scene requires us to draw attention to two key figures who have left their mark on the philosophical developments of the past century: while Nietzsche emphasises embodiment as opposed to the Idea, Wittgenstein draws attention to the particular in contrast with the general. These ways of thinking may help us to understand the aspects of education on which this paper focuses.

As argued above (see Chapter 5) for Nietzsche Socratism amounts to a denial of life. He means to show how we resist the meaning that we find in the world. He replaces the basic Socratic notion of responsibility (which in his view expresses philosophical dissatisfaction with life) with a notion of responsiveness (the 'will to power'). What is most important for us cannot be grounded either by metaphysics or by science. It is the lesson of tragedy that what we most care about surpasses our possibilities. His claim against Socratism is not that we must learn to live without reasons, but rather that we must come to see where it no longer makes sense to ask for reasons. The kind of philosophy he is criticising amounts, in his view, to only a spectator's way of making sense. The values Nietzsche envisages arise out of the creative process itself, involving an ever-renewed engagement with the flux of phenomena, with perpetual birth and death, and new birth of existence. Instead of rushing to judge phenomena these values are held at a distance, thus inspiring us and making us wonder. One looks for ways to overcome nihilism which enable us to affirm this world. And it can be seen how that which moves and motivates is part of a larger structure that creates certain objects of desire – though knowing these is of course not being free from them.

Sheridan Hough (1997) accentuates the receptive or passive in Nietzsche's philosophical stance. On the one hand one finds an articulate perspective which provides a reflective account of some sort; on the other hand there is also the embodied perspectives in which we dwell (or which dwell in us). They exist prior to their articulations, both in an individual's life and in the life of the culture. The *Übermensch* is, on Hough's view, not the 'Overman' but a hybrid: he is a free spirit (and so not one who suffers from a restless inability to stop overthrowing norms) joined with a 'higher man' (not burdened with his past) who joyfully celebrates his cultural inheritance. It is therefore not the highest human type; it is not a goal, a being that does not yet exist. Instead it is the *Übermensch* of the *Augenblick* for whom the world has become perfect:

We might therefore conclude that 'the Moment' is the moment of self-acceptance, the moment when Zarathustra can say 'yes' to himself and find himself annealed, completed, quenched, and finished: his yearning for humanity's distant goal is satisfied.

(Hough 1997: 94)

This *Übermensch* is a 'whole', completed being and in this essential respect seems at a remove from the process of self-overcoming. Hough characterises self-overcoming also in terms of an aesthetic aspect (the active dimension, a creative activity that focuses on what can be made of a person) and of a historical dimension, which focuses not on what a person can become, but what a person has become, and so is 'receptive' in its recognition of whatever the self has assimilated and emulated from the many materials it has encountered or experienced. Thus a particular kind of dualism is retained. The *Übermensch* is the human who is 'overcome', the person who is momentarily divested of self in a flash of insight or rapture but who must return to the exigencies of her life, to the particular projects and concerns of which her life is made. The desire to stay in that moment, however, is an invitation to panolepsy, madness, the ultimate denial of her humanity.

In Wittgenstein's work too one finds a parallel anti-metaphysical stance and he too discusses the boundaries of what makes sense. His attention is however much more focused on the micro level of language. His way of doing philosophy provides us with a model of detailed analysis for educational discourse. In the determination of the meaning of a word the context fulfils, according to Wittgenstein, a crucial role. The idea of a 'language-game' is used to express this. Within a system of thinking and acting there occur, up to a point, investigations and criticisms of the reasons and justifications that are employed in that system. We bring this inquiry to an end when we come upon something that we regard as a satisfactory reason, and that we do so shows itself in our actions; then we stop asking questions. The end, Wittgenstein says, 'is not certain propositions' striking us immediately as true, i.e. it is not a kind of *seeing* on our part; it is our *acting*, which lies at the bottom of the language-game' (Wittgenstein 1969: section 204). It is by our actions that we fix a boundary to the 'language-game'. Not only does the meaning of a word turn on the context in which it is learned, but, obviously, there are different contexts in which the word is used, or to put this more technically, there are different 'language-games'. The use of a concept cannot be described without a context and language-games themselves are part of the 'form of life' (see below). Wittgenstein's 'theory' of meaning advocates neither a position of pure subjectivity nor of pure objectivity. From the beginning, what one could call an element of risk is present in the way communication is conceived. In order to be understood (that is, to make sense), the present use may not be radically different from former ones. It is thus within the normal context that the meaning of a concept is determined. As there is no absolute point of reference (neither internal nor external), the community of language speakers forms the warrant for the (consistency) of meaning. With the concept of the 'form of life', Wittgenstein indicates what he considers to be the bedrock of our 'language-games'. These unjustified and unjustifiable patterns of human activities can be seen as the complicated network of rules which constitute language and social life. This 'given' is a whole: it is the 'language-and-the-world'. We cannot place ourselves outside it. Our acting is embedded in a matrix of certainty that precedes our knowledge (the matrix of knowing-and-doubting and knowing-and-'making a mistake'). 'I said I would "combat" the other man – but wouldn't I give him reasons? Certainly; but how far do they go? At the end of reasons comes persuasion. (Think what happens when missionaries convert natives)' (Wittgenstein 1969: section 612). If we try to doubt everything, Wittgenstein argues, we do not get as far as doubting anything: 'The game of doubting itself presupposes certainty' (Wittgenstein 1969: section 115).

It will be clear that Wittgenstein's criticism of the longing for crystalline purity does not only concern epistemology, but also has far-reaching implications for the domain of ethics. The ethical problem confronts us with the claims of other persons. To say that the meaning of 'good' or of 'human' is not once and for all determined, does not mean that it doesn't matter what we do. It is precisely the fact that we have options that means that it is not always evident that we will follow this or that option. Convincing someone on the ethical level is not (simply) a matter of giving them reasons. It is more like a practice in which other people are interactively involved. Being moved by a person seems to be crucial here. It will be recalled that Wittgenstein quoted Goethe: '*Im Anfang war die Tat* (In the beginning was the deed)' (Wittgenstein 1969: section 402). To reach understanding and agreement, one should first of all try to involve one's opponent in a particular 'language-game'. As James Edwards says: 'by playing it to understand its telos from within; to feel for himself its attractions; and thus to recognise the game's internal standards of excellence' (Edwards 1982: 157). This actual participation is important before the opponent can be engaged. A new way of acting is therefore the first requirement.

Both Nietzsche and Wittgenstein thus free us from the meta-physical stance of Platonism. Both insist that we run up against the limits of our language, that we cannot look around our own corner. As Hough believes, Nietzsche's position indicates also the longing for completeness, just as Wittgenstein's directs us to Emersonian perfectionism. There is a line of thinking here that follows from the philosophies of Nietzsche and Wittgenstein and that bears both on educational possibilities in general and on the position of the educator in particular. Before taking up the subject of eros again, we will indicate how in general their position highlights particular educational matters.

Interpreting education

As argued above (see Chapter 5) Nietzsche holds that education aims through devotion at bringing out the very best in someone. It is not defined by the acquisition of facts or skills or technique, but is the transmission of passion and will from teacher to student. What the teacher has to teach is simply not transmissible to a crowd. The educator is to serve as a model for her students, and authority and discipline are considered to be indispensable. Education is not the determination of who the student should be, but of how she might become.

Nietzsche's hostility toward formal, institutionalised education can be understood as expressing his battle against all justificatory tendencies based on firm foundations. His warning can be seen as a way to help us to overcome our insecurity and the rationalisations this generates. He makes it clear that we do not operate in a vacuum of power relations but that these are masked by quasi-arguments. Making sense, overcoming, both refer, though not necessarily, to accepting and acknowledging the world as it is. It is a perpetual task, one of struggling against our unwillingness to let ourselves be intelligible. That all knowledge presupposes experience and that all experience is individual lies for him at the start. But far from being a champion of subjectivism and arbitrariness, Nietzsche is doing more than simply making a logical point about the subject as the locus of giving meaning. Nietzsche's language is rhetorical and necessarily visionary. For education it expresses a mission as urgent as ever: in the end all education crosses over into (what is perhaps not adequately expressed by the concept of) 'self-education'.

From a Wittgensteinian position 'education' can be conceived as a dynamic initiation into a 'form of life'. The educators offer the child the truths by which they themselves live: what moves them, what appeals to them, what supports the idea of 'human being' they offer to the child hoping that he will participate. Of course, what is considered to be important is liable to change, and it could have been different, but it is thus and thus now. Precisely because of the particularity of the context I am answerable for what I do. The lack of an ultimate foundation makes me long for a universality which would free me from this burden and give me certainty. But the kind of absolute certainty that is longed for will reveal itself as a fraud. It haunts my existence and asks for an answer that cannot be given because we cannot live but in the particular. The Wittgensteinian position is threatening to the individual, as it confronts her or him with the fact that not the, but only a, solution is possible; that things are very complicated, that no simple answer will do and that all solutions are conditional; it leaves her or him very literally alone. The only way to deal with this un-groundability consists, according to Wittgenstein, in the acceptance of this unavoidability and, with that, its correlative: one's engagement. That we cannot but act out of what speaks to us and that we cannot answer questions of ultimate justification is the essence of our tragic human existence. It is difficult but not impossible to live with this kind of uncertainty, in the midst, moreover, of the irreconcilable desires of others and what appeals to them. The combination of the 'third person perspective' with authenticity generates a challenging legacy for education.

In Nietzsche's position too there is attention to what someone could in this third person perspective mean for someone else. He views excess as healthy and replaces Aristotelian prudence with extravagance, thus shifting attention from giving material goods to giving of ourselves. Thus, Nietzsche's most completely generous individuals seek greatness of character so that they may give of their moral bounty (cf. Kupfer 1998). Robert Solomon (1998) claims that Nietzsche defends a version of 'virtue ethics' in which not only virtue but passion would take a primary place and emphasizes not aesthetics but 'energy', 'enthusiasm', 'strength', and 'self-mastery' (not, that is, a conquest of the passions but their cultivation). In his opinion Nietzsche has mainly creative power in mind, the power of the artist, the poet: in other words, in some sense a strong self, a passionate but disciplined self, a self that follows its powerful 'instincts' but has 'overcome itself' sufficiently to 'give style to its character', a matter of becoming what you are. Notoriously absent, according to Solomon, are such philosophical virtues as rationality and reflection. A Nietzschean virtue is first of all a kind of fullness, a sense of oneself on top of the world. For him the good life consists not of humility (of wanting no more) but of exuberance, passions, eros, of what he calls simply life.

Building on these insights, Solomon defends the virtues of a passionate life, defined by emotions, by impassioned engagement and belief, by one or more quests, grand projects, embracing affections. The enthusiasm born of love's attachments is the most obvious example of the kind of virtue that it generates. Love of this kind tends to build on itself, to amplify with time, and one tends to find ever more reasons to love – the fact that love often ends does not undermine the thesis that it is an emotional process that is or can be intensified and deepened with protracted intimacy, familiarity, knowledge and understanding, and shared experiences. Though objectively love may be contrary to everything that philosophical ethics likes to emphasise – objectivity, impersonality, disinterestedness, universality, respect for evidence and arguments – it seems that such 'irrationality' constitutes one of our most important and charming moral features. For instance, we care for each other prior to any evidence or arguments that we ought to, find each other beautiful, charming and desirable without reference to common standards. This kind of love is blind; it resembles aesthetic fascination, being in the grip of what enchants. This position echoes Nietzsche in *Twilight of the Idols*: 'The spiritualization of sensuality is called love; it is a great triumph over Christianity' (*TI*, 'Morality as Anti-Nature': section 3). It is erotic love or eros (and not *agape*) that provides the exemplary case for the defence of the passionate life – in the proper sense of both words, for eros has been degraded and reduced to crudest sexual desire, and *agape* has been idealised to the point where it becomes a possible attribute of God alone. But Nietzsche warns us too that our pleasure in ourselves seeks to maintain itself, by always transforming something new into ourselves. Thus sexual love betrays itself most plainly as a striving after possession: the lover wants the unconditioned, sole possession of the person he or she longs for. But Nietzsche also points to another possibility, where that covetous longing of two persons for one another has yielded to a new desire and covetousness, to a common, higher thirst for a superior ideal standing above them whose right name is (reminiscent of Plato) friendship.

To think of love, Solomon further argues, as a virtue is first of all to expand the domain of eros: in the prevalence of self-interested desire it differs from *agape*, but it is not thereby selfish and the desire is not just sexual. It may therefore include a more general physical desire to 'be with' the loved one, as well as such personal desires as 'to be appreciated' and 'to be happy together', such inspirational desires as 'to be the best for you', and such altruistic desires as 'to do anything I can for you'. Solomon argues that the derogation of eros is due to the common mistake of thinking of the other person in the sexual relationship as a mere object of desire (or as degraded to it). He holds that the passionate attachment of one person for another is a virtue because it embodies a form of respect, and because sexuality is the most intimate form of attachment we might say that in sexual love one passionately loves the other person as such. Love, unlike most of the virtues, is exciting, and some of this excitement is sexual (but not seen as simply reduced to arousal). Much of the excitement of sex might better be understood in terms of our vulnerability, our openness to others in an obviously more basic way than specified by many of the recognised virtues. The ultimate reason for the excitement of sexual love can be put in the terms of self-identity, as love might be conceived as defining oneself in and through another person.

How then do educative relationships with one's pupils look from such a stance as this?

Epilogue: Man lernt nur von dem Jenigen, den man liebt[3] (J.W. Goethe)

These reflections may elicit the reaction 'Where will it all end?' It could be taken as a permit, even as a recommendation, for sexual relationships with pupils and students, more generally for a promiscuous life-style in educational contexts. Clearly, this would be an over-simplification. As in all contexts where human beings are involved with each other, ethical issues arise and have to be dealt with. Whether or not one has sex with another person is one of these issues. To deny the proximity of sexual relationships to education – amongst adolescent and older students, and sometimes between students and staff – is obviously absurd. And although legislation may be put in place to deal with what is considered inappropriate behaviour and courts may discipline offenders, this is unlikely to change this particular human inclination. Incidentally, although in many cases educators are surely the instigators, in some the initiative is taken by pupils or students. As in other areas, society will construct (and change) boundaries through legislation and will reflect in this the spirit of its time. But surely the issue of eros in education is altogether broader and more important than this. In so far as education concerning the whole person is at stake, and not just the way one is equipped to function in this or that society as reflected in demands for particular outcomes, in terms, that is, of performativity, it seems that eros is its real nature. We distinguished the body of knowledge from the bodies involved. Our argument goes a lot further than erotetic teaching as it is defined by MacMillan and Garrison (1988): 'it is the intention of teaching acts to answer questions that students ought to ask concerning the subject matter with which the teacher and student are engaged' (ibid.: 15–16). We agree that the subject being taught has to be seen in 'seductive terms', but we also accept that there is some role for learners in determining the content of what is taught, so that, as it is argued by many, hitherto unheard voice will find their place.

In the history of western thought, the mind/body dichotomy has certainly privileged the mind as that which defines human being while the body has been interrogated as the excess baggage of human agency. It is not so much that the human body as a physical essence has been ignored – educators have certainly stressed its importance in relation to the training of young people, a healthy mind in a healthy body – but the body's importance has been perceived generally in terms of the necessity of its careful management in order to enhance, or to avoid distracting from, the mental. With the recovery of 'the body' (understood both as the body of a human being and as a subject, a discipline of study), it comes to be seen how 'desire' has been excluded from rational discourses. Understanding that sex, gender, race, skin, blood are indeterminate and unstable signifiers of the differences and similarities between bodies requires attention not to the issue of the real make-up of bodies, but to how the idea of the body is constructed. Bodies become relational, territorialised in specific ways, made up through the production of their spatial registers, through relations of power. Contrary to Plato for whom the content of education and the way the position of the educator was conceived were closely linked – both necessarily aimed at what is beyond them – contemporary ways of thinking enjoin us to distinguish fundamentally, if not radically, the content and the position of the educator.

That the body of knowledge is taught by someone to someone else and that, within this, attraction and dislike (among other things such as power) inevitably play their part is not necessarily to be deplored. In dealing with education, Nietzsche speaks of the transmission of passion and will from teacher to students. And although the Nietzschean educator is not looking for the love of her pupils, it follows from her position that she is not afraid of seeing the pupils in their full humanity, and this includes the carnality of the body. The teacher is the person who captures desire and turns it into a desire for the subject. It is difficult to see how this could be otherwise, how else than through love and trust for someone one would find the energy and the 'lust' to engage oneself in something difficult, demanding and new. From the fact that there are dangers in relationships it is not quite right just to forbid them: where there is danger, there is also potential.

Changes in demography, economic structure and lifestyle in contemporary society have led to diminished opportunities for adults to be meaningfully involved in the lives of children. As it is difficult now to find time to spend with young people, inter-generational bonds are difficult to form and without these, as Judith Deiro (1996) argues, the older generation has a hard time playing a key role in shaping the emotional and social development of young people. Teachers are potentially a rich resource for rebuilding the network of supportive, caring adults needed by young children, and for this reason we educators may need to reframe our primary professional responsibilities to include the development of stimulating and healthy relationships with students. Healthy influential relationships are characterised as focused on the promotion of growth and change, fostering independence through encouraging the internalisation of learning, and respectful use of the asymmetry of power. Referring to Nel Noddings and other authors, Deiro claims, contrary to the traditional position referred to in the beginning of the paper, that teachers ought to take a more active role in nurturing students. But altering the purpose of the relationship more along the lines of an expressive or emotional relationship – a relationship formed for the purpose of friendship, romance, love and marriage – is, she argues, inappropriate and unhealthy (Deiro 1996: 14). Thus, she advises: 'Only when two individuals who were involved in an influential relationship are separated for a significant period of time, usually two years, and then meet again on an equal footing is the development of an expressive-emotional relationship ethically defensible' (Deiro 1996: 15). One may wonder whether what is going on here is a denial at the cognitive level of the situation teachers and students find them-selves in as if just by issuing this commandment possible emotional involvements cease to exist.

A more balanced view that does justice to the nature of things is argued for by Stuart Piddocke, Romulo Magsino and Michael Manley-Casimir (1997). Exploring the normative character of teaching in the book *Teachers in Trouble* they distinguish 'inherent necessities' of teaching from 'adventitious content'. To the first belong, for example, that the teacher must be respected by the student if the teacher's messages are to be positively accepted and learned; to the latter subjects and skills on the one hand and moral or social habits on the other. Particularly when the teacher has to teach values such as appropriate attitudes to authority, the duties and rights of citizenship, appropriate attitudes concerning gender, and the like, her off-the-job conduct might well be expected to illustrate these attitudes and ideals. Because the teacher is in a position of authority over the pupil and could use that authority to impose sexual activities upon or to induce sexual favours from the pupil our confidence in the integrity of the teaching becomes shaken. They refer to the case of 'Come sleep with me and I'll give you a good grade in the exam', as well as to the situation of the pupil who is 'street-wise' and aware of the teacher's desire, where the pupil may try to seduce the teacher and exchange sexual favours in return for preferential treatment: 'If you give me a good grade on my exam, I'll sleep with you'. Concerning sexual liaisons with students they advise:

> Sexual liaisons with students, in which the student is a consenting partner to the relationship, imply that the student is older than in the preceding class of cases [paedophilia]. Because the teacher is responsible to persons other than the student, sexual relations between teacher and student will necessarily interfere with the teaching. When such liaisons involve consent by a student who is fully informed of the implications of the liaison, this offense is less heinous than paedophilia.
>
> (Piddocke, Magsino and Manley-Casimir 1997: 100)

In a footnote, the basic rationale of their position is made clear:

> This is because the teacher, besides to the students, is in fact responsible to the school, the community, the profession, the state, and so on, to ensure that the student gets a certain training and that examination results reflect the actual attainments of the student. If the teacher/student relationship was between only the teacher and the student, and both were consenting adults, an exchange of sexual favours in return for the teacher's skill and knowledge would be a fair bargain. But this situation does not happen in the public schools, or in any institution which issues certificates that are to be respected in the general society.
>
> (Ibid.: 278)

Far from thus denying what may happen, they make clear that the code of conduct refers to particular professional and societal demands which reflect the *Zeitgeist*.

For Nietzsche, as incidentally for Wittgenstein, embeddedness is our natural condition and looking for crystalline purity leads to idle talk and makes us go astray. Both go beyond dualism and scepticism, both accept the necessary materiality of a particular culture. Wittgenstein's insights make abundantly clear how it is that practice determines meaning (and thus a particular body of knowledge – Giroux's analysis demonstrates this in exemplary fashion). They also confront us with the threat they pose for the individual in terms of a particular 'way of looking at things'. Wittgenstein also points to the fact that doubting comes after belief, and he insists on the unavoidability of persuasion.

Will McNeill (1998) argues that the art of philosophising as practised by Michel Foucault is nothing other than the attempt to be attentive to the wonder we 'see' in the eyes of another human being (in his or her living embodiment, in their ethos – which originally refers to where one dwells ontologically, the place from which we emerge and to which we return in showing ourselves in a particular manner of being in each case), as a radiance, a shining whose provenance is obscure and which may itself become largely concealed. To experience wonder in one's existence is to pause, to hesitate before something unknown, to have time to dwell for a moment in the presence of other beings, to deliberate, to think, to hesitate amid the commitment of one's existence, to pause before rushing headlong, to cultivate perhaps a sense of time (cf. McNeill 1998: 61–2). This ethical dwelling has to be cultivated through the experiences and practices of the self. These abilities cannot simply be taught; they must be learned or acquired by practices of self-formation, exercises in which one's own singularity is engaged, renewed, and where necessary transformed. Unlike the ordinary citizen who settles into a routine way of being, the philosopher is unwilling to let the relationship with himself stagnate or become complacent. His existence is nomadic, and therefore to say that the appropriate care of the self is a philosophical task is simply to reiterate that ethical existence has never been accomplished by anyone. But Foucault also describes in *The Use of Pleasure* (1985) how for the elite of classical Greece desire was merely one element in a dynamic ensemble that also included pleasure and action: this aphrodisia consisted of learning to manage one's life so as to be respected in the *polis* and to be fit to lead, so as to shape a beautiful life, one's own and others'. In his opinion it is bodies and pleasure, therefore, that make better rallying points for counterattacking the normalised correlate of desire (that is, sexual object) than the way sex and desire are institutionalised.

There are many kinds of love affairs and there are no universal rules that define the roles of lovers. Having sex or not, living together or not, giving special consideration or not to one another's interests and needs, wanting a relationship to become public or permanent, sharing financial resources, the issues could be extended almost indefinitely. There are lovers who want permanence and there are lovers who don't; there are lovers who are best friends, and there are lovers who aren't. Perhaps education could be seen as a love affair of a particular kind in which 'pleasure' is sought on both sides and on different levels. Instead of a detached enterprise focused on performativity and skills, it might be a personal fulfilling relationship with its own intrinsic ends. And would it be so preposterous to suggest that it is through this personal involvement that one finds the resources and energy to enjoy more mundane relationships, and – to express this in more utopian terms – to challenge and change society's practices of inclusion and exclusion?

A philosophical problem is for Wittgenstein among others things characterised by 'a problem someone has'. Here one is confronted with what touches the heart of all education. In so far as we care for the one to be educated we will necessarily want the best for her – wise teachers see the possible beyond the constraints of the actual – which is in a Hegelian and Lacanian way also 'the best for us'. Clearly a genuine education will be philosophical, as it is philosophy as love of wisdom that puts the big questions and uncertainties of human life on the agenda. Is it surprising then that dealing with this in the lusty enthusiastic way with which Socrates approached the subject (joyful wisdom) is itself erotic? For Nietzsche too philosophers create themselves by virtue of their signature practices of self-experimentation as artworks of surpassing beauty, and so as objects of eros. The genuine philosopher lives unphilosophically, unwisely, above all imprudently, feels the burden and the duty of a hundred attempts and delights in these: he is both an experimenter and a seducer (cf. *BGE*: section 205). As Daniel Conway argues, 'Only when engulfed in madness of eros would human beings ever attempt to overcome or transcend their natural limitations' (in Kemal *et al.* 1998).

To give shape to what is of such importance indeed keeps desire going. It would be foolish to give that up by bringing an end to all the ambiguity that surrounds it – a satisfaction we would not want to deny ourselves.

Notes

1 While eros is discussed in the *Phaedrus*, it is its explicit association with education in the *Symposium* that is central to the discussion here.
2 Diotima is the non-historical character of the Priestess of Mantinea whose doctrines belong to the Platonic Socrates.
3 'One learns only from someone whom one loves'.

Chapter 12

Taking ignorance seriously

Ignorance is an evil weed, which dictators may cultivate among their dupes, but which no democracy can afford among its citizens.
W.H. Beveridge, *Full Employment in a Free Society*, 1944, Pt. 7.

'There is a vast deal of difference in memories, as well as in everything else, and therefore you must make allowance for your cousin, and pity her deficiency.
And remember that, if you are ever so forward and clever yourselves, you should always be modest; for, much as you know already, there is a great deal more for you to learn.'
'Yes, I know there is, till I am seventeen . . .'
Jane Austen, *Mansfield Park*, Ch. 2

Whenever you hear a man speak of 'realism', you may always be sure that this is the prelude to some bloody deed.
attrib. Sir Isaiah Berlin (Ignatieff 1998: 225)

'I know nothing, except that I know nothing', said Socrates, at least according to Diogenes Laertius in the *Lives of the Philosophers*. If this is supposedly the best known dictum of the fountainhead of western philosophy, surely it deserves to be taken seriously, not least by educators, who are principally concerned with knowledge.

Notoriously, Nietzsche set himself against everything that Socrates seemed to him to stand for. In particular, he viewed the dialectic as a practice of systematic evasion of any serious engagement with the tragic urgency of existence and the imperative of action. Minute dissections of argument, he believed, functioned principally as distractions from commitment.

Today, we are perhaps more cautious than Nietzsche in distinguishing the historic Socrates, glimpsed rather vaguely in the earlier Platonic dialogues, from the fiction who is Plato's own mouthpiece in his later writings. We might feel Nietzsche's proper target is Plato rather than Socrates. In this famous throwaway remark, we find perhaps a Socrates much closer to Nietzsche than Nietzsche expected. We suggest that they share at least one important virtue, that they both take ignorance seriously. And our first motive in thinking for a while about Socrates here is the light it might shed on this Nietzschean theme; this seems to us more helpful than struggling with melodramatic Nietzschean overstatement. So how might a modern philosopher try to make sense of Socrates' claim? As we will argue, contemporary educators would benefit from a serious answer. There are a number of possibilities.

Socrates' understanding of ignorance, and our own

The simplest approach should be noted first. 'Poor Socrates', it might be said, 'here was a man yearning for an education, at a time and in a place where none (or none that would satisfy us) was available. Academic study just wasn't sufficiently advanced for him.' Now this is obviously naïvely inappropriate as a response – there is surely something ethically more challenging that Socrates has in mind – but it highlights the attitude to ignorance which is arguably fundamental to all modern education of any kind. Ignorance is seen today as just a lack, a gap to be filled in, a debility to be cured. This attitude seems as fundamental to any progressivism as to the most rigid educational conservatism: the difference lies only in the scope and nature of the knowledge they want. If we call this dismissive antagonism to ignorance a 'modern' attitude, we root it in the optimistic assumptions about knowledge and ambitions for its use and dissemination of the eighteenth-century Enlightenment.

A second approach might be more of a tetchy rebuke to the Master. 'Look, Socrates, this just cannot be the case. When we say of someone that they don't know that p, that is an assertion that stands in need of evidence, just as much as any other claim. And evidence is knowledge of some sort or it just isn't evidence at all. So to claim you are ignorant of one thing is also in itself to lay claim to some other kind of knowledge.' For instance, we know that the world's great biotech companies just don't know what will be the ecological effects of genetically modified crops because we know that they haven't done enough appropriate research. We know of their (and our) ignorance because we know something else about them. By the same token, but paradoxically, Socrates would have to know a very great deal indeed in order to be able to risk such a sweeping statement, that he 'knows nothing', and thus this statement must be taken as self-refuting. (And indeed, modest claims of everyday fact do actually litter the Socratic dialogues, contrary to his claim. How could it be otherwise?)

Now this approach too would be absurdly unsympathetic to Socrates, but it isn't irrelevant to our debate – we will come back to it. However, it may get rather nearer the mark to take Socrates' aphorism as an early groping after that repudiation of foundations or the sense of unlimited fallibility of knowledge claims that characterise contemporary epistemology. Perhaps this is Socrates (not Plato) registering a sense of futility in the ambition of proving any knowledge claims at all, just as Lakatos has argued that a fact is in principle not the kind of thing that can be proven (Lakatos 1970: 91–196), or as Quine has argued that no proposition is ever beyond correction, because there is no such thing as analytic truth (Quine 1960). After all, Socrates' practice is dramatically different from that of earlier Greek thinkers who can properly be seen as reductionists and thus foundationalists of some sort, arguing for instance that 'fundamentally' everything is water (Thales) or fire (Anaximander). Perhaps he was the first to glimpse the inevitable failure of foundationalist projects – an insight long overlooked in western philosophy.

If this were the right interpretation, Socrates' claim would be cademically intriguing yet would have lost its ethical potency for us. Neither Lakatos nor Quine nor any other major post-foundationalist thinker is in business to argue to the position of 'Ignorance, all is ignorance'. (On the contrary, both are devoted to scientific progress.) The interest of postfoundationalist claims lies elsewhere, and this is not the place to pursue it.[1] But we have been 'playing dumb' so far. All philosophers know that the real interest of this claim of Socrates – if indeed he made it – lies in its relation to his practice in dialogue, dialogue as philosophy and as pedagogy. As we all know, his brilliance as a teacher and his seminal influence for western civilisation lay not in the things he told people but rather in the questions he asked them. His ambition was not so much to clarify the epistemological status of the things being told (though this was often incidentally necessary for him), but primarily not to 'tell things' at all. His practice was not strictly even a form of fallibilism. When he puts a counter-instance to a friend who has made a generalisation, his aim is not to knock the generalisation into a more precise, modest and defensible (scientific) form, but typically to get the friend to stop making that kind of generalisation at all, and to start looking for a better way to answer the question, typically by pursuing a sort of conceptual analysis (rather different from our own, of course). Plato's Socrates – we aren't sure about the real one – is a sophisticated methodologist. To have made a whole civilisation self-conscious about the kinds of question it asks was in itself a titanic intellectual achievement.

But important as it is to learn to take questions seriously, this still doesn't seem like getting to the heart of Socrates' thinking about ignorance. We have to ask why this methodological scruple seemed imperative. It's a good question for us today, because methodological scruple has never seemed more imperative to the way we think and thus to the way we live. Perhaps Socrates' reasons may help us to better understand our own.

There are unlikely to be definitive answers here – certainly we offer none ourselves, but speculation is valid at this point. It seems wrong to take Socrates' claim of ignorance as simply an early version of scepticism. His practice in dialogue is too seriously committed to finding answers to important questions – usually ethically important. And as we hinted above, usually Socrates actually does have simple claims of fact to make. As Wittgenstein would put it, in dialogue he often 'assembles reminders for a purpose', points out to his friends familiar and relevant facts or reasonable assumptions which they have typically overlooked. So Socrates' remark is not well taken as an expression of epistemological scepticism.

We suggest it is better viewed as a reminder of an important aspect of the human condition. Knowledge does not fall readily into our lap, nor is 'the real' so easily distinguished from the unreal. Socrates is not sure he has ever achieved knowledge: it might be fairer to say that he fears that he 'knows nothing', rather than that he knows it. After all, it seems obvious that we lead much if not most of our lives more or less in a state of partial or relative ignorance. (For instance, if we have any sense, we read our newspapers with a sceptical eye. Do they really tell us just what's going on? Often we know that they cannot do so and sometimes they admit it themselves.) Yet if our lives are the worse for our ignorance, they are not, for all that, impossible or worthless. After all, if Socrates himself 'knows nothing', he is hardly one of life's dupes or villains but rather the contrary. And surely there is more integrity in admitting our ignorance, as he did, than pretending too easily to conquer it. Perhaps we are not even quite sure, then, why ignorance is actually a problem?

(These questions and attitudes, let us notice immediately, are utterly remote from the practice of contemporary professional educationists, who are much too busy to play thought games about ignorance. Ignorance is what you put right, as quickly and efficently as possible. As we noted, with dissent, in Chapter 1, David

Reynolds, for instance, calls uninhibitedly for a 'risk-free' (i.e. error-free) education for all. 'We can do it!')
    But why should we see ignorance as just part of the human condition? And what does it imply for education if we do? What's wrong with the Enlightenment ambition of conquering ignorance in pursuit of the maximum possible social and individual happiness – not a trivial or contemptible ambition, notwithstanding Nietzsche's disdain?[2] And first, how might a perception of ineradicable ignorance inform philosophic and pedagogic practice?

Ignorance as the human condition or as lack?

Socrates believes in learning. The dialogues are exercises in a kind of teaching, after all. But as object lessons, they demonstrate that knowledge itself is hard won, provisional and easily misunderstood, forgotten or mislaid. (Never utterly and helplessly mislaid of course – the immortality of the soul and its memories is guarantee against that, or at least so Plato thought.) Over and again in the dialogues, Socrates takes his partners back to first principles. It is rarely, if ever, a case of, 'Remember what we learned when we were talking some time ago?' and taking off from there. To rely on what we think we already know is to rely on something unreliable. Socrates' project is not the modern one of 'forcing back the boundaries of knowledge': the idea of 'cutting edge research' would have made no sense to him. And even for Plato, with his very un-Socratic interest in programme-building and social engineering, the business of the Philosopher Kings is not to be one of an accumulation of wisdom, as in case law, for instance, but rather of an intensification in contemplation of the Good, and of just action 'illuminated' by this apprehension. Better judgement is achieved not through judicial practice and experience, but through deeper contemplation of the abstract Idea or Form of the Good. The value of contemplation lay as much in a personal abstraction from delusion, trivia, fantasy, opinion and private interest as in anything we might call propositional knowledge. (Indeed, language itself could be delusory, an inappropriate 'medium' for knowledge.) Knowledge of the Good is for Plato a personal and moral state of being rather than a propositional inroad on ignorance. Knowledge of the Good does not edge forward as each scientific paper adds minutely to the sum of human wisdom. *Theoria* was not theory.
    Thus, to know that you know nothing was, for Plato and probably for Socrates, to understand the inherently delusory nature of the world in which one lives. Knowledge, for Plato, is knowledge of a realm beyond the mundane, which shows knowledge in the

mundane world itself to be at best true opinion. It was thus to recognise an inescapable constraint on one's exercise of the intellect. And these were predicaments deeper than mere fallibility. Ignorance was more than a 'lack' of precision or accuracy or the simple absence of knowledge yet to come. Therefore it was morally imperative to understand this when entering into thoughtful discussion of the most urgent questions of how we are to live. (Compare too the moral impulse which arguably drives Kant's, and indeed Hume's, wish to investigate the limits of human understanding: the wish to avoid the perils of overwheening confidence in spurious knowledge claims.) All such exercises must begin by acknowledging ignorance. Ignorance, for Socrates and Plato, is a constant companion whose presence must be honourably acknowledged in any serious dialogue.

Does such a picture of life have anything to say to us today? After all, unless we are extreme sceptics (and most philosophers have learned not to be), we now know that we do know something, just as Socrates did, if only at a modest level and despite his claim to the contrary. In fact, we know that we know a very great deal. Hawking speaks incautiously of 'reading the mind of God'. Biologists begin to read the human genome and seem poised to create new life in the test tube. We could go on at length here. So is there any room left today for any conception of ignorance as fundamental to our lives and which might be important for education? What this question comes to, we suggest, is whether it is reasonable to continue to think of ignorance as simply some kind of lack, waiting to be made good, or whether it still has some more positive significance, even for us. Is it still helpful to acknowledge ignorance as inevitable and as a perennial constraint on our thinking?

An initial move in questioning the view of ignorance as mere 'lack' could be to query whether the balance of knowledge and ignorance forms a 'zero sum game' – whether every advance in knowledge should be thought of as constituting a corresponding erosion of ignorance. We are actually all familiar with the idea that this is wrong, that the more we learn, the more aware we also become of the extent of our ignorance. For instance, in discovering America, Columbus literally discovered a continent of things unknown (to Europeans!). This phenomenon needs no explaining: it is easily understood. But perhaps we find it less remarkable than we should. Are we not too easily tempted to think of both our knowledge and our ignorance as having potentially some objective designation and thus an ontological reality independent of our own thinking, as if some God's eye view could specify the extent of our ignorance, without reference to our own estimate of it? If so, we could tell ourselves that even though advances in knowledge make us subjectively aware of a larger extent of ignorance, nonetheless the 'real' balance is simply shifted in favour of knowledge and away from ignorance, however things might otherwise appear. It may not look like a 'zero sum' to us, but really it is. More knowledge equals less ignorance.

But if we take a more constructivist view of knowledge, which post-foundationalists arguably must do, then we can't sensibly talk about the 'real' extent of an ignorance of which everyone is nonetheless wholly unaware. Unless we have some awareness of a set of valid questions to which, as it happens, we have no answers, then we can't even talk about ignorance in those respects. If we think of ignorance like this, we see it as being at least partly constructed by our understanding of valid but unanswered questions. And then we might be well advised to think that sometimes processes of learning actually create ignorance as part and parcel of the creation of new knowledge, and of ignorance as the inevitable shadow of knowledge. For instance, until Röntgen discovered X-rays, we could not even describe our ignorance of their properties; so that along with the construction of some knowledge of them there also came a construction of a degree of relative ignorance of them.

So perhaps we should think not just of the advance of know-ledge, but of knowledge and ignorance both advancing hand in hand. And if so, perhaps we can begin to glimpse a value in the advance of ignorance, as part and parcel of the advance of knowledge. Phenomenologically, someone who knows how much she doesn't know lives in a 'bigger, wider world' than someone who has no such awareness of ignorance. And perhaps this changes for the better the kind of person she is. Nietzsche sometimes uses the figure of a man climbing a mountain, which vouchsafes to him the inspiration of wider horizons. But the climb reveals to him an ignorance of a yet wider terrain beyond the broader horizon. Similarly, we can begin here to glimpse the positive aspect of ignorance, if only as a kind of 'higher order' knowledge, of 'knowing what you don't know'. And this at least seems wholly compatible with a modern world view.

Ignorance banished from education

We can begin to see useful educational implications here. 'Knowing what you don't know' doesn't come easily or unreflectively. It is not an immediate corollary of what you do know. A science specialist has a much richer, wider and more articulated conception of what she might not yet know about X-rays, for instance, than the layman.

Educating other specialists in appreciation of the nature and extent of this ignorance is a significant educational task. It is likely to involve drawing comparisons and analogies with what is known or not not known in other areas. It is also likely to involve an understanding of why this or that particular aspect of ignorance is important, and the possible implications of finding answers.

We would not claim any great profundity in this insight, but as we begin to see, the shift in perspective might have an educational value. Many will share the perception that ours has become a remarkably incurious society in recent years. We seem to have become so used to the luxuries of knowledge that areas of ignorance begin to seem almost scandalous. 'They' ought to know the answers to any questions our day-to-day lives throw up. It is just a bit of an embarrassment that the medics still have no cure for Alzheimer's or that the economists have no agreed understanding of the effects of free trade on Third World poverty. 'They' just ought to get together and sort them out, pronto. Besides, isn't 'everything out there on the Web', as we're superstitiously told? How can there be any excuses for ignorance, now that 'we have the technology'?

If society seems in danger of 'dumbing down', then perhaps our new superstitions promote not so much an encroachment of ignorance, but rather a glib new underestimation of its relative intractability. Knowledge actually remains hard to get, however easy it becomes to publish it, and we might live in a better world if this were better understood. A shared picture of knowledge and ignorance coming forward together and inextricably intertwined would surely have a salutary educational effect.

Or is this straining at a gnat? Is contemporary educational practice really so inhospitable to a proper appreciation of the nature and value of ignorance that it makes any difference to actual educational practice? We do think so, in fact. Consider the new emphasis on targets, outcomes and accountability, or the new approaches to study in higher education and the ongoing divorce case between teaching and research.

Take first the contemporary emphasis, widespread in the developed and developing world, on outcomes and targets in education. Educators at every level are increasingly pressured to specify the 'learning outcomes' they seek to secure for their pupils or students. But from our point of view here, this is immediately worrying. To specify the intended outcomes of a course of study is to specify some termini of it. It does not look beyond the course to the further uses or interests which the student might draw from the study – that's just not the educator's business. It takes little interest in the nature of the remaining ignorance or what, if anything, the student might be educated to do about it or why they might care, beyond a facile nod towards the ideal of 'learning to learn'. Julia, from *Mansfield Park*, would be at home with this outlook. She has much to learn, indeed, 'until I am seventeen'. But having 'learned to learn' will be one more obsolete achievement for her, come her birthday. Thus this approach betrays the contemporary indifference to the nature and structure of ignorance. Who cares what our modern Julias don't know? It's what they do know that matters, and little else.

But this is rarely seen as objectionable, except by those who resent the deep encroachment of bureaucracy that specification of outcomes involves. And these objectors in turn are immediately suspected of at best woolly-mindedess and, perhaps more likely, evasion of responsibility. After all, the universal aim in education today is indeed supposedly 'raising standards'. This is an insincere ambition, a desultory aim, it seems, unless one sets explicit targets for improvement. But whether or not we 'hit the target' can only be gauged by statistical monitoring of learning outcomes. (This is a transparency model, aiming at maximised accountability. Again, Reynolds' ambition for an error-free education comes to mind.) And besides, why should target-setting be seen as objectionable? After all, it is only a 'modernised' version of the axiom that education needs aims and objectives if it is to be a worthwhile and justifiable activity – isn't it?

Well no, in fact, it isn't. The traditional request for more or less explicit aims requires the educator to answer the question, 'Why are you teaching this course?' And this allows an answer in terms of the general value of the discipline in the development of mind or in the furtherance of vocational and instrumental knowledge. These are appropriate aims for education. And this kind of answer can be refined to justify the more specific topic or area under disscussion. If objectives are also demanded for a course, these can be specified as ideal minimum achievements for the student. And all this is fair enough, because none of it specifies any terminus. This way of conceiving education is quite compatible with the concern that the best educators always used to have, that their teaching should not just lodge in the mind but transform the student to some degree, and send her off on a journey of her own of indefinitely rich development, for either vocational or purely personal or indeed social and moral reasons.

All this is lost when the question of aims is recast as a question of intended outcomes. For 'Why are you teaching this?' we now substitute the quite different question 'Why do you want the student to know this?'. Attention becomes narrowly focussed on the 'positive' of what is taught, to the neglect of what hasn't been or can't be taught here and now but might be investigated by the student at a later date, and which used to be seen as the prime interest which a successful student took away from her education: understanding of her own ignorance and of how she can fruitfully trim it back in some ways, whilst inevitably and fruitfully extending it in others, along with an eagerness to do so. Without appreciation of ignorance, the necessary and inspiring shadow of knowledge, the hectic accumulation of knowledge becomes a sophisticated form of stupidity. The student finds herself barricaded in a world of knowledge (increasingly often renamed 'information', of course), bereft of curiosity or the potential for development. She loses autonomy. (And quite how this is supposed to enhance 'flexibility' in a new globalised economy is wholly unclear.)

This degradation in the conception of education which subtends the supposed drive for higher standards is reflected in the language we now use to describe the process of higher education. We speak now of 'teaching and learning' and, what's more, seem increasingly apologetic about the 'teaching' side of it. Learning is all. Learning is what 'really' matters. Higher education does not exist for the benefit of teachers (what a scandalous idea! – as if teachers' interest in the future of the knowledge they hand down were legitimate or selfless!). Teachers' intrusion on the sacred process of student learning had better be shown to be entirely necessary, or it will look like a narcissistic or ideologically motivated imposition on the learner's freedom.

But what is lost in this newly antiseptic language of higher education is attention to less easily monitored and measured aspects of advanced study – interpretation, evaluation, critique and judgement, not to say actual engagement in debate. None of these modes of engagement with a subject can properly be assimilated to learning, not least because, for all their importance, they all necessarily lack determinate 'outcomes'. (We can be sure that some zealous apparatchik somewhere will be fiddling definitions to 'prove' that this is 'of course' part and parcel of 'teaching and learning'. But there are some things casuistry just can't buy.)

One way of describing the problem posed for the New Accountability by interpretation, evaluation, critique and judgement, for instance, is that they all require engagement as much with what we don't know as with what we do know – with the extent and nature of our ignorance. And public ignorance can only be indefinitely specified and never measured. (Of course one might measure private ignorance of a circumscribed realm of public knowledge, but that's not our problem.) The focus on teaching and learning is just as inimical to taking ignorance seriously as the narrow concern with outcomes. (It also dictates the worrying and increasingly wide divorce between the realm of teaching, intellectually ever more closed, and the intrinsically open-ended realm of research.)

If we see the inadequacy of these educational practices and values, perhaps we can begin to see why it would be valuable to reinstate a view of ignorance as fundamental to our lives and important in education.

A modern view of the condition of ignorance

If we see how knowledge creates correlative areas of ignorance, but remember too the anti-sceptical point made near the beginning of this essay – that necessarily we must know something and probably quite a lot – then it seems a necessary feature of the human condition to be not simply knowledgeable or simply ignorant, but to partake of a great deal of both knowledge and ignorance, each mixed up with the other. But this remains so far a speculative picture, to a degree. For of course, after the construction of our ignorance of X-rays, for instance, comes the construction of more and deeper knowledge of them. It seems reasonable to expect to find ourselves continually confronted with ever more challenges to knowledge, ever-expanding areas of ignorance which then contract, and yet then, for some unanticipated reason, expand again. But we do not have an argument yet to show why this must be so. We seem to be dealing with contingent wisdom about ignorance rather than philosophical assurance. And the concept of ignorance as lack, and faith in its eventual fulfilment, still seem intrinsic to knowledge in this picture. Ignorance is still seen fundamentally as something that can in principle be 'filled in'.

Perhaps we can get nearer to a view of ignorance as inherent in life, and edge further from the idea of mere lack, first by taking more seriously the notion of the construction of knowledge. We do not mean here that knowledge is arbitrary or that we can construct 'knowledge' of the world as however we might wish it to be. We do not think of knowledge as unconstrained in its construction. On the contrary, in talking of 'construction' we see the primary constraint as that of critique by competent fellow investigators. And where such critique rests on claims of fact, we agree with Wittgenstein that the only ultimate guarantee of fact is 'agreement in judgements' by users of the language in question. Since no such agreement is guaranteed, this need for agreement in itself is a constraint. 'What knowledge isn't' in such a picture is anything passively read off from the world, as if the world were a library of mosaïc tablets, handed from God to Man in the furnace of the Burning Bush. We accept, with both Wittgenstein and Gadamer, that such processes of argument and incidents of agreement take place within historical and traditional contexts of language, discourse and interpretation. And, with Habermas, we might point to an internally necessary ethic of discourse which distinguishes rational from coerced consensus, genuine from forced agreement in judgements. Thus, the construction of knowledge is not in any way an exercise in irrationality. But the point in insisting on the constructed nature of knowledge is to emphasise its necessary partiality on the one hand, determined by the interests of human beings, be they fundamental or fleeting, and on the other, the intrinsic role of human creativity in the extension of knowledge.

From within such a view, it becomes easier to see ignorance as intrinsic to our condition. There might be a number of ways of doing so. We will indicate a possibility for the sake of argument rather than as proof. One might start by turning to Chomsky for a guarantee of the nature of human creativity. Chomsky's fundamental contribution to epistemology is the insight that competent linguistic performance, our ability to construct grammatically correct sentences which we had never heard others use before us, could only be understood on the hypothesis that we understand a grammar of 'deep' rules which can be applied iteratively. But since their output is mathematically indefinitely large, it must be an implication of our competence in using language that we can always say something new. And insofar as this iterative ability seems also to be an aspect of semantics (Seuren 1974), then the conceptual content of the new things we say seems also indefinitely extendable.

Having said this, we might then turn back to Quine or Lakatos for arguments to fallibilism, to the impossibility of defending any claim against the remote possibility of disproof. Between Chomsky on the one hand and Quine on the other, the potential for advances in ignorance, no less than in knowledge, does begin to seem highly plausible. We seem to have an indefinite capacity to entertain thoughts whose truth we do not know. Moreover, we could never know all we might want to know because fallibility is ineradicable. If we desist from saying this thesis is 'guaranteed', it's because that would generate a self-refuting paradox. We would be claiming to know securely that knowledge was never secure. But happily we don't need a guarantee and so we can avoid the paradox. Reasonable belief in ineluctable ignorance is reasonable enough.

Socrates showed us that we need to take ignorance seriously. And it can seem to be as pervasive for us as for him. The difference is that we get our ignorance with heavy admixtures of knowledge too, and this changes the problem for us. Socrates can't give us everything we need now to think responsibly about the problem.

Ignorance as psychologically necessary

So we need to look more closely at 'ignorance in action', taking its ineluctability as given, just as Socrates did, but for somewhat different reasons. We need to ask what kind of constraint it is for us and what that implies for education. But the epistemological emphasis of the argument so far is not educationally helpful. It focuses on knowledge claims taken in a somewhat abstracted way, lifted out of their context in human interaction. In doing so, it sounds like an argument which might illuminate the teaching of the sciences or perhaps some reductive versions of history, for instance – an education focussed on 'facts'. (We shall return to ths kind of curriculum later, to see it as problematic in its indifference to ignorance.) But education just will not fulfil its most important functions unless it also has to do with the worlds of personal and social relations, explored in history (on a richer model), literature and the other arts, religious and ethical studies, in social and cultural activities such as music, drama and sports, in sociology and other kinds of social studies, including economics and geography, and doubtless much else. And the point fundamental to all these kinds of study is that whilst our relationships, personal and social, have aspects of 'facticity' or ontological objectivity about them, they remain nonetheless in a sense our own creations. Occasionally they may be private creations, but more usually, of course, they are socially constructed and with reference to histories, societies, discourses and traditions. What's intriguing, we suggest, is to investigate the ignorance we construct alongside and intertwined with our knowledge of the realm of the social, the personal and the psychological. Is this ignorance simply another lack? Or is it rather a kind of constraint which is integral to these realms of experience: a constraint which must be properly understood and respected, if education is not to be mis-education?

The three 'Masters of Suspicion' in European culture each viewed ignorance as unavoidable. Nietzsche we have noted already. But Marx too saw ignorance as inevitable in anything less than a fully communist state, though unlike Nietzsche he saw this as purely a negative matter. Once labour relations were fully released from alienation, then 'false consciousness', ignorance in the form of active delusions, could be escaped. Certainly each of the three 'Masters' shared the Enlightenment view that where ignorance reigned, there too power operated and played 'dirty games'. (Michel Foucault is the one who added, 'not just where ignorance reigns – perhaps knowledge itself is even worse implicated in the ploys of power'.) But you do not have to align your views with any particular philosopher to accept that there are problems which intertwine knowledge and ignorance with problems of power. We want to turn to the third of the Masters of Suspicion. Perhaps Freud can inform our view of the workings of ignorance in a way that illuminates its presence as a worthwhile constraint in our lives, and not just a mere lack. We have found Adam Phillips' essay 'The Death of Freud'[3] (Phillips 1999) richly suggestive here.

The central theme of Phillips' essay is Freud's lifelong loathing and hatred for biographers. For Freud, the biographer was an opportunistic intruder on his own territory. Part of the task of a psychoanalyst is to help her client come to terms with his past in a way that makes possible a more autonomous future: to replace, as Freud said, neurotic (compulsive or constraining) misery with ordinary human unhappiness. Thus the psychoanalyst shares with the classic educational theorist a concern with personal autonomy – a reason, surely, for attending to what he has to say.

The biographers also want to grasp an individual's past. Yet Freud detested their manner of doing so. And it was not simply that their own methods were shallow and undisciplined. (Phillips contrasts two very different biographical interpretations of the actual death of Freud, those of Ernest Jones and Peter Gay, a contrast which seems to support Freud's own scepticism.) More deeply, it was a matter of what Phillips calls 'Freud's early ambivalence about knowing [others] and being known' (Phillips 1999: 72). Freud feared some biographer coming along, later in his life, to tell him who he was. (Note the young Freud's confident assumption, correct as it turned out, that not only would he have a biographer but before he were even dead! As early as his twenties, he destroyed a whole raft of his papers to deny them to later biographers.)

Now isn't this apparently inconsistent? Isn't this precisely what the analyst does with her client? Doesn't she tell the client who he is? On the contrary, for Freud, personal enlightenment follows from recognition, in the process of analysis, of areas of ignorance about ourselves which must remain impenetrable, in particular the history of the unpredictable workings of instinct in contexts governed tragically by chance. Psychological emancipation is in part emancipation from ill-founded assumptions of knowledge about ourselves and our lives.

Ignorance, reinterpretation and autonomy in personal narrative

The problem is not simply that instinct and chance are difficult to know about. More profoundly, the problem follows from the fact that our lives are constructs, partly of our own making and partly of others' making (importantly, of course, our parents'). For our own part, our motive in constructing our life is to obtain various satisfactions, some no doubt more legitimate than others. What we are not truly doing, even when guided by conscience, is trying to get our life 'right', according to some independent criterion or valid script. It is worth reminding ourselves, for instance, why the Freudian Superego (a mythic way of conceptualising actual psychological events) is a problem in Freud's terms. Not, certainly, because he was any kind of immoralist, but quite the contrary. The Superego is not in fact conscience, but the collection of our fantasies about independent arbiters of our lives, modelled on those original arbiters, our parents – or rather our fantasies about our parents. This is why the truly conscientious person does not want to be controlled by the Superego. The Superego tells us false stories about ourselves (and about others too). But the alternative is not to tell true stories instead, but rather to stop relying on such stories altogether for moral guidance, for none of them can ever be authoritative. No story is authoritative because none is ever complete. Our life stories are always and necessarily available to us to remake – to alter the sense of earlier events by the way we connect them with later ones, including actions yet to come. Only once we stop relying on stories which can only be provisional can conscience proper hold sway.

But this is not to say that stories or personal narratives have no function, much less that they are eradicable. Whilst remaking our own stories robs them of authority, nonetheless stories are our way of making sense of life, and their re-creation remains an important part of the very process of living autonomously and satisfactorily. As Phillips says,

> It is part of our own life story to try and keep control of the stories people tell about us (there is always the story of the stories I don't want people, including myself, to tell about myself).
>
> (Phillips 1999: 71)

As we have argued, the construction of knowledge entails the construction of ignorance too, as a kind of necessary shadow. Freud points out ways in which the construction of areas of ignorance, intertwined with our lives and relationships, is intrinsic to the maintenance of our autonomy – a very different notion from the Enlightenment idea of ignorance as an inevitable constraint on autonomy. (The difference is not one of simple contradiction, however. Where Enlightenment thinking emphasises knowledge of the public world in sustaining autonomy, Freud looks at the necessary role of ignorance in the realm of subjectivity.) If we are to maintain our own autonomy, we must not be captives of the past, of course. But neither can we simply flee from the past, for that is just an indirect way of continuing to be governed by it. (We let it dictate what we must run away from.) Freedom consists in coming to terms with the past, reappropriating it by reinterpretation, in a way that helps us move forward from it. It is not a matter of denying things which we know to have happened. But it is a matter of realising how much we really don't know. And that, in part, is a matter of freeing ourselves from deceptive ways of 'packaging' the past in narratives which actually lack any unique authority. We are free only inasfar as our lives are open to our own indefinite reinterpretations of them. And since our lives are inherently intertwined with those of others, the maintainance of others' partial ignorance of us is a precondition of our not foreclosing on our own creativity in constructing our own lives.

In turn, this inherent element of mutual ignorance reinforces, in circular fashion, the inevitable ambiguity of our past experience itself, ensuring it always remains open to interpretation and reinterpretation. Because we are inevitably unsure about others in relation to ourselves, to that degree we must remain unsure about ourselves in relation to them. We are not transparent to ourselves, any more than to others. (This does not mean that personal knowledge is arbitrary, but that it is never final, as Quine for instance would expect.)

It begins to seem that taking ignorance seriously may be part of taking autonomy seriously – a possibility that must surely give pause to us as educationists. And Freud is clear that this particular kind of ignorance is more than just a lack. His later inventions of the ideas of Eros and Thanatos, Life Instinct and Death Instinct, can be seen as ways of capturing in myth the inherent struggle between the necessity of making some kind of sense of one's life versus resistance to being captured by any spuriously authoritative story, reflected in his ambivalence noted above, about knowing and being known. Freud noted those patients who seemed to have made a nonsense of their own sense of self, and began to suspect there was some covert benefit to them in having done so:

Freud was to suggest that the ways in which we tried to destroy our lives (and our life stories) were integral to our life stories. That we were always, as it were, tampering with the evidence of ourselves. Indeed, it was the function of what he would later call the death instinct to make narrative coherence impossible; to spoil our life stories and put a stop to them. To spoil the connections we, or other people, might wish to make.

(Phillips 1999: 71)

But the well-adjusted person is not the one without any Death Instinct at all, but rather the one for whom the Life Instinct is constantly in play with it. Neither exists independently of the other.

If we think of these instincts as characters in Freud's drama – as useful fictions but improbable facts – then the death instinct . . . does not, for example, believe that life is an epistemological project in which we strive for better and better knowledge of ourselves and others. Instead it promoted the idea that not knowing things [e.g. by repressing knowledge of them] will get us the life we want. The parodist of our truth-seeking, the saboteur of our will to be good, the death instinct becomes the silent unsettler of our lives, and not merely the nihilist lurking in our souls.

(Ibid.: 74)

And being unsettled is essential to us. Settlement is death itself (cf. Nietzsche, *GS*: section 285). It is not that we do not seek truth at all nor wish to be good in any way. But the Life Instinct needs the Death Instinct, just as knowledge needs ignorance. It is not that we give up trying to make sense – the Life Instinct spurs us on to revise our stories yet again – but that we recognise the impossibility, and indeed undesirability, of finality in doing so. Knowledge is good, but finality in knowing – certainty – is worrying. Other people's necessary inability to know us finally is good for us: it keeps us free. And so too does a measure of our own ignorance of ourselves.

Why we might want to believe that we are intelligible to ourselves and others was what preoccupied Freud from the beginning, and not merely how we could get better and better at doing it. It is as though he is asking, even in [an] early letter: What is this wish for understanding a wish for? And if understanding isn't our best currency, our most useful project, then what is? . . . A life, for example, might become a search for experiments in living, rather than a quest for recognitions. It might be more about finding pleasurable ways of getting on with people than good ways of knowing them.

(Ibid.: 72–3)

And Adam Phillips further comments:

> It's not that we misunderstand each other, that we keep getting it wrong, it is that we put so much belief – false belief – in the whole notion of knowing and understanding [other people].
>
> (Ibid.: 73)

> It is not merely that we might be endangered by people's assumed knowledge about us, our assumed knowledge about them – as in racist and sexist fantasy – but that it is misleading to assume that it is knowledge that we want or that we have of people, any more than it is knowledge we get from listening to music.
>
> (Ibid.: 74)

Now of course Phillips is not saying that we know nothing of each other. Rather, as with other forms of knowledge, knowledge and ignorance of ourselves and others come ineluctably wrapped up together. The deeper point is that merely shifting the balance between the two can in some ways miss the point, just as Socrates was ultimately not interested in simply shifting the boundaries of supposed knowledge. In Freudian psychoanalysis itself, the point is rather to effect a satisfactory 'transference' and 'counter-transference'. In analysis, the client achieves and then transforms her relationship to the therapist, and by extension and implication her relationships with others too. The analyst is reciprocally bound up in this process, making and modifying her own relationship with the client (counter-transference). The reinterpretation of the past which goes on in the psychoanalytic dialogue is governed, not by 'the facts' or 'the past' but by the requirements of these shifting relationships. The reinterpretation is only as good as the quality and sustainability of those relationships themselves. None of this would be possible, however, if the resources of ignorance could be exhausted and all 'unknowns' exposed and made clear to us. Where there is some encompassing 'truth' to be definitively known, leeway for reinterpretation is nullified, and unlikely to accomodate succesful transference and counter-transference, except by lucky chance.

Autonomy, ignorance and education

Is there any useful analogy here for education? After all, in education too we have always taken autonomy seriously, or so we like to think. The new managerialists who now govern education would probably claim to epitomise this concern, precisely by 'forcing up standards' and promoting educational choice, but do they? Has their indifference to ignorance restricted the scope for autonomy in education? Do they inhibit what children and students might make of or do with their education, in the same way that the possibility of personal transparency would undermine the recreation of the ways the analytic client is able to live her life? What is knowledge to the pupil or student if it is not knowledge for some purpose? And more to the point, what is a purpose to them if it cannot ultimately be seen as their own, and not just willed upon them?

We suggested in an earlier chapter that a more fundamental aim for education than rational autonomy might be plain realism. But the kind of realism we need is arguably of a Freudian sort, one that importantly includes acknowledgement of ignorance. Consider for a moment how one might suppose that simply learning more and more about the social and subjective world, most broadly conceived, could enhance our autonomy, notwithstanding hostile indifference to the structure and content of our supposedly ever-diminishing ignorance. Autonomy here would increasingly approach the condition of consumer choice, a choice which must increasingly seem objectively arbitrary. For in such a world (which would favour Reynolds' project of an error-free education), the ideal educational *telos* would be that ignorance were expunged, and thus that everyone shared the same knowledge as everyone else. The less-than-ideal actuality would be an increasing assurance that, if this person doesn't know *x*, then someone else does, and can tell them. As education progressed, people would increasingly lose sight of the still-remaining fact that their world was open to divergences of re-interpretation. Autonomy under such circumstances would be experienced as complete freedom of choice, but nothing more. This freedom itself would eventually cease to be informed by any particular understanding or view of the world. It might be informed only, at best, by commitment to personal values.

But debate about values itself would be at best increasingly limited in scope. Moral argument in turn would be less and less informed by personal experience, because experience itself would be increasingly bereft of that very scope for interpretation which makes it personal. Moral commitments would become less constrained by any sense of moral ambiguity or uncertainty which might be garnered from lived personal experience, and more completely dependent on abstract ratiocination, accepting or rejecting particular moral arguments solely on grounds of internal logical coherence. And since questions of validity are easy to mistake – why else do we have debates in philosophy? – moral argument too, in this radically limited and idealist form, would begin to seem at best a veil for an underlying arbitrariness in choice (since validity is always open to question), in a world where knowledge of facts had come increasingly to seem cut-and-dried and secure. The only morally relevant experience might be that which commanded consensus as to fact. This in turn could only be as relevant as avoidance of the Naturalistic Fallacy allowed it to be – necessary to practical decision on occasion, but never sufficient. The neo-Marxist view of moral debate as covert ideological manœuvre would ironically seem more reasonable than ever in this supposedly ideology-free world.

This scenario should not seem like fantasy to us, either. It would mark quite simply the return of the world view of positivism, familiar from the 'end of ideology' ideologists of the 1950s and 1960s, for whom moral choice was characterised as a practice which Habermas describes as 'decisionism'. Along with the narrowest interpretation of the Naturalistic Fallacy comes the characterisation of all normative commitments as ultimately arbitrary choices, with the consequent trivialisation of the moral, the religious, the political, the cutural, the aesthetic. And such a revived positivism is patently of a piece with the renewed hegemony of free market ideology, dismissive of all pretensions to objective validity of any good other than unrestricted freedom.

Most of us are likely to recoil from the prospect of return to those arid assumptions. But mere distaste is no reply to those who would say, 'But this just happens to be what autonomy amounts to, in a world that values knowledge and doesn't value ignorance. If your objections depend on either committing the Naturalistic Fallacy or a commitment to revaluing ignorance, then they are contemptible – an irrationalist assault on autonomy in its own right'.

But we can say much more than this. Our discussion of Phillips and Freud alerts us to the problem that the pursuit of knowledge and maximal transparency, disregarding ignorance, has reflexive effects on us ourselves. A world in which we all concur in our interest in knowledge and our disregard for ignorance, in the subjective no less that the objective sphere (of maths, science and so on), is a world in which others disregard, *inter alia*, their own ignorance of us and we, *ex hypothesi*, see things, including ourselves, the same way they do. To that extent we become ourselves ever more tightly limited and constrained. We have less and less freedom as we are increasingly led to agree with and accept others' view of 'the facts' about ourselves (shades of Foucault and panopticism), becoming less and less inclined to consider what we don't know, and can't know about ourselves because we haven't finished constructing ourselves yet. It is a world in which we would be increasingly distracted from the reconstruction of ourselves, the more we are fed supposedly authoritative and ever more complete stories about ourselves. It is a world in which our choices become not merely objectively arbitrary but increasingly subjectively pointless: a world in which our own autonomy begins to cease to matter to us anyway, however it were conceived.

However, these fears may seem just excessive and melodramatic. Surely, it might be said, the kinds of generality that we have to do with in education, and in the culture more generally, are not the specifics which might become so oppressive if mistaken for adequate knowledge of ourselves. But this is unperceptive. We should remember that we cannot but frame the things we think we know about individuals in terms of concepts and generalisations drawn from elsewhere. So we need to take care with these concepts and gneralisations if we are to deal freely with each other. Surely we are all familiar with the way in which the clichés of newspapers, magazines and soap operas become reductive and trivialising ways of thought, yet some people patently come to reconceive their knowledge of themselves in such foolish terms. TV chat shows, currently promoting preposterous parodies of the language of psychotherapy, ironically show us the results. It would be grossly snobbish to say of the denizens of this world that they are incapable of autonomy. But it arguably reflects a real decline in the culture to say that these are people for whom autonomy is not even subjectively valuable. Yes, they want their freedom of choice. But their problem is precisely that they think they know who they are because they share a general ignorance of our ignorance of ourselves; and choose accordingly. The problem is not that the stereotypes are bad, but that we forget how much ignorance they gloss over. And the facile generalisations which sustain these delusions are themselves derived from disciplines which are often the content of education at some level (if not school). And these disciplines are increasingly misconceived in terms of positive knowledge and disregard of ignorance, in ways such as we discussed earlier. Bad contemporary educational theory, with its prattle of outcomes, targets and accountability, is part and parcel of all this.

So how could a revived and invigorated theory and practice of education release us from the encroaching panoptic nightmare, and free us from the ever less ignorant ministries of truth? Arguably, the role of education is not to substitute superior stereotypes for vulgar ones, but to reinforce our appreciation of the inherent inadequacy of thinking in terms of generalisations mistaken for adequate knowledge. Emphasis on our own ignorance of people, including ourselves, is essential here. (Nor should this be glibly equated with any call for recognition of 'the spiritual dimension' or the mysterious in life. It is not that we lack a special kind of knowledge, but that we need to acknowledge ignorance at a quite mundane level, and to value its positive side as well.)

To recognise our ignorance of people, and to celebrate their partial ignorance of us, is to conceptualise with greater moral realism the great majority of the disciplines which inform, if they do not constitute, the curriculum at every level. As we glimpsed earlier, the natural sciences, powerful as they are, are an untypical corner of the map of knowledge in their autonomy from human relationships and institutions. The objectivity which comes with this autonomy is suitable for science, but in no way a model outside the sciences. A disregard for the autonomy-sustaining ignorance, which can and should characterise the social and subjective spheres, would not improve non-scientific disciplines but destroy their very subjects and rationales. And at the same time, it would undermine our best justification for education.

The point, then, is not to marginalise the sciences but to insist on the importance for so much of the rest of the curriculum of understanding the importance of ignorance and of the openness of narratives for personal autonomy. In turn, to understand this is to realise how radically inapposite so many of our current educational concepts, aims, practices and self-imposed constraints must be in optimising the value of 'the pursuit of knowledge' for both individuals and society. For this pursuit entails the pursuit of ignorance too: its recognition, its description, understanding, in some ways its maximisation, and respect for it as the guarantor of our future freedom. And correlatively we must learn to fear contemporary emphases on the 'positives' of education. It is a deep form of foolishness to underrate ignorance.

We are told over and again that knowledge is power, and that herein lies part, or perhaps even all, of its value. And the equation of knowledge and power is true, and has proven vitally important to social progress down the last three hunded years. But power is problematic. Power is too often a threat to freedom. Whilst we all need and deserve power, it is also easily abused, unbalanced, illegitimate or excessive. However much it may be a good, power needs constraint. So perhaps may knowledge need constraint, if it is itself power. But we are all too familiar with the deceit and plain corruption which results when knowledge and its pursuit are subject to extraneous constraints – constraints such as censorship, ownership, sponsorship, bias and so on. These are problems significantly worse than plain ignorance. If knowledge needs constraint, these extraneous impositions are quite the wrong kinds of constraint. What, then, might more legitimately 'keep knowledge in order'?

If the power which is knowledge is to be properly marshalled without damage to knowledge itself, then it can only be by full recognition of our concomitant ignorance and by understanding the value of the ignorance of others in securing our own autonomy, especially our autonomy as knowledge-seeking beings. For to repeat, ignorance is not extraneous to knowledge. It is its undetachable shadow. Ignorance itself is not power. But as Socrates understood so well, a true appreciation of ignorance is the deeper part of wisdom. If knowledge is power, to counterpose other powers – censorship and so on – can only mean war (as Foucault understood). Rather, knowledge, as power, must be properly deployed in the first place, not resisted in combat. It takes wisdom to deploy knowledge well, and wisdom appeals to our ignorance. Socrates knew this. So too, we have seen, did Hume and Kant, when they sought the limits of understanding. Appreciation of ignorance is still deeply embedded in the philosophical traditions which refer back to these avatars, contrary to occasional appearance. Therein lies the importance of philosophy for education.

Notes

1 For an attempt to do so, see Blake *et al.* 1998.
2 'Man does *not* strive after happiness; only the Englishman does that': F. Nietzsche, *Twilight of the Idols*, Maxims and Arrows 12.
3 Phillips is a practising psychoanalyst and writer on psychoanalysis. But much of what he has to say is arguably as much philosophy as empirical study – and none the worse for that.

FRAGMENT VIII

Nietzsche tells us that there are no values waiting for us ready-made:

> No one *gives* a human being his qualities: not God, not society, not his parents or ancestors . . . *No one* is accountable for existing at all, or for being constituted as he is, or for living in the circumstances and surroundings in which he lives . . . *this alone is the great liberation* – thus alone is the *innocence* of becoming restored.
>
> (*TI*, 'The Four Great Errors': 8)

There is no value to be discovered in the world, but for that reason we must bestow value upon it. This is unsettling to a certain cast of mind, which wrongly imagines that nihilism is here being recommended, rather than diagnosed.

Such a mind will see all the more reason to fill the world with structures and lists, in order to keep primeval chaos and panic at bay.

If we are not accountable . . . we shall wander the world seeking someone to explain ourselves to, someone to absolve us and tell us we have done well.

In the end *effectiveness* is a charm to reassure ourselves, to keep the nightmares at bay.

FRAGMENT IX

Top tips for education managers:

1   Ensure all staff are familiar with the mission statement.
2   Always be alert for what you can learn from the world of business.
3   A good manager is a calm manager.
4   Our handy Management Walletbooks are just the thing for a train journey or while waiting at the airport. Just out: *50 Ways to Motivate your Workforce*.

An alternative programme:

1   Listen to people, attend carefully to the world.
2   There are no answers that save creative effort.
3   Irony and self-deprecation are good qualities.
4   Laugh a lot, especially at the latest idiocies.

Nietzsche writes:

> *Iche wohne in meinen eignen Haus,*
> *Hab Niemandem nie nichts nachgemacht*
> *Und – lachte noch jeden Meister aus,*
> *Der nicht sich selber ausgelacht.*
>
> **Ueber meiner Hausthür**

> I live in my own house,
> have never copied anybody else at all,
> and I laugh at any manager who cannot laugh at himself.
>
> **Over the door to my house**

(Prefix to *The Gay Science*; our translation)

There is nowhere else to live.

References

Abinun, J. (1977) 'Teaching and personal relationships', *Educational Theory* 27: 297–303.

Adey, P. and Shayer, M. (1994) *Really Raising Standards: Cognitive Intervention and Academic Achievement*, London: Routledge.

Aloni, N. (1989) 'The three pedagogical dimensions of Nietzsche's philosophy', *Educational Theory* 39: 301–5.

Altieri, C. (1994) *Subjective Agency*, Oxford, Blackwell.

Alvarez, A. (1962), *The New Poetry*, an anthology selected and introduced by A. Alvarez, Harmondsworth: Penguin.

Anton, J.P. (1974) 'The secret of Plato's *Symposium*', *Southern Journal of Philosophy* 12: 277–293.

Arcilla, R.V. (1995) *For the Love of Perfection: Richard Rorty and Liberal Education*, New York: Routledge.

Austin, N. (1975), *Archery at the Dark of the Moon: Poetic Problems in Homer's Odyssey*, Berkeley and Los Angeles: University of California Press.

Aviram, A. (1991) 'Nietzsche as educator', *Journal of Philosophy of Education* 25: 219–234.

Bearn, C. (2000) 'Pointlessness and the university of beauty', in P. Dhillon and P. Standish (eds), *Lyotard: Just Education*, London: Routledge.

Bennett, J. (1996) '"How is it, then, that we still remain barbarians?" Foucault, Schiller, and the aestheticization of ethics', *Political Theory* 24: 653–672.

Berlin, I. (1990) *The Crooked Timber of Humanity*, London: Murray.

Beveridge, W.H. (1944) *Full Employment in a Free Society*, London: Allen & Unwin.

Blake, N. (1997) 'Spirituality, anti-intellectualism and the end of civilisation as we know it', in R. Smith and P. Standish (eds), *Teaching Right and Wrong*, Stoke-on-Trent: Trentham Books.

Blake, N. (1999) 'The machine stops: education and autonomy in a mature global economy', in 'Globalisierung: Perspektiven, Paradoxien, Verwergungen', Special Number of the *Jahrbuch für Bildungs- und Erziehungsphilosophie* 2.

Blake, N., Smeyers, P., Smith, R. and Standish, P. (1998) *Thinking Again: Education After Postmodernism*, New York: Bergin and Garvey.

Borgmann, A. (1992), *Crossing the Postmodern Divide*, Chicago and London: University of Chicago Press.

Byatt, A. (1978) *The Virgin in the Garden*, London: Chatto & Windus.

Carr, K.L. (1992) *The Banalization of Nihilism. Twentieth-Century Responses to Meaninglessness*, Albany: State University of New York Press.

Cavell, S. (1990) *Conditions Handsome and Unhandsome: The Constitution of Emersonian Perfectionism*, Chicago: University of Chicago Press.

Cavell, S. (1995) *Philosophical Passages: Wittgenstein, Emerson, Austin, Derrida*, Oxford: Blackwell.

Conway, D.W. (1997) *Nietzsche's Dangerous Game. Philosophy in the Twilight of the Idols*, Cambridge: Cambridge University Press.

Conway, D. (1998) 'The genius as squanderer. Some remarks on the *Übermensch* and higher humanity', *International Studies in Philosophy* 30: 81–95.

Cooper, D.E. (1980) *Illusions of Equality*, London: Routledge and Kegan Paul.

Cooper, D.E. (1983a) 'On reading Nietzsche on education', *Journal of Philosophy of Education* 17: 119–26.

Cooper, D.E. (1983b) *Authenticity and Learning. Nietzsche's Educational Philosophy*, London: Routledge and Kegan Paul.

Cooper, D.E. (1995) 'Technology: liberation or enslavement', in R. Fellows (ed.), *Philosophy and Technology*, Royal Institute of Philosophy Supplement 38, Cambridge: Cambridge University Press.

Corradi Fiumara, G. (1990) *The Other Side of Language: A Philosophy of Listening*, trans. C. Lambert, London and New York: Routledge.

Crainer, S. (1996) *Key Management Ideas*, London: Pitman.

Danto, A.C. (1980) *Nietzsche as Philosopher*, New York: Columbia University Press.

Deiro, J.A. (1996) *Teaching With Heart. Making Healthy Connections With Students*, Thousand Oaks: Corwin Press.

Deleuze, G. (1983) *Nietzsche and Philosophy*, trans. H. Tomlinson, New York: Columbia University Press.

Derrida, J. (1983), 'The principle of sufficient reason: the university in the eyes of its pupils', *Diacritics*, Fall.

Derrida, J. (1992) *The Other Heading*, trans. P.-A. Brault and M.B. Bloomington, Ind.: Indiana University Press (original work published in 1991).

DfEE web page: http://www.dfee.gov.uk/read/index.htm.

DfEE (1997) *Excellence in Schools*, London: HMSO.

Dhillon, P. and Standish, P. (eds) (2000) *Lyotard: Just Education*, London: Routledge.

Edwards, J. (1982) *Ethics Without Philosophy. Wittgenstein and the Moral Life*, Tampa: University of South Florida Press.

Edwards, J.C. (1990) *The Authority of Language. Heidegger, Wittgenstein, and the Threat of Philosophical Nihilism*, Tampa: University of South Florida Press.

Emerson, R.W. (1982) *Selected Essays*, Harmondsworth: Penguin.

Ervin, E. (1993) 'Plato the pederast: rhetoric and cultural procreation in the Dialogues', *Pre/Text. A Journal of Rhetorical Theory* 14(1–2), 73–98.

European Commission (1995) *Teaching and Learning: Towards the Learning Society*, Brussels: European Commission, Website http://www.cec.lu/en/comm/dg22/dgss/ html.

Fellows, R. (ed.) (1995) *Philosophy and Technology*, Royal Institute of Philosophy Supplement 38, Cambridge: Cambridge University Press.

Foucault, M. (1987) *The Use of Pleasure*, Harmondsworth: Penguin.

Frege, G. (1984 [1892]) 'Sense and reference', in G. Frege, *Collected Papers on Mathematics, Logic and Philosophy*, ed. B. McGuinness, London: Blackwell.

Freire, P., Giroux, H.A. and Simon, R.I. (1989) *Popular Culture, Schooling and Everyday Life*, Westport, Conn.: Bergin & Garvey.

Fuller, T. (ed) (1989) *The Voice of Liberal Learning: Michael Oakeshott on Education*, London: Yale University Press.

Gage, N. (1963) *A Handbook of Research on Teaching*, Chicago: Rand McNally.

Gergen, K.J. (1972) 'The healthy, happy human being wears many masks', *Psychology Today*, Lewes: Sussex Publications Inc.

Giroux, H.A., and Simon, R.I. (eds) (1989) *Popular Culture. Schooling and Everyday Life*, New York: Bergin & Garvey.

Goleman, D. (1996) *Emotional Intelligence*, London: Bloomsbury.

Goleman, D. (1999) *Working with Emotional Intelligence*, London: Bloomsbury.

Golomb, J. (1985) 'Nietzsche's early educational thought', *Journal of Philosophy of Education* 19: 99–109.

Gordon, H. (1980) 'Nietzsche's Zarathustra as educator', *Journal of Philosophy of Education* 14: 181–92.

Haydon, G. (1999) *Values, Virtues and Violence: Education and the Public Understanding of Morality*, Oxford: Blackwell.

Heidegger, M. (1968) *What is Called Thinking?*, trans. J.G. Gray, New York and London: Harper & Row.

Heidegger, M. (1977) *The Question Concerning Technology and Other Essays*, trans. W. Lovitt, New York and London: Harper & Row.

Heidegger, M. (1991) *The Principle of Reason*, trans. R. Lilly, Bloomington Ind.: Indiana University Press.

Helm, B.W. (1996) 'Integration and fragmentation of the self', *The Southern Journal of Philosophy* 34: 43–63.

Hillisheim, J. (1973) 'Nietzsche's agonistes', *Educational Theory* 23: 343–53.

Hough, S. (1997) *Nietzsche's Noontide Friend. The Self as Metaphoric Double*, University Park: The Pennsylvania State University Press.

Hutchins, P. (1968) *Rosie's Walk*, London: Bodley Head.

Ignatieff, M. (1998) *Isaiah Berlin, A Life*, London: Chatto & Windus.

Ihde, D. (1979) *Technics and Praxis: A Philosophy of Technology*, Dordrecht: D. Reidel.

Johnston, J.S. (1998) 'Nietzsche as educator: a reexamination', *Educational Theory* 48: 67–83.

Kelly, U.A. (1997) *Schooling Desire. Literacy, Cultural Politics, and Pedagogy*, New York: Routledge.

Kemal, S. Gaskell, I., and Conway, D.W. (eds) (1998) *Nietzsche, Philosophy and the Arts*, Cambridge: Cambridge University Press, 287–309.

Kierkegaard, S. (1985) *Fear and Trembling*, trans. A. Hannay, Harmondsworth: Penguin.

Kipling, R. (1994) *Stalky & Co.*, Ware, Herts.: Wordsworth Editions.

Kupfer, J. (1998) 'Generosity of spirit', *The Journal of Value Inquiry* 32: 357–68.

Lakatos, I. (1970), 'Falsification and the methodology of scientific research programmes', in I. Lakatos and A. Musgrave (eds), *Criticism and the Growth of Knowledge*, Cambridge: Cambridge University Press.

Leiter, B. (1997) 'Nietzsche and the morality critics', *Ethics* 107: 250–85.

Lyotard, J.-F. (1984) *The Postmodern Condition: A Report on Knowledge*, trans. G. Bennington and B. Massumi, Manchester: Manchester University Press.

Lyotard, J.-F. (1993) *Libidinal Economy*, trans. I.H. Grant, London: The Athlone Press.

Lyotard, J.-F. (1997) *Postmodern Fables*, trans. G. Van Den Abbeele, Minneapolis: University of Minnesota Press.

MacMillan, C.J.B., and Garrison, J.W. (1988) *A Logical Theory of Teaching. Erotetics and Intentionality*, Dordrecht: Kluwer.

Margolis, M. and Resnick, D. (1999) Online: hhttp://firstmonday.dk/issues/issue4_10/margolis/index.htm

Marshall, B. (1998) 'English teachers and the third way', in B. Cox (ed.), *Literacy is not Enough: Essays on the Importance of Reading*, Manchester: Book Trust and Manchester University Press.

Maskell, D. (1999) 'Education, education, education: or, what has Jane Austen to teach Tony Blunkett?' *Journal of Philosophy of Education* 33 (2): 157–174.

McNamara, D. (1994) *Classroom Pedagogy and Primary Practice*, London: Routledge.

McNeill, W. (1998) 'Care for the self. Originary ethics in Heidegger and Foucault', *Philosophy Today* 42: 53–64.

McWilliam, E. (1996) 'Seductress or schoolmarm: on the improbability of the great female teacher', *Interchange* 27: 1–11.

McWilliam, E. (1997) 'Beyond the missionary position. Teacher desire and radical pedagogy', in S. Todd (ed.), *Learning Desire. Perspectives on Pedagogy, Culture and the Unsaid*, New York: Routledge, 217–35.

Meek, M. (1994) *Learning to Read*, London: The Bodley Head.

Mills, C.W. (1970) *The Sociological Imagination*, Harmondsworth: Penguin.

Neiman, A. (1995) 'Pragmatism and the ironic teacher of virtue', in J.W. Garrison and A.G. Rud (eds), *The Educational Conversation. Closing the Gap*, Albany: State University of New York Press, 61–83.

Nicholson, L.J. (ed.) (1990) *Feminism/Postmodernism*, London: Routledge.

Nietzsche, F. (1909) *On the Future of Our Educational Institutions*, Vol. VI of *The Complete Works*, ed. O. Levy, trans. Kennedy, London: T.N. Foulis.

Nietzsche, F. (1962) *Twilight of the Idols*, New York: Viking Press.

Nietzsche, F. (1979) *Ecce Homo*, trans. R.J. Hollingdale, Harmondsworth: Penguin.

Nietzsche, F. (1993) *Thus Spoke Zarathustra*, trans. T. Common, revised with an introduction by H. James Birx, Amherst, New York: Prometheus Books.

Nietzsche, F. (1996), *On the Genealogy of Morals*, trans. D. Smith, Oxford: Oxford University Press.

Nussbaum, M.C. (1994) 'Pity and mercy. Nietzsche's stoicism', in R. Schacht (ed.), *Nietzsche, Genealogy, Morality. Essays on Nietzsche's 'Genealogy of Morals'*, Berkeley: University of California Press, 139–67.

O'Hear, A. (1995) 'Art and technology: an old tension', in R. Fellows (ed.), *Philosophy and Technology*, Royal Institute of Philosophy Supplement 38, Cambridge: Cambridge University Press.

Peters, R. (1965) *Ethics and Education*, London: Allen & Unwin.

Phillips, A. (1999) *Darwin's Worms*, London: Faber and Faber.

Phillips, M. (1996) *All Must Have Prizes*, London: Little Brown.

Piddocke, S., Magsino, R., and Manley-Casimir, M. (1997) *Teachers in Trouble: An Exploration of the Normative Character of Teaching*, Toronto: University of Toronto Press.

Plant, S. (1997) *Zeros + Ones*, London: Fourth Estate.

Plato (1955) *The Republic*, trans. H.D.P. Lee, Harmondsworth: Penguin.

Plato (1964) *Symposium and Other Dialogues*, intro. J. Warrington, London: Dent.

Pratt, D. (1980) *Curriculum Design and Development*, New York: Harcourt Brace Jovanovich.

Quine, W. van O. (1960) *Word and Object*, Cambridge, MA: MIT Press.

Reginster, B. (1997) 'Nietzsche on *Ressentiment* and valuation', *Philosophy and Phenomenological Research* 57: 281–305.

Reynolds, D. (1997a) *Times Educational Supplement*, 27 June: 21.

Reynolds, D. (1997b) 'School effectiveness: retrospect and prospect', *Scottish Educational Review* 29 (1): 97–113.

Reynolds, D. (n.d.) 'Better teachers, better schools', on the Teacher Training Agency's website, http://www.teach-tta.gov.uk/speech.htm.

Richardson, J. (1997) 'Is there a Nietzschean post-analytic method?' *International Studies in Philosophy* 29: 29–36.

Rosen, S. (1969) *Nihilism: A Philosophical Essay*, New Haven: Yale University Press.

Rosenow, E. (1973) 'What is free education? The educational significance of Nietzsche's thought', *Educational Theory* 23: 354–70.

Rosenow, E. (1986) 'Nietzsche's concept of education', in Y. Yovel (ed.), *Nietzsche as Affirmative Thinker*, Dordrecht: Martinus Nijhoff, 119–31.

Rosenow, E. (1989) 'Nietzsche's educational dynamite', *Educational Theory* 39: 308–16.

Sassone, L. (1996) 'Philosophy across the curriculum: a democratic Nietzschean pedagogy', *Educational Theory* 46: 511–24.

Schacht, R. (1998) 'A Nietzschean education: Zarathustra/'Zarathustra' as Educator', in A.O. Rorty (ed.), *Philosophers on Education. New Historical Perspectives*, London: Routledge, 318–32.

Schatzki, T. (1994) 'Ancient and naturalistic themes in Nietzsche's ethics', *Nietzsche Studien* 23: 146–67.

Schneider, J. (1992) 'Nietzsches Basler Vorträge "Ueber die Zukunft unserer Bildungsanstalten" im lichte seiner Lektüre pädagogischer Schriften', *Nietzsche Studien* 21: 308–25.

Sennett, R. (1998) *The Corrosion of Character: The Personal Consequences of Work in the New Capitalism*, New York: Norton.

Seuren, P.A.M. (1974) *Semantic Syntax*, Oxford: Oxford University Press.

Shaffer, P. (1976) *Three Plays (Equus, Shrivings, Five Finger Exercise)*, Harmondsworth: Penguin.

Sharp, A.M. (1984) 'Nietzsche's view of sublimation in the educational process', *The Journal of Educational Thought* 9: 99–106.

Simon, R.I. (1992) *Teaching Against the Grain*, Westport, Conn.: Bergin & Garvey.

Simons, M. (1988) 'Montessori, superman, and catwomen', *Educational Theory* 38: 341–9.

Smith, R. and Standish, P. (eds) (1997) *Teaching Right and Wrong: Moral Education in the Balance*, Stoke-on-Trent: Trentham Books.

Solomon, R.C. (1986) 'A more severe morality. Nietzsche's affirmative ethics', in Y. Yovel (ed.), *Nietzsche as Affirmative Thinker*, Dordrecht: Martinus Nijhoff, 69–89.

Solomon, R.C. (1996) 'Nietzsche *ad hominem*: perspectivism, personality and *ressentiment*, in B. Magnus and K.M. Higgins (eds), *The Cambridge Companion to Nietzsche*, Cambridge, Cambridge University Press.

Solomon, R.C. (1998) 'The virtues of a passionate life. Erotic love and '*The Will to Power*', *Social Philosophy and Theory* 15: 91–118.

Solomon, R.C. and Higgins, K.M. (eds) (1991) *The Philosophy of (Erotic) Love*, University Press of Kansas.

Spender, D. (1995) *Nattering on the Net: Women, Power and Cyberspace*, North Melbourne: Spinifex Press.

Standards and Effectiveness Unit's web page: http://www.standards.dfee. gov.uk/literacy/whatisliteracy.

Stringfield, S. (n.d.) *Attempting to Enhance Students' Learning through Innovative Programs: The Case for Schools Evolving into High Reliability Organisations*.

Swanton, C. (1998) 'Outline of a Nietzschean virtue ethics', *International Studies in Philosophy* 30: 29–38.

Thiele, L.P. (1990) *Friederich Nietzsche and the Politics of the Soul*, Princeton, NJ: Princeton University Press.

Ungar, S. 'The professor of desire', *Yale French Studies* 63: 81–97.

White, J. and Barber, M. (1997) *Perspectives on School Effectiveness and School Improvement*, Bedford Way Papers, Institute of Education, University of London.

Williams, B. (1993) 'Nietzsche's minimalist moral psychology', *European Journal of Philosophy* 1: 4–14.

Williams, J. (2000a) *Lyotard and the Political*, London: Routledge.

Williams, J. (2000b) 'For a libidinal education', in P. Dhillon and P. Standish (eds), *Lyotard: Just Education*, London; Routledge.

Wittgenstein, L. (1958) *Philosophical Investigations*, Oxford: Blackwell.

Wittgenstein, L. (1960) *Tractatus Logico–Philosophicus*, London: Routledge and Kegan Paul.

Wittgenstein, L. (1969) *On Certainty/Über Gewissheit,* ed. G.E.M. Anscombe and G.H. von Wright, trans. D. Paul and G.E.M. Anscombe, Oxford: Blackwell.

Woodhead, C. (1995) *Education: The Elusive Engagement and the Continuing Frustration,* Annual Lecture at Royal Society of Arts, London.

Woodhead, C. (1998) *Blood on the Tracks: Lessons from the History of Education Reform,* Annual Lecture at Royal Society of Arts, London.

Index

KING ALFRED'S COLLEGE
LIBRARY